GLOBALITY

GLOBALITY

COMPETING WITH EVERYONE
FROM EVERYWHERE
FOR EVERYTHING

**Harold L. Sirkin, James W. Hemerling,
and Arindam K. Bhattacharya**
with John Butman

**BUSINESS
PLUS**

NEW YORK   BOSTON

Business Plus
Hachette Book Group USA
237 Park Avenue
New York, NY 10017
Visit our Web site at www.HachetteBookGroupUSA.com.

Business Plus is an imprint of Grand Central Publishing.
The Business Plus name and logo are trademarks of Hachette Book Group USA, Inc.

Printed in the United States of America

First Edition: June 2008
10 9 8 7 6 5 4 3 2 1

Library of Congress Cataloging-in-Publication Data

Sirkin, Harold L.
   Globality : competing with everyone from everywhere for everything / Harold L. Sirkin, James W. Hemerling, and Arindam K. Bhattacharya.
      p. cm.
   Includes bibliographical references and index.
   ISBN-13: 978-0-446-17829-7
   ISBN-10: 0-446-17829-2
   1. Competition, International.   2. International trade.   3. Globalization—Economic aspects.
I. Hemerling, James W.   II. Bhattacharya, Arindam K.   III. Title.

   HF1414.S57 2008
   382—dc22

                                                                                                    2007039682

Book design by Giorgetta Bell McRee

To my parents, Arthur and Benita; my wife, Eileen;
and our children, Jessica and David
Hal

To my parents, Bill and Ruth; my wife, Nicola; and our sons,
Nicholas, Christian, Mitchell, and Alexander
Jim

To my parents, Kshitindra and Basanti; my wife, Sujata;
and our sons, Ishaan and Dhiman
Arindam

Contents

GLOBALITY

CHAPTER 1

WHAT IS GLOBALITY?

"We are in a new economic order.
Who will survive and who will go down?"
A.M. Naik, L&T

Globality is not a new and different term for globalization, it's the name for a new and different global reality in which we'll all be competing with everyone, from everywhere, for everything.

We three, management consultants turned authors, are partners in The Boston Consulting Group (BCG), and we have been studying the change in the global business environment—and working with companies involved in it—for more than twenty years. The extensive research that we and our colleagues have conducted over the past five years set us on a path that led to this book.

When we started out in our international travels, globalization was just getting under way. It was a cavalcade that traveled from West to East—big multinational companies centered in Europe, Japan, and the United States marching out from their corporate fortresses to foreign lands in search of low-cost manufacturing and low-end markets.

Today we look forward and see a new era emerging. We call it globality, a different kind of environment, in which business flows in every direction. Companies have no centers. The idea of foreignness is foreign. Commerce swirls and market dominance shifts. Western business orthodoxy entwines with eastern business philosophy and creates a whole new mind-set that embraces profit and competition as well as sustainability and collaboration.

Globality is a blockbuster new script—action, drama, suspense, and road picture all packed into one—with a sprawling cast of characters and locations in every corner of the earth. We have met, worked with, and had extensive conversations with many of the key figures in this unfolding scenario.

Ratan Tata, chairman of India's largest conglomerate, the Tata Group, is unquestionably one of the "everyone" who will be players in the world of globality. He graduated from Cornell with a degree in architecture in 1962, flew back to India, and went to work for the family firm, which was founded as a trading company in 1868 by Ratan's great-grandfather, Jamsetji Nusserwanji Tata. Ratan Tata was named chairman in 1991, when Tata Group was a jumble of local companies, and India was still essentially closed to foreign business and investment. Ratan Tata made it his mission to modernize and internationalize his company and, along the way, help India open its borders and its mind to worldwide business.

Today the Tata Group is a decentralized family of companies grouped into seven sectors, including information and communication technology, chemicals, hotels, automotive, and steel. When Ratan Tata negotiated the $13.1 billion deal to buy Corus Group, an Anglo-Dutch steelmaker, in 2007—India's biggest-ever foreign acquisition—Tata flashed onto the world's radar in a big way. Today, Tata Group has market capitalization in excess of $50 billion, and more than 50 percent of its $50 billion annual sales comes from outside India. "We no longer discuss the future of India," said Kamal Nath, the country's minister of commerce. "We say: 'The future is India.'"[1]

Tata Group is a "global challenger," one of the hundreds, even thousands, of companies that have their origins outside the established world of Western commerce in the rapidly developing economies (RDEs)—Argentina, Brazil, Chile, China, the Czech Republic, Egypt, Hungary, India, Indonesia, Malaysia, Mexico, Poland, Russia, Thailand, and Turkey—and that are bursting their way onto the big stage. They're fast growing, hungry, and have access to all the world's markets and resources. They're showing up everywhere—in each other's markets throughout the world, in markets that are less developed than their own, and, increasingly, in the developed markets of Japan, western Europe, and the United States.

A few years back, Glenn Tilton, chief executive officer of United Airlines, spoke over breakfast about the Embraer 170, a new regional jet made in Brazil that United had put into service on the Chicago–Santa Fe route, which we often fly. At the time, we weren't fans of the small, narrow-bodied jets in service to secondary cities. "Regional jet, as in no overhead bin space and knees banging up against the guy in front, right?"

Tilton smiled. "Try it," he said. "I think you'll like it." We did. He was right. The seventy-seat, twin-engine jet has all the comforts of the big planes with none of the drawbacks, especially the dreaded middle seat. In 1995, Embraer was virtually bankrupt. Today it's the world's leading manufacturer of commercial jet aircraft of up to 120 seats, surpassing the Canadian producer Bombardier in deliveries and sales volume, yet constantly vying for supremacy with its archrival. And Embraer grew up in a South American country much better known for coffee, oranges, diamonds, and steel—and supermodel Gisele Bündchen—than for the kind of engineering and high-tech manufacturing you need to build state-of-the-art aircraft.

Embraer, like all the challengers, will increasingly be competing with everyone from everywhere for everything. And by everything, we mean just that—all the world's resources and markets. Everybody will be trying to grab the same things that everybody else wants, especially the most precious and limited ones: raw materials, capital, knowledge, capabilities, and, most important, people: leaders, managers, workers, partners, collaborators, suppliers. And, of course, customers.

In 2007, attendees at the Detroit Auto Show may have been a little perplexed when they strolled by the display booth where Changfeng, a Chinese automaker, was showing off its prototype SUV, the Liebao. The company sold about 100,000 vehicles in 2006, mostly to customers in China's Hunan Province. Could Changfeng really be serious about going up against the likes of Toyota (2,542,525 light vehicles sold in the United States in 2006) and Ford (2,901,090 light vehicles sold in the United States in the same year) in the U.S. market? If so, it would have to come up with more, and better designed, models than the Liebao. But most automakers work with independent design firms, and—as every executive at the show knew—the leading European design shops, like Giugiaro in Italy, are completely sold out for years to come. (Many of them are working with other Chinese auto companies.)

But Changfeng thought they had that one covered: They had lured a former Ford engineer, Chinese-born Allen Han, to be their head of product development. Why would Han jump from a high-paying job in Detroit, Michigan, to a lower-paying one in the industrial city of Changsha, Hunan? "In Detroit, the working conditions and the pay are much better," explained Li Jianxin, chairman of Changfeng. "But the city lacks energy and passion. We have plenty of that in China."[2]

Companies have been battling each other for talent for years, of course. But there's no doubt in our minds that competition among everyone from everywhere for everything is going to get much more intense. We're going to see people vying with each other for everything from palm oil in Malaysia to English-speaking office staff in Shanghai, shipping containers in Shenzhen, shelf space in Monterrey, factory workers in Bratislava, pellets of iron ore in São Paulo, natural gas in Moscow, customers in Dhaka, cotton in Kampala, senior managers in Warsaw, and business-class seats on the flight from London to Beijing.

In the spring of 1976, *The New Yorker* ran a cover illustration called "View of the World from Ninth Avenue" by Saul Steinberg that has become famous, iconic of the parochial mind-set. Do you remember it? Manhattan looms large in the foreground, the rest of the United States occupies a greenish rectangle in the middle distance, and on the faraway horizon lurk three low-lying blobs labeled China, Russia, and Japan. India doesn't even make the cut.

That cover would never run now because China and Russia, along with India, Mexico, Brazil, Turkey, the Czech Republic, and the other rapidly developing economies, crowd into our everyday lives from every direction at every minute of every hour. We all know about the global sourcing of products and services—that our shirts are stitched in Romania, our apricots harvested in Turkey, the computer help-line staffed from India, and laptops assembled in China. But shirt labels and Indian accents are just the tip of the very large iceberg that is the challengers' presence in our everyday lives.

Have you heard of Johnson Electric? Sounds like a midsize maker of switches and junction boxes, based in, let's say, Tyler, Texas? Wrong. Johnson Electric is a major player in the world market for micromotors. When you adjust the rearview mirror on your car or attack your carpet with a vacuum cleaner equipped with a spinning brush bar, the family of Wang Seng Liang smiles another profitable smile. In 1959, Wang founded Johnson Electric in Hong Kong to churn out the tiny motors that propelled the cheap toy boats and airplanes exported by Chinese traders to the United States. (The name Johnson Electric was chosen for use outside China so the company wouldn't sound "too Chinese.") Today, Johnson Electric is number one in motion actuators, the little engines that whirr around us constantly, powering hospital beds, surveillance cameras, foot spas, toothbrushes, coffee grinders, juicers, joysticks, toilets, printers, blood pressure pumps, headlight washers, seat adjusters, and cooling fans.

Does the name Cemex ring a bell? When you drive through the Channel Tunnel on your way from London to Paris, climb the steps of Turner Stadium in Atlanta, touch down on the tarmac at Sondika Airport in Bilbao, or lounge on the patio for drinks with your friends in El Dorado, California, that gray stuff in the walls or beneath your feet is supplied by Cemex of Mexico, the world's largest ready-mix concrete player.

Unless you're in the micromotor or cement business, it's pretty easy to get used to—and, in fact, enjoy—the incredible cornucopia of goods and services available to you from around the world, but the implications of competing with everybody from everywhere for everything get more personal when you think about, for example, college admissions.

It's already tough enough competing with the best students from across the country for admission into one of the top-ranked schools in the United States, but today you're in the race with the finest students from around the world. At the twenty top business schools in the United States, international students now account for 20 to 30 percent of all enrollees. At the University of California, 23 percent of the undergrads were born outside the United States. Not many years from now, sons and daughters raised in the United States may be the ones traveling out of their home country for an MBA, obsessing about whether to attend the China Europe International Business School (CEIBS) in Shanghai (one of the top fifty business schools in the world, so they claim) or the Skolkovo School of Management, outside Moscow.

And finally, let's get down to one of the most important activities of all: baseball. In the 2007 season, the best pitcher for the New York Yankees was not the comeback kid Roger Clemens, who contracted for as much as $28 million for the season, depending on the number of games pitched, but Chien-Ming Wang, born in Taiwan. In 2005, 242 of the 829 players—29 percent—on the opening-day rosters of the thirty Major League Baseball clubs were born outside the United States, in such countries as Cuba, Mexico, and Venezuela.[3]

Now baseball is starting to catch on in Africa, too. During the off-season of 2007, the New York Mets took a four-day goodwill tour to Ghana, where they conducted a clinic for kids in the capital city of Accra. "Not everyone's going to play soccer, not everyone's going to play tennis," said George Ntim, president of the African Development Foundation, "so there has to be another sport for them. Why not baseball?"[4] Will American baseball end up like tennis at Wimbledon has for the British? Will Americans desperately hope, year after year, that a U.S.-based team will make it to the World Series?

Globality will affect everyone, everywhere, everything. And that means you. One day, it may be your company that Tata Group wants to acquire, your child calling home from Shanghai, your job moving to Mexico City, and your brand-new Changfeng gleaming in the driveway.

It's just a matter of time.

THE TSUNAMI

Or is it?

Remain calm. This is hardly the first time that a set of competitors from developing economies has risen up and challenged the established players—the companies we call "incumbents"—of the developed markets. In the early 1900s, they sprang up from the United States to challenge the dominance of the stodgy European manufacturers. In the 1970s, Japanese manufacturers pounced on the U.S. market with their low-cost, high-quality products. In the 1980s, with help from NAFTA, Mexico fielded its set of challengers. In the 1990s, the contenders hailed from Korea.

You can go back even further if you like, to the wave of upstart European enterprises that, in the early 1500s, sailed out to the established societies of India and China to trade silver for spice.

However, although all those previous waves had tremendous impact on the world, this wave of global challengers from the rapidly developing economies is far bigger and much more significant, and will have a far greater effect on the world than any of the previous ones. This one is more like a tsunami—a series of low, powerful waves caused by an undersea disruption that crash against the shore and surge far inland—than the single sharp crest of a tidal wave.

Why? Three reasons:

- *The unique origins of the challengers*
- *The unprecedented global access they have enjoyed*
- *Their insatiable hunger for achievement*

The country origins of China and India, in particular, are very different from those of the United States, Japan, or Korea. They are massive countries with huge populations. Not only does that mean they have abundant (low-wage) workforces, it also means they have astounding potential as markets and, what's more, that they are important providers of resources as well. The combined population of India and China is about 2.6 billion people, or 37 percent of the planet's humanity. Add in 200 million Brazilians, 143 million Russians, 110 million Mexicans, and 150 million eastern Europeans, and you have a total of more than 3 billion people in the rapidly developing economies. That's three times the number of people in the combined populations of western Europe (400 million), the United States (300 million), and Japan (127 million). And that's not even considering the hundreds of millions more people in Southeast Asia, the Middle East, and Africa.

The second key factor is the unprecedented access to everyone, everywhere, and everything that the challenger companies have enjoyed—thanks to, among many other developments, worldwide communications nets and international laws and policies favorable to commerce. Information, data, talent, organizations, capital, systems—it's all available at the click of a mouse, at the other end of the cell phone connection, or within a day's plane ride. Everyone from everywhere can get access to everything.

That was far from true in the sixteenth century, when Portuguese merchants in Macao had to build their own ships on the spot and when French traders were forced to borrow silver from moneylenders in the local markets, a situation guaranteed to drive up interest rates. Nor was it true in the Japanese wave of the 1970s, well before the Internet played a major role in communications and commerce, and when the only way to scout the U.S. markets and study the habits of the natives was to send in undercover product-development teams. (That's still the best, but hardly the only, way.) Even in the 1990s, when Korea staged its challenge, the World Wide Web was not yet the force it is today, and the world had not opened so widely.

The third factor that makes this wave so remarkable is the unrelenting hunger that people in the rapidly developing economies have for learning, improvement, achievement, success, and recognition. You have to remember that Russia, India, and China were virtually out of the world economy for most of the twentieth century. With the opening of their societies, and then the growing success of their economies, people and companies are more and more driven to achieve at higher and higher levels.

People in the rapidly developing economies see the world fundamentally differently than it is viewed from the developed ones. The United States, Japan, and western Europe are slow-growth economies characterized by wealthy consumers, well-established companies, well-defined markets, and (relatively) well-functioning infrastructures. China, India, Russia, Brazil, and the others are fast-growth economies with young and poor populations, companies inexperienced in modern business, overburdened infrastructures, and markets of unknown dimension.

Everybody in the rapidly developing economies is hurrying to catch up, grab hold of opportunities, improve their fortunes, and help their countries take their deserved place in world society. That's why business books are selling like hotcakes in China, why farmers in the villages of India are working second jobs in business-process outsourcing, why retail malls are sprouting up in Ekaterinburg, Russia, and why executives and workers alike routinely put in long work-days, sometimes seven days a week.

THE SEVEN STRUGGLES

Who are these challengers?
   How did they achieve their success?
   How do they think?
   What do they do?
   Where are they going?
We know from observing their progress, visiting their companies, working with them, and talking with their leaders that the

challengers are well versed in the principles and practices of Western business orthodoxy. After all, many of their senior executives were educated in the West. Anand Mahindra holds a Harvard MBA. Baba Kalyani did his postgraduate work at MIT. Patrick Wang studied electrical engineering at Purdue. Shi Zhengrong has a degree in physics from the University of New South Wales.

But these leaders did not return home and instantly apply to their companies what they had learned from the case-study method. They synthesized Western ideas with attitudes, practices, and concepts from their own and other cultures, which causes them to take actions and make statements that, to incumbents, can seem heterodox, counterintuitive, even baffling—but also enticing and provocative, and we'll provide many examples in this book.

Not only have we gotten to know dozens of challenger companies in the rapidly developing economies and talked with their leaders about what it means to compete with everyone from everywhere for everything, we have also worked closely with incumbents as they have worked to adjust their thinking and adapt their operations to the new global reality.

Based on our experience and analysis, and on a wealth of data and knowledge, we have to conclude that, in general, the challengers are learning faster about how to succeed in the age of globality than most incumbents are. This should not be surprising, given the different starting points of the challengers and the incumbents and the vast gap between their current positions. The challengers have everything to gain. The incumbents, it often seems, have a great deal to lose.

That does not mean, however, that the rapid rise of the challenger companies will lead to the certain fall of the incumbents. That is not what happened in any of the previous waves of global change. Some incumbents will lose their current positions (some already have), but some will not. Some challengers will become world leaders; others will drop off the radar completely.

To survive, compete, and succeed in the age of globality, every company will have to face and work its way through a set of challenges and difficulties that we call the seven struggles of globality.

In a world that often prefers simple answers and bullet-point solutions, we at first balked a little at the word *struggles*. Isn't that word kind of negative? Won't people be put off by the thought of a business activity that doesn't have a clear resolution? Maybe. But anyone who has set foot on the stage of international business knows that performing there is often complex and always dynamic.

So, we decided that the word *struggles* is the most descriptive and accurate one, because these issues are decidedly different from tasks or projects that can be neatly defined, handily addressed, and checked off the to-do list. They are ongoing and often complex concerns that rarely have simple, one-off answers and that need to be constantly revisited. They can be more or less under control, but never really get solved. They are:

- *Minding the Cost Gap*
- *Growing People*
- *Reaching Deep into Markets*
- *Pinpointing*
- *Thinking Big, Acting Fast, Going Outside*
- *Innovating with Ingenuity*
- *Embracing Manyness*

No company—challenger or incumbent—can compete in globality without engaging in one or more (and probably all) of these struggles. But do not turn back! There are many actions that companies can take as they engage in the struggles, and we discuss them in detail in the chapters that follow.

MINDING THE COST GAP

The first struggle involves cost.

Low cost is the great lever that enabled small, local companies in the rapidly developing economies to evolve into global challengers, and their access to low-cost resources—first and foremost labor, but also equipment, raw materials, and components—continues to give them a great advantage over incumbents in developed economies.

However, globality is more than a never-ending battle to achieve the lowest cost in every aspect of every business. The challengers—especially as they seek to move from commodity suppliers to full-fledged global competitors—will not have such complete control over their costs and will find that their focus on low cost will be a disadvantage in some areas, especially when competing for talent. Allen Han went for the Changfeng offer, but he was a mid-level engineer at Ford. No matter how much passion there may be in Changsha, not everybody will fall for that city's allure.

To overcome their disadvantage in cost, incumbents can build on a number of other advantages—such as innovation and brand legacy—to offset the cost difference. The issue, therefore, is not so much about achieving the absolute low cost but about keeping a vigilant eye on the cost differential. No competitor will be able to succeed if its costs are significantly higher than others in its industry—except in those rare cases when it is able to completely transform a category or process through innovation. Even then, its advantage likely will not last for long.

The struggle for incumbents—and increasingly for challengers—will be constantly minding the cost gap. The most important actions they can take are:

- *Optimizing with Labor*
- *Clustering*
- *Superscaling*
- *Simplifying*

GROWING PEOPLE

According to various analyses, there is a huge reservoir of talent available worldwide. The rapidly developing economies are supposedly flooded with educated and skilled workers and managers while, in the developed economies, the talent pool shrinks and wages rise.

That may be, but there's still a talent struggle involved in globality, and that's aligning the right talent with the work to be done—getting the optimal number of people with the right capabilities to do the required tasks in the right places at the right times. It's partly an issue of quantity. Despite the great numbers of workers, there often aren't enough qualified people available to meet demand. In India, the attrition rate in the outsourcing industry has been as high as 50 percent annually.[5] That's why Infosys Technologies, the giant Indian outsourcing firm, is looking to hire six thousand Chinese employees over the next five years.[6]

Sometimes, the work is located in places where there aren't enough workers available to do it. That's one of the reasons why China has some 140 million migrant workers, people who leave their homes and families to do itinerant work in distant cities. The problem is acute in eastern Europe, where workers have been emigrating to the West by the millions to find higher-paying jobs, forcing some companies with facilities in Poland to increase wages, recruit from Africa and the Middle East, or shut down their operations altogether.

The struggle is mostly, however, about quality, because even people who have what seem to be the right credentials for the job (like an engineering degree or a training certificate) don't always have the actual skills needed or at the right level, or the ability to perform as required. For example, a great percentage of people in India who have college-level training in English are not truly fluent.

Companies, therefore, will find themselves struggling with the issue of alignment and, with frustrating frequency, the misalignment of the many players involved. The successful ones focus on developing their methods of recruitment, development, and deployment. They are making their own talent, rather than just fitting people into boxes, by focusing on these key actions:

- *Recruiting for Rapid Growth*
- *Developing for Depth*

   • *Deploying for Early Results*
   • *Letting Leaders Build*

Reaching Deep Into Markets

Much of the history of globalization within domestic markets has been about incumbents doing business with a very small percentage of the large populations in these markets, if they sold into them at all.

Now incumbents are targeting, much more aggressively than ever before, the rapidly developing economies as the enormous and valuable markets they are—attracted not only by the size of their populations but also by the increasing wealth and sophistication of both industrial customers and general-market consumers. Rather than play on the surface of these enormous markets, the challenge is to go deep and reach the hundreds of millions of potential buyers waiting there.

However, incumbents are often confounded in their efforts to reach deep by many factors, including their inadequate understanding of consumers, the many cultural differences that exist—not just in comparison to developed markets but within a single market—infrastructural lacks, brand legacies, and complex and often unfathomable distribution and retail systems.

These issues make it difficult enough to capture the "easy" segments of the markets in the rapidly developing economies, which are only the tip of the population iceberg. At least another billion people in China, India, and eastern Europe have yet to join the global consumer society—and, over the next several decades, have the potential to do so.

The struggle for incumbents (and for challengers as they expand into other rapidly developing economies) is to achieve penetration of the well-defined and easily accessible pockets of populations and then reach deep into the mass markets beyond, by executing on one or more of the following:

- *Creating New Categories*
- *Finding the Sweet Spot*
- *Localizing*
- *Distributing Amid Chaos*
- *Doing Business with Business*
- *Stepping into Other Markets*

PINPOINTING

Over the years, many international players have worked to offshore some elements of their operations, primarily to reduce costs. But the challengers have begun to completely rethink their value chains, disaggregating and modularizing them, then siting the various elements in the optimal locations around the world and, as a result, creating compelling advantages of both cost and scale.

Incumbents have typically thought of the rapidly developing countries as low-cost locations that can support only low-cost work and don't differentiate sharply enough the particular advantages (or disadvantages) of one location in comparison to another.

But many challengers have shown themselves to be more relentless and even ruthless about scrutinizing the elements of the value chain, breaking them into discrete elements, relocating them—and then folding them into their business processes in a way that makes distance and location seem almost irrelevant.

As conditions change within the rapidly developing economies, and as other developing economies (e.g. Vietnam, Malaysia, Pakistan) improve their skills, incumbents and challengers alike will struggle to constantly reevaluate which locations are best for which activities now and in the future, to support the following actions:

- *Connecting with Customers*
- *Distributing Complexity*
- *Reinventing the Business Model*

Thinking Big, Acting Fast, Going Outside

In the Western business orthodoxy, mergers, acquisitions, partnerships, and joint ventures are pursued for many reasons, such as to increase scale, extend geographical reach, add capabilities and, yes, occasionally for less-than-strategic purposes, such as whim, revenge, or adventure.

For the challengers, acquisitions provide a speedy way to catch up with the incumbents. The challengers are young companies, or former state-owned bureaucracies, or midsize companies with few resources and out-of-date systems. Acquisitions, mergers, and collaborations enable challengers to make the great leaps forward they need to bring themselves into the contest. As a result, they tend to place the opportunity for knowledge building higher on the list of reasons to make acquisitions than incumbents do.

Part of the reason for this is the hunger the challengers feel. They want to move as fast as possible, which often means they don't want to take the time to build a capability or acquire the knowledge they need by themselves. As a result, both the number and the size of merger and acquisition deals completed by the challengers have soared in the past five years.

Readers may be familiar with post merger integration (PMI), the process of rationalizing and integrating two companies that have joined forces in a merger or an acquisition. In the developed economies, post-merger integration is often an exercise in cost cutting, staff reduction, facilities rationalization, and the force-fitting of one company into the template of another.

Challengers, however, are more likely to work to truly understand what it is the acquired company has to offer and learn what it has to teach as they pursue the following actions:

- *Scaling Up*
- *Building Brands*
- *Filling Capability Gaps*
- *Bartering*

INNOVATING WITH INGENUITY

Incumbents labor mightily to innovate and worry about innovation as much as they achieve it. Great research labs and creative departments pursue new ideas and technologies, materials, and processes. Engineers, designers, managers, and marketers constantly think about new products and services that could and should be created and how existing ones might be improved or refined to add a new twist or feature.

The challengers generally have not been associated with breakthrough innovation. Rather, they have become known as expert copiers, interpreters, simplifiers, and adapters of technologies, products, and services created elsewhere by others.

But the challengers, more and more, are practicing their own particular style of innovation. They have not had big R&D budgets or heavyweight development talent. They don't have enormous databases filled with knowledge, shelves stacked with prototypes, or thousands of patents on file. They rarely disrupt an industry with a blockbuster breakthrough.

What they do have, however, is ingenuity. They're quick-witted and resourceful, able to quickly whip up new variations on a theme with whatever resources are at hand. They have deep local knowledge—of what people want and need, what resources are available, and what limits are constraining their choices—that enables them to introduce to the marketplace reimagined, reinvented, and reconfigured technologies, products, and services that can win. And if they don't win, they can cook up another ten possibilities in no time.

The struggle in globality is achieving the right combination of formalized innovation and on-the-fly ingenuity. These actions characterize ingenious innovation:

- *Adapting*
- *Leveraging*
- *Rapid-fire Inventing*

Embracing Manyness

Incumbent companies have a bias toward standardization. One-world strategies. Centralized authority. Home office. Alignment of people and ideas.

The struggle of globality is learning to live with and thrive on manyness.

Globality implies many countries, economies, markets, locations, facilities. There are no centers. No home markets. No foreignness. No hierarchy of location.

Globality encompasses the use of more than one strategy or approach for different cultures, products and services, customers, times, and competitive situations.

Globality takes advantage of many kinds of backgrounds, skills, talents, ideas, organizations, systems, and states of being.

Manyness is an unfamiliar and even uncomfortable concept for those who are looking for the single best way, the ideal organizational structure, the signature leadership style.

Although challengers operate using organizational structures and practices that are quite different from those of most incumbents, it's not that they have fundamentally reinvented management science. Rather, they have taken from the knowledge and wisdom that's been accumulating for nearly a century in the developed markets, adapted it to the operating models of their own economies, and created interesting syntheses that are particularly suited to the age of globality.

The struggle is to determine which management practices from developed markets can be successfully transplanted or adapted for each developing market and situation, which ones must be (sometimes painfully) rejected, how to take advantage of manyness in all its forms, and how to manage these key actions:

- *Choosing Global Presence*
- *Retaining Local Character*
- *Polycentralizing*

IMPLICATIONS: RECOGNIZE THE URGENCY

Are you ready for the era of globality? Is your company prepared to enter the environment in which everybody, everywhere, is competing for everything?

Many companies in the West and Japan continue to act as if they are unaware of how quickly things are changing and bask in a state of blissful denial of the emerging reality. Many leaders still adhere to a Western-centric view of the world, as if they expect that things will eventually snap back to the "way it was" in 1991 or 1982 or 1967 or whatever their worldview default date may be.

Most businesspeople we know and work with, however, are well aware that the global landscape of business has been fundamentally altered and that the tsunami of change is roaring in.

The problem is that they don't know exactly what to do about the changes they discover around them. How should they meet and beat competitors on the competitors' home turf? How can they fend off the challengers' attacks on their customers? Will speed and flexibility always trump size and legacy assets? When low-cost, high-quality products are taken for granted, how can a company create advantage?

The leaders of the challenger companies will feel in their guts that they have a tremendous amount to gain in the era of globality—that they can become the new global players, call the shots, gobble up markets, and stride boldly across the world. The leaders of incumbents will sense that they have much more to lose than the challengers do: share, stature, dominance, talent, intellectual property, and jobs—their own included.

During the earlier phases of globalization, many companies saw "going global" as a choice; they could make a decision to participate in the phenomenon by operating in low-cost countries, seeking out foreign markets, and availing themselves of global supply-chain resources—or not.

Globality, however, allows less room for choice. It may be possible for some companies to achieve success by staying small, serving limited markets, or connecting with the world through intermediaries, but most companies will not have that option. They must join the game on the global playing field or face the possibility of being pushed to the sidelines, perhaps never to return.

Our goal is to help companies shift their mind-sets in light of the new global realities so they can successfully take advantage of the vast opportunities that globality offers.

When we discussed these issues with one executive of a large company, he said, "We don't have to move too quickly. We've got five or six years to figure that out." Twiddling their thumbs will likely prove to be a mistake for his company, as it will for most companies throughout the world. By the time they realize they're in trouble, it will be too late. The only way to succeed is by competing with everyone from everywhere for everything.

Starting now.

CHAPTER 2

TSUNAMI

"It is our destiny to go global."
*Juan Antonio Alvarez, Compañía Sudamericana
de Vapores (CSAV)*

A weekly newspaper in Wenzhou Province, one of the most prosperous regions in China, posed this question to readers: "If forced to choose between your business and your family, which would it be?" Sixty percent of the respondents chose business. Twenty percent chose family. Twenty percent couldn't make up their minds.[1]

No wonder the global challengers have risen up like a tsunami.

A tsunami begins with the sudden shift of the earth's crust or the eruption of an undersea volcano. The location of the shift and the power of the shock determine just how potent the tsunami eventually will be. After all, not every seabed crack and volcanic sputter catalyzes a worldwide wave of change.

The tsunami of the challengers had its origins in some of the world's largest and most important countries and was created not just with a single, shuddering bump but by a whole series of societal shocks and economic eruptions over a period of several decades.

One of the most significant came in 1978, just a year after the death of Mao Zedong, chairman of the Chinese Communist Party, when the great gate to China began to swing open, allowing a freer flow of business into and out of the country.

The opening of China—which on its own was probably enough to cause the tsunami—was followed in 1986 by the restructuring (perestroika) and move toward openness (glasnost) of the Soviet Union, which eventually helped to bring about its implosion in 1991 and the subsequent tumbling down of the walls that had isolated the countries of eastern Europe.

Hungary had been busily privatizing since 1968, so it hit the ground running when Communist rule collapsed there in 1989. The modern Czech Republic and Slovakia came into being in 1993.

In that same year, India instituted a number of fundamental reforms that produced its own burst of internal growth and international expansion, after decades of fitful attempts to get its economy moving with one five-year plan after another and an economic crisis in 1991.

In 1997, Brazil passed several constitutional amendments that allowed for greater participation by private companies in different sectors of the national economy, opened up opportunities in all segments, redefined corporate structures for local companies, and altered the monopoly status of Telebrás, the telecommunications leader, and Petrobras, the national oil and energy giant.

Bulgaria, after a long period of instability, pulled itself together and was admitted to the European Union in 2007.

In the last five years, Turkey, which has traditionally served both East and West, has experienced 7-percent annual growth of its gross domestic product, and its exports have more than doubled.

These shocks and shifts, one after another, kept adding force to the wave of change. Then, just as a tsunami can be further kicked up by the surrounding weather conditions, this surge was further intensified by two environmental factors: first, the unprecedented availability of global resources of all kinds and the challengers' easy access to them, and second, a remarkable state of being the challengers developed over time that can best be characterized as hunger—a practical hunger to improve, an intellectual hunger to learn, and an emotional hunger to achieve.

Already potent due to its origins, made even more powerful and greater in scale as a result of external factors, the tsunami rapidly concentrated in force as it approached the shore of international business.

Now people could see its dimensions much more clearly. Suddenly, they realized that, inevitably, it would hit. Assets that had seemed well protected, looked as if they could be broken loose. Positions that had felt completely secure, suddenly felt vulnerable.

No one could accurately predict just how deep into the landscape the tsunami would penetrate or how long it might keep thundering in.

But don't worry too much. It's only a metaphor.

THE BCG CHALLENGER 100

The challengers, however, are the real thing. There are at least three thousand challenger companies that have achieved a healthy measure of success and prominence in their rapidly developing markets and beyond. Of those, we selected a hundred of the biggest, most successful, most influential, and most interesting ones to study further, learn from, and understand. Many of them are featured in this book.

The BCG Challenger 100, as we call them, come from fourteen countries: Argentina, Brazil, Chile, China, Egypt, Hungary, India, Indonesia, Malaysia, Mexico, Poland, Russia, Thailand, and Turkey. Sixty-six of them are based in Asia—forty-one in China, twenty in India. Thirteen come from Brazil, seven from Mexico, six from Russia. (See the complete list in the Appendix.)

The BCG Challenger 100 companies participate in all kinds of industries. Thirty-four provide industrial goods; fourteen make consumer durables; seventeen are resource extractors; fourteen of them offer food, beverage, and cosmetics products; four make technology equipment. The remaining seventeen operate in a wide variety of fields, including pharmaceuticals, mobile communication services, shipping, and infrastructure.

Total revenue of the BCG Challenger 100 group of companies reached $1.2 trillion in 2006. That sum may seem small in comparison to the sales of Fortune 500 companies (Wal-Mart, Exxon-Mobil, and General Motors, after all, had a combined 2006 revenue of $900 billion), but the challengers are growing extremely fast. Total revenue for the BCG Challenger 100 grew 30 percent a year for the 2004–2006 period, three times that of companies in the S&P 500 and Fortune 500. International revenues for the BCG Challenger 100 grew at 37 percent between 2005 and 2006, faster than total revenues. In 2006, the BCG Challenger 100 companies generated 34 percent of revenues offshore, up from 32 percent in 2004.

What's more, these companies are highly profitable. The BCG Challenger 100 earned 17-percent operating profits in 2006, in comparison to a margin of 14 percent for the S&P 500 U.S.-based companies, 8 percent for Japan's Nikkei companies, and 7 percent for Germany's DAX companies.

And their stock performed well, too. The seventy-five publicly traded companies had a market capitalization of $680 billion in March 2006. We calculated the total shareholder return (TSR) and market capitalization for sixty-four of these companies, excluding eleven that are traded on exchanges that make it difficult to gather reliable data. The group of sixty-four achieved a TSR of 418 percent from January 2002 through June 2007. This compared to 221 percent for the MSCI Emerging Market Index and 47 percent for the S&P 500 Index. As of June 2007, total market capitalization for the sixty-four had increased 447 percent, reaching $954 billion.

Clearly, the vendors have become serious contenders.

COUNTRY ORIGINS

The countries that the challenger companies come from had been isolated from the world of international commerce for long periods of time during the twentieth century. (India and China had, for centuries prior, been two of the most important economies in the world. In 1700, the combined income of those two countries was about half the world's total.) For the most part, these fourteen countries missed out on the growth of industry, rise of technology, accumulation of business ideas and practices, and building of experience through market competition that took place in the twentieth century.

So when their economies began to open, the world was rather startled at how different the business environment looked in these countries. Where were the big corporations? the modern factories? the sprawling R&D labs? the branded retail chains? the distribution networks? the industry associations? Where, for that matter, were the eight-lane highways, mighty bridges, international airports, vast computer networks, and nationwide telephone systems?

There were none. At least none that Westerners could recognize or think of as modern. Rather, across these economies, there was a maze of state-owned enterprises and politically constipated bureaucracies, tens of thousands—perhaps hundreds of thousands—of mom-and-pop shops and street kiosks, antiquated factories (Changfeng was founded in No. 7319 Factory of Chinese People's Liberation Army, which had originally been equipped for gun repair), distribution systems that relied as much on rickshaws and donkeys as they did on motorized vehicles, companies operating in schools with teachers as managers, entrepreneurs set up in abandoned structures (Johnson Electric's first factory outside Hong Kong was in a Shenzhen village grain shed), people working with their hands where there should be automated production lines, and machines still in operation that would have been retired by the incumbents decades ago.

When the period of globalization began, these too-young or over-bloated, inexperienced or outdated, almost completely disconnected companies suddenly found themselves working with the most sophisticated and demanding businesses from all over the world—companies from the United States, Europe, and Japan that had arrived on their shores in search of low-cost labor and materials.

It seemed natural that the local companies would serve the incumbents as vendors, jobshoppers, and low-cost suppliers. It seemed inevitable that the incumbents would think of them as "locals" and expect little more of them than to accomplish a few specific tasks—bending some metal, stitching some seams, assembling a few parts into a subcomponent—on time, on spec, and on budget.

For two decades or more, the incumbents and the locals found that the arrangement worked to the benefit of both (although there were downsides) and there was little, if any, direct competition between them. How could there be? How could Bajaj of India, maker of motorbikes with 100cc engines, compete with Honda and Kawasaki, Harley-Davidson and Triumph? How could BYD of China, a tiny start-up maker of batteries, match its products with those of Sony and Sanyo? How could Embraer of Brazil, a little-known producer of propeller and turbo-prop planes, play on the same field with Cessna, Beechcraft, and Bombardier?

The incumbents found their arrangements with the locals to be quite satisfactory. They were able, in fact, to reduce their costs substantially and, quite quickly, to produce at the quality levels they required. Some of the incumbents also discovered that their products were suited for sale into the local markets, as tricky and uncharted as they might be.

For their part, the locals learned a lot, fast. They steadily improved and expanded their operations, built expertise, and added capabilities. They grew in size and profitability. They gained confidence.

Some incumbents encouraged and supported their suppliers in their efforts to grow and improve; others didn't notice or care. After all, there was an unspoken agreement about how to slice up the global pie, and it worked well, so long as everybody kept to the script.

Then the locals started the big rewrite. Not only did they get better at what they did, they got really good. Some of them gained world-class expertise, built tremendous volume, improved quality, and made serious profits in their home markets. They expanded regionally. Went national. Created brands. Expanded into other developing economies.

They were no longer content with anonymity, subservience, and isolation. At last, some of them set their sights on the developed markets. "We proved, in the developing markets, that we were able to succeed," Sanjiv Bajaj, executive director of Bajaj Auto, told us. "That gave us the guts to go to bigger markets."

Overnight, it seemed, the locals had ceased to be locals and had become global challengers. And that's when the incumbents really sat up and took notice.

No longer could the challengers be ignored, avoided, or explained away. Hey, when did that BYD company in Shenzhen become the planet's largest maker of nickel-cadmium batteries? Who are these Russian oligarchs, and how did Lukoil get so skilled at oil exploration? Am I crazy not to get a bid from Cemex for our make-or-break construction project? Should I really be thinking about outsourcing my information processing to Wipro, based in what city is it—Bangalore? If I need photovoltaic cells, is Suntech Power in China really the number-one supplier? Can it be right that the best regional jets are made by a Brazilian company called Embraer? Wait a minute, when did the Ritz-Carlton Boston become a Taj Hotel?

Well, at least we still know who the richest man in the world is. That's right: Carlos Slim, Mexican tycoon. Estimated worth: $60 billion. (Or is it India's Mukesh Ambani?)

GLOBAL ACCESS

But how did the challengers change the scenario so quickly and successfully?

Unlike the challengers of previous waves, the companies of the rapidly developing economies had amazing access to the wealth of resources the world had to offer—knowledge, intellectual property, services, talent, capital, and much more—as well as to the markets from which they could buy and into which they could sell.

Perhaps the most important and fundamental of the resources is knowledge. The challengers have been able to seize on an incredible array of educational opportunities—which, for many, has meant studying abroad. For example, several members of the current generation of

Wangs who run Johnson Electric were educated in the United States. Patrick Wang, currently chairman and chief executive officer, studied electrical engineering at Purdue University in Indiana and joined the family business after graduating in 1972. Winnie got her bachelor of science degree from Ohio University, in Athens, Ohio, and is now vice chairman. Richard also studied electrical engineering, at the University of California, and is currently an executive director and adviser to the CEO.

Over the years, the Wangs have imported the best management and manufacturing philosophies and practices from Western and Japanese companies, including kaizen, kanban, self-directed teamwork, lean organizations, and employee stock-option plans. Every year, Patrick attends an intensive one-week program for young executives at Harvard Business School.[2]

Anand Mahindra, vice chairman and CEO of Mahindra & Mahindra, received his undergraduate education at Harvard University and earned his MBA at Harvard Business School. "If you look at my psyche," he told us, "you have to understand that my education has been abroad. There are two dimensions of an aspiration to go global. One is a strategic logic. The other is an internal or personal conviction, and I cannot deny the existence of the latter. We can pretend that we are all automatons and we work according to algorithms which are purely logical. But clearly sometimes it's aspirations that determine what you will do."

Mahindra & Mahindra was founded on the belief that Indians are second to none in the global arena and that education is key to their success. "If we use the power of the people after education," Anand Mahindra said, "then there is no reason why we can't build a company that is equal to the best."

The MBA degree has become one of the most coveted courses of study for aspiring businesspeople in the rapidly developing economies. The number of applications to U.S.-based business schools has risen steadily throughout the tsunami period of the 1990s, and students born outside the United States account for about 30 percent of the enrollment in the twenty top schools.

The demand is so intense that several universities, including Harvard Business School and Columbia's Graduate School of Business, along with others from developed economies, are planning to open management/executive education programs in India. "If you're in business, or business education, you cannot ignore India any longer," says Julian Techer, director of the Graduate School of Business at Australia's Monash University. Monash already has campuses in Malaysia and South Africa and intends to form a partnership with an Indian school soon.[3]

And, in the face of such demand, the rapidly developing economies are building or improving their own systems of business education. At the Indian School of Business, Ajit Rangnekar, deputy dean, says the institution has expanded from 128 students to 418 in the last five years. "The difficulty from now on lies not in finding good students but people to teach them and affordable places to house them. We don't have any more hostels to put the students in," he said. "Until we can find more land, we'll have to pause."[4]

In China, Shanghai's China Europe International Business School (CEIBS)—a Shanghai-based joint venture between the Chinese government and the European Union—is joining with Harvard Business School and Barcelona-based IESE Business School to create a global CEO program. "It is the first time business schools from three continents have cooperated on a common executive MBA (EMBA) program for training top managers," said Zhang Weijiong, vice president of the school. In 2005, the school's EMBA program jumped from twentieth to thirteenth in the annual *Financial Times* business school rankings, up from forty-second in 2002.[5]

Russia, too, has recognized the importance of a good business education. In 2007, President Vladimir Putin announced an initiative to improve the quality of life in his country that included some $3 billion earmarked for education.[6] An important part of Putin's program is the establishment of the School of Management in the town of Skolkovo, near Moscow, to provide business education for future executives and managers. "The demand for high-class managerial personnel is really big," President Putin said.[7]

He got that right.

But formal education has been only one source of knowledge for the challengers. They have also been able to tap into many other sources of general knowledge—as well as more specific and well-defined knowledge in the form of intellectual property—through contacts with profit and not-for-profit research labs, scientists, and patent holders around the world. They have been able to contract with suppliers possessing specialist knowledge, license it from various types of owners, or acquire companies with important intellectual assets.

In fact, as we'll discuss in chapter 7, the challengers often make acquisitions primarily for the purpose of gaining knowledge. Hindalco Industries Ltd., the flagship company of the Indian business conglomerate Aditya Birla Group, agreed to take over the Atlanta-based aluminum company Novelis Inc. for $6.4 billion in 2007. As one company executive put it, "The acquisition will help Hindalco to shorten the learning curve for technology."[8]

The challengers have also had unprecedented access to a huge range of services of every kind and description—including consultants and advisers, lawyers, engineers, architects, communications agencies, logistics providers, and design firms.

In recent years, the challengers have tapped into the global talent pools far more aggressively than ever before, bringing people with knowledge and expertise into their companies. In India, there are some fifty thousand expatriates working for Indian companies, most of whom are from the United States or the United Kingdom.[9] According to Deepak Gupta, managing director of Korn/Ferry International in New Delhi, "Everybody wants to be part of the India growth story." The company says that there were about 1,000 foreigners holding executive positions in India as of early 2007, compared to just 143 in 2005. Korn/Ferry projects that the number will double by 2009.[10] There are thousands of eastern Europeans working in the United Kingdom and other western European countries, thousands of Chinese working in Poland and other countries in eastern Europe, hundreds of thousands of Taiwanese working in Shanghai, and on and on.

The challengers have also have greater access to goods than ever before. They have purchased components, equipment, systems, and even entire facilities from suppliers abroad.

In some industries, such as energy, the challengers have been aided in their efforts to gain access to raw materials by the governments of the rapidly developing economies in which they operate. According to a report called "The Changing Role of National Oil Companies in International Energy Markets," by the Baker Institute Energy Forum, "Asian and Russian national oil companies have increasingly begun to compete for strategic resources in the Middle East and Eurasia, in some cases knocking the Western majors out of important resource development plays. Russia's Lukoil is becoming a major international player in key regions such as the Middle East and Caspian Basin. Firms such as India's ONGC and IOC; China's Sinopec and CNPC; and Malaysia's Petronas have been successful in Africa and Iran, with eyes now on investments in Saudi Arabia, Kuwait, and Iraq. Many of these emerging national oil companies are bankrolled or have operations subsidized by their national governments, with geopolitical and strategic aims factored into investments rather than purely commercial considerations."[11]

And the scope, speed, and ease of the access to all these resources—and many others we haven't discussed—have been increased substantially by a number of other factors, including new communications technologies, the falling of trade barriers, streamlined and favorable regulations, and the rise of intermediaries whose role is precisely to make connections between companies and the resources they need, worldwide.

Not only have the challengers enjoyed access to global resources, they have also been able to enter global markets with remarkable ease and efficiency, thanks to international trade agreements like the World Trade Organization (WTO), the rise of distributors and big retailers, the emergence of sophisticated shipping and logistics facilitators, and the role of the Internet in connecting everybody from everywhere with everything.

The challengers have sold tangible goods, from natural resources to components to finished products, by working with established distributors, retailers, and private labelers in both developed economies and developing economies outside their own. The megaretailers—such as The Home Depot, Lowe's, Circuit City, Best Buy, and Target in the United States—have provided especially speedy entrée into developed markets. If a challenger can crack into even a single one of these retailers, it can gain virtually immediate access to the entire U.S. market and quickly leap to a 10- to 15-percent market share. This route simply was not available to challengers of the previous waves.

The global markets have been just as open for the sale of services, including business-process outsourcing and IT offshoring, usually facilitated by intermediaries in developed countries and by the Internet.

Access to markets was fundamental in getting the Chinese economy going in the early stages of the tsunami. The first companies to rise in China were exporters, mostly based in the special economic zones in the south of the country. Much of China's infrastructure—power generation, roads, port capacity, rail, telecommunications—has been developed to support the exporters.

Access to global markets also helped jump-start the Indian economy. Although the Indian challengers were service providers rather than exporters, their success in meeting the demands of overseas customers created a virtuous circle similar to China's.

Similarly, access to global markets has enabled Russia's energy companies to expand into western Europe and gain a dominant position (politically as well as commercially) in many countries there. Embraer (Brazil) has built a global position with its aircraft, Cemex (Mexico) with cement. And the list goes on.

INSATIABLE HUNGER

Even with this virtually unlimited availability of and access to global resources and markets, the locals might not have taken advantage of it without the remarkable hunger they felt for achievement, success, and worldwide recognition. This hunger infused the culture, and people in the rapidly developing economies developed a remarkable business-mindedness—an intense entrepreneurial spirit and a near obsession with work and commercial affairs—that seems even more intense than that of the most business-minded of developed countries, the United States.

The hunger is tangible for many people. There are many mouths to feed, and wages are so low there is little money to fill them. The hunger is also intellectual and emotional. People see tremendous opportunities in their home economies, as well as abroad. They have a strong desire to prove themselves and are keen to take a role on the world stage. What's more, as their societies gain success and stature, individuals and companies have become increasingly confident. And so the virtuous cycle feeds itself.

Peter Hessler wrote about this business fever in an article called "China's Boomtowns" that appeared in *National Geographic*. "The government motto of the Lishui Economic Development Zone is 'Each person does the work of two; two days' work is done in one,'" he writes. "The slogan may be too modest. From 2000 to 2005, the city's population went from 160,000 to 250,000, and the local government invested 8.8 billion dollars in infrastructure for the region it administers. During those five years, infrastructure investment was five times the amount spent in the previous half century. In money terms, what was once 50 days' work is now done in one."[12]

Similarly, many office workers in Shanghai are so driven by the desire to improve their lot that they work after hours as street vendors. One woman, a clerk at a travel agency, sells lollipops in the evenings after dinner and makes an average of 500 yuan (about $65) a week. According to an article in *China Daily*, "Most of the vendors regard roadside vending not just as a way to make extra cash, but rather as a good way to build their experience of running a business, which might benefit them later in life should they decide to set up a more traditional company."[13]

Such an obsession with work and commerce has its downside. According to a study of white-collar professionals conducted by Beijing Normal University, up to 70 percent of white-collar workers in China put in an average of ten hours per day and take no vacations. "The study of professionals in major cities showed most white-collar workers are stressed at the thought of losing their jobs or being able to 'survive' in the fierce employment market."[14]

Central Europeans also demonstrate a remarkable drive to put in work hours. Poles work an average of 1,984 hours a year, in comparison to 1,777 for American workers and 1,362 for Germans. "These people are really hungry," says Stefaan Vandevelde, managing director of Delphi Europe. "They work day and night."[15]

Indian businesspeople also work long hours. According to the Grant Thornton International Business Report 2007, Indian business leaders—along with their counterparts in Argentina—work the longest, at 57 hours a week, and were the third most stressed in the world, behind China and Taiwan, in 2006.[16]

Even so, the survey shows that India tops the chart when it comes to optimism. Most people in the rapidly developing economies, it seems, are looking up and forward, while many in the developed countries are looking over their shoulder.

CHAMPIONS OF CHINA

The challengers have done a lot of catching up. And, as they have risen, each country has developed its own particular strengths. China has focused more and more on manufacturing (rather than on services as India has, or natural resource development as Russia and Brazil have) and has, as a result, created the most diverse set of challengers of all the rapidly developing economies, with leading manufacturers in consumer electronics, household appliances, tele-communications and information technology equipment, and autos.

And steel.

China is obsessed with steel. The Chinese government has long considered the steel industry to be vital for national security and economic development and critical to the growth of key industries like construction, automaking, shipbuilding, oil and gas production, as well as for major infrastructure projects like the Three Gorges Dam and facilities for the Beijing 2008 Olympic Games.

In 2005, China was by far the world's largest steel consumer, with a consumption of 350 million tons of crude steel, double the demand of all the NAFTA countries combined. China's consumption rose by about 20 percent a year from 2001 to 2005, in comparison to the demand in the thirty countries of the Organization for Economic Cooperation and Development (OECD), which rose by only about 2 percent during the same period.[17] And China's voracious appetite for steel will not be sated soon. America consumed some 7 billion tons of steel to develop its economy. Japan consumed 4 billion tons. So far, China has consumed only 2 billion tons.

For all its love of steel, China lacks the crucial raw materials for steelmaking and must import virtually all the iron ore it needs to feed its massive steel industry. As a result, China has become the world's largest importer of iron ore, bringing in some 325 million tons in 2006—40 percent of the world's transcontinental iron ore trade.

What's more, China's steel industry has long been composed of hundreds of small domestic players—most of them located in northern China, close to the country's coal-mining centers—that produce low-grade products, with productivity and profitability far below global industry standards. Chinese steel companies require, on average, thirty man-hours to produce one ton of steel, in comparison to four hours per ton in developed countries.[18] Because of their low profit margins, most of the small producers have been unable to modernize or innovate.

In 1978, seeking to satisfy China's hunger for steel and further

President Deng Xiaoping's program of economic development, a small group of government officials decided it was time to start a government-sponsored steel company that would produce high-quality products and give it the support it needed to become a world-class company.[19]

They decided to build from scratch, rather than buy an existing facility or convert another type of factory, and selected a greenfield site in Baoshan, a suburb north of Shanghai.[20] The group favored Shanghai because they did not want the new company to be associated with the small steel producers that were clustered, along with dozens of small coal-mining companies, in northern China. Shanghai had many experienced technical workers and was also well equipped with port facilities and direct shipping links to Brazil and Australia, all the better to support Baosteel's planned forays into international commerce—facilitating the import of raw materials and the export of finished goods. Most important, the east China area is filled with industries that require steel, including the makers of home appliances and automobiles.

Thanks to the continued support of the government and strong leadership under Xie Qihua, China's "Iron Lady," Baosteel has, in fact, developed into one of the world's most successful steel companies. In 1996, the Chinese government designated Baosteel as one of the country's National Champions—one of a handful of companies that the Chinese government intended to build into globally competitive multinationals by the year 2010.

As a National Champion, Baosteel has received a variety of benefits, including rights for stock-market listings, decision-making autonomy, access to state assets, and rights to conduct foreign trade. The company has also benefited from the creation of proprietary research centers funded by the government, special financial assistance (including an annual grant of RMB 20 million for R&D), direct state investments, and protective tariffs.

As National Champion, Baosteel has also sometimes been obliged to bite the bullet for the greater good of its industry and for the society as a whole. In 1998, for example, the government required

Baosteel to merge with four loss-making companies, among them Shanghai Metallurgical Holding Group Corporation and Shanghai Meishan Group Co., Ltd. The mergers left Baosteel with eighty thousand redundant workers, but the company could lay off no more than ten thousand a year.

In general, though, the National Champion status has paid off for Baosteel. Today, it is the world's sixth-largest producer of steel, with 112,000 employees, revenues of $21.5 billion in 2005, and a high-quality product mix—including cold-rolled and hot-rolled steel products, steel tubes, billet, and wire rod.[21] Baosteel commands market shares of around 50 percent in the lucrative automotive and household appliances segments and is the only Chinese steel company with the ability to compete on the global stage.

Baosteel went public in 2000, with an initial public offering on the Shanghai Stock Exchange that raised $1 billion—the largest-ever IPO in China at the time. The listed entity, Baoshan Iron & Steel Co., has emerged as one of the most profitable steel enterprises in the world. Revenues rose an average of 33 percent per year from 2000 to 2005, with an earnings before interest, taxes, depreciation, and amortization (EBITDA) margin on sales of 24 percent in 2005, twice the EBITDA margin of global steel giant U.S. Steel in the same year.[22] Productivity has also surpassed the average level in developed countries—the company needs 2.5 man-hours to produce one ton of steel.[23]

Baosteel is a source of national pride for China, an example of how economic reform, modernization, and participation in the world markets can be accomplished—and just one demonstration of China's manufacturing prowess.

STARS OF INDIA

While Chinese companies like Baosteel have made manufacturing their forte, many Indian challengers have specialized in delivering services, often demonstrating a flair for self-reinvention along the way.

Take Bangalore-headquartered Wipro. Incorporated in 1945 as Western India Vegetable Products Limited, Wipro started out producing cooking oils, bakery shortening, and edible cakes, selling its wares to households throughout Maharashtra, one of India's largest states.

In 1966, Azim Premji—Wipro's chairman and managing director today—took the company's helm when his father died suddenly. Just twenty-one years old, the young man was about to finish his engineering studies at Stanford University when he got word of his father's death and rushed back to India to take over the firm. (He eventually completed the degree by correspondence.) As the years unfolded, Premji pushed Wipro into new business lines, including the manufacture of hydraulic and pneumatic cylinders.

In 1980, the company launched an information-technology services business for the domestic market. It began developing operating systems, financial and accounting applications, databases, and systems-integration services for small- to medium-size Indian companies, procuring hardware and software from suppliers such as Intel, Motorola, Novell, and Unix Labs.

To reflect its broadened focus, the company changed its name to Wipro Limited in 1982. Today, though it still has divisions that sell other products (such as consumer care and lighting equipment), Wipro is primarily known as a global provider of IT consulting and services, outsourced R&D services, infrastructure outsourcing, and business-process services. Wipro was the first Indian company to embrace Six Sigma, the first software services company in the world to achieve Software Engineering Institute (SEI) Capability Maturing Model (CMM) Level 5 (a model of best practices for software providers), and the world's first company of any kind to achieve the People CMM Level 5.

How did this local consumer-goods manufacturer transform itself into a global IT services powerhouse? The journey started somewhat fortuitously in the late 1970s, when several multinational companies—IBM was one of them—pulled their operations out of India due to nationalistic policies adopted by the Indian government. In the early 1980s Wipro bought technology from the United States and adapted it for use in India. Within a year, Wipro produced a "made in India" multi-user mini-computer, and quickly became the leading computer company in the country. In the early 1990s, India liberalized its business regulations and some of the multinationals that had left the country returned. Indian companies found themselves competing head-on with much larger and more experienced companies in the research and development of both hardware and software, and most chose to exit the business. Wipro, finding itself with a large group of engineers who had little business to keep them occupied, sensed a business opportunity. The company approached its erstwhile suppliers and partners and established a new relationship with them—selling its engineering expertise to these companies as an engineering lab for hire. Wipro was soon collaborating with the likes of AT&T, Tandem Computers, Sun Microsystems, Novell, and Intel.

Since that time, Wipro has executed a blend of strategies centering on innovation—not only of key business processes such as building scale and managing talent but also of business models. For example, since 2000, Wipro has scaled up by acquiring sixteen companies—including mPower Inc (accounts payable), NewLogic (wireless and radio-frequency identification technology), AMS (energy consulting), Spectramind (business-process outsourcing), and Enabler (Oracle retail solutions)—that have expanded its service lines and brought it niche technology, a global footprint, industry knowledge, and business expertise. The company has paired this inorganic growth with organic expansion; for instance, through the proliferation of its global delivery centers. Its newest centers opened in Monterrey, Mexico, and Atlanta, Georgia, in 2007.

Wipro also excels at talent management. Among other approaches, it has identified its most critical strategic roles and established a succession process to ensure that there are always three to four people ready to occupy any one of those positions. And in conjunction with BITS Pilani, a premier engineering institute in India, its Wipro Academy of Software Excellence (WASE) provides a master's degree in IT/software engineering for recent college graduates holding non-IT degrees. In 2007, Wipro engaged some twenty-five hundred WASE graduates—up from fewer than thirteen hundred in 2006.

Wipro has also reinvented its business models to drive its world-wide expansion. In its domestic IT business (which grew 46 percent in fiscal year 2006-07), Wipro has positioned itself as a provider of a wide range of IT services, while in overseas markets it combines R&D services with IT outsourcing for global customers.

Sudip Nandy, Wipro's chief strategy officer, likens the domestic business model to an ever-present army that handles everything for its constituencies—supplying hardware, integrating and managing systems, developing applications. Nandy contrasts Wipro's domestic "army" with its global "air force." "We fly people over there, we parachute them into the different countries," he said. "We solve the problem and give aid where required, leave local experts in charge, and come back and give support-on-demand remotely."

These and other strategies have paid big dividends for the company. More than 95 percent of its EBIT comes from IT business and software services, which it delivers from forty-six development centers worldwide. Wipro's IT business boasts a global workforce of more than 76,000 employees, who represent more than thirty nationalities and serve more than six hundred and fifty global clients. Twenty-one percent of its revenues are generated in India (which includes revenues from its non-IT businesses), while 50 percent comes from the United States, 25 percent from Europe, and 4 percent from the rest of the world. In 2006, Wipro IT business recorded revenues of $3 billion and after-tax profits of $600 million. Wipro is currently the world's largest provider of outsourced R&D services and is among the top three offshore BPO service providers. Over six decades, Wipro's compounded revenues and net income have grown 22 percent and 31 percent, respectively.

Even though companies like Wipro and many others have achieved great success as service providers, India has been less attractive as a location for global manufacturers because of its not-so-rich domestic market, frustrating infrastructure, bureaucratic red tape, and restrictive labor policies. Between 1990 and 2005, manufacturing's contribution to the economy remained more or less stagnant, edging up from 25 percent to 27 percent. In 2005, India's manufacturing exports were only 6 percent of GDP ($37 billion), compared to 35 percent for China ($712 billion).[24]

However, as India's domestic market has developed and there has been an increase in the number of low-cost workers with advanced technical skills, more incumbents have established manufacturing operations in India. Ford, Hyundai, and Suzuki export cars from India in significant numbers. LG, Motorola, and Nokia all either make handsets in India or have plans to start doing so, with a sizable share of production being exported. Schneider, Honeywell, and Siemens have set up plants to manufacture electrical and electronic products for domestic and export markets.[25]

In addition, a clutch of globally competitive Indian manufacturing companies—many of them in the automobile industry—have inserted themselves into the global supply chain. Sundram Fasteners makes radiator caps for General Motors. New Delhi–based Moser Baer has established itself as a global manufacturer of data storage media such as DVDs and CDs.

Similarly, an aggressive group of pharmaceutical companies— India has about sixty plants that meet the stringent quality standards of the U.S. Food and Drug Administration, the largest number outside the United States itself—is opening new markets around the world.[26]

THE PROXIMITY ADVANTAGE IN MEXICO, EASTERN EUROPE, AND TURKEY

Labor costs in Mexico and parts of eastern Europe are sometimes double or triple those of the rapidly developing economies in Asia, so challengers in those countries can rarely compete on price alone, but they can offset the higher cost of labor with the lower costs of doing business that come with having proximity to customers and their markets. Supply chains get shorter, and transportation costs go down. Relationships are cheaper to manage, and communications get easier.

Genpact, a business-process outsourcing company spun off from General Electric, has a processing center based in Budapest, Hungary. Gross pay for a worker at the Budapest facility is between $950 and $1,400 a month, which is about four times the pay scale for similar workers in its centers in India. But Genpact's many European clients want their outsourcing company to be located in the same time zone as they are. "The nice thing about Hungary and Romania is that they are a two- or three-hour flight from anywhere in Europe," says Patrick Cogny, president and chief executive officer of Genpact Europe.[27]

SHORTER SUPPLY CHAINS

Between the time an order is placed with an Asian manufacturer and the time it shows up at a loading dock in the United States, sixty to ninety days have passed. The product has spent up to four weeks of that time in the hold of a cargo ship.

Supply-chain costs, including transportation, add 10 to 30 percent to the cost of manufacturing, which effectively eliminates a large portion of the cost savings. Many factors can drive up supply-chain costs, especially rush and emergency shipments.

In industries where product design and demand are relatively stable, the two- to three-month cycle is generally not a problem. Demand and supply can be planned for and managed. But in industries where designs and styles change quickly or demand is unpredictable—such as in the fashion business and consumer electronics—long supply chains can be a major disadvantage. Three months can be longer than the entire life cycle of a new dress.

Fashion delivery from eastern Europe to the United States takes half as long as it does from Asia—four to six weeks, including a day or two for delivery by truck[28]—and substantially less time to western European markets. That's why many incumbent purveyors of "fast fashion"—garments ordered and manufactured to respond to fast-changing trends—trade off the low-cost of Asia with the speedy delivery of eastern Europe. Ralph Goodstone, a U.K.-based textile entrepreneur who brokers deals between low-cost suppliers and customers in developed countries, figures that fast fashion adds a few dollars per piece when delivered from central or eastern Europe rather than from Asia. "But customers are prepared to pay," he says.

The advantages of proximity can be so significant that firms in more distant rapidly developing economies are investing in operations in central Europe. Both Infosys, the Indian software giant, and Li & Fung, the Hong Kong–based trading company, have opened offices in central Europe.[29]

Similarly, many electronics-manufacturing services (EMS) incumbents like to manufacture in Mexico to supply their customers in North America. "It was very fashionable to talk about China in 2004," said Jan Lindholm, director of corporate marketing for Elcoteq, a telecom EMS based in Finland with plants around the globe. "But in 2005 we had questions from people who had outsourced to China and were deciding to pull back closer to their markets."[30]

Airfreight can shorten the cycle time, but it's expensive and can largely negate labor savings. For example, Hewlett Packard, based in Palo Alto, California, constantly weighs the cost implications of the proximity of its suppliers in building high-end enterprise servers and storage systems—avoiding airfreight whenever possible.

When HP's customers have special requirements, like a particular software configuration or custom racking, it can be more efficient and less costly to build the systems in the regions where they will be sold. "There is a significant landed cost issue," said Jack Faber, supply-chain vice president of enterprise storage and servers for Hewlett-Packard. "We have the capability in many cases to take a product and have it built in another region, but it's likely you'd have to airfreight that product to the customer. These products have a lot of cubic feet, so that can be costly."[31]

Better Relationships

Incumbents who work with suppliers and partners offshore devote a good deal of time to managing their relationships, which can be expensive and can cause a lot of wear and tear on the people involved. Travel to Asia from locations in the United States can be difficult, time-consuming, and exhausting. A journey from a U.S. city to China or India can take twenty hours (if all goes according to schedule). If you fly out on a Monday-morning flight for China, you arrive there Tuesday evening, at a cost of several thousand dollars for a business-class seat. And you're dealing with a thirteen-hour time difference. It's inevitable that you will fade out at some point in a meeting or during dinner with a client.

As a result, U.S.-based executives seek to optimize their visits, packing as much activity as they can into the fewest days. Even so, the average stay is seven to ten days, with three or four of those days spent traveling. Although executives tend to think of a long-distance flight as useful "plane time," the reality is that the concentrated work time is often offset by long spans of inactivity as well as periods of low output, when communications are not available or jet lag kicks in.

Typically, starting up a relationship with an Asia-based vendor and launching a product consumes at least three of these prolonged trips, and maintaining the relationship once it is in operation requires frequent contact. Because of the time differences, telephone calls must often take place early in the morning or late at night, extending already-extended workdays even longer—and cell phone coverage can be spotty. E-mail messages sent at the start of a workday in China or India may arrive after the executive in the United States has signed out for the evening and may not be answered until the next day. Given the complications of travel and the difficulties of communication involved, we estimate that as much as 1 percent may be added to product cost as a result of lost time and productivity.

By contrast, flight time from Chicago to Mexico City can be as short as four hours on one of several available nonstop flights and costs less than $1,000. You can leave Chicago Monday morning, arrive in Mexico for an afternoon of work, and return Friday afternoon in time for a late dinner at home. No time difference, no jet lag.

Solectron, an electronics-manufacturing services company, worked with a customer to set up manufacturing operations in Mexico because all of the customer's engineers were located in the northeastern United States, which meant just a one-hour time difference between the engineers and the manufacturing people. The two groups could regularly and easily communicate during seven of the eight hours in a normal workday.[32]

Proximity also brings greater understanding of the customer and its markets. Central Europe has become a center for automobile manufacturing not only because costs are reasonably low but because countries there have carmaking clusters. Incumbents from Japan and Korea like to build cars in central Europe because of the proximity to western European customers. "If we try and do everything from South Korea, we cannot know what exactly European customers want," says Bae In-Kyu, the boss of Kia's plant in Slovakia.

FOUND ADVANTAGE IN BRAZIL AND RUSSIA

Brazil and Russia have built their economic rise not on low-cost work and workers or on proximity (Peter the Great knew that Russia had a proximity problem; that's why he pursued his own massive infrastructure project, the construction of Saint Petersburg, starting in 1703)—but on the abundance of low-cost natural resources.

Brazilian companies share access to a broad base of resources ranging from iron ore to agricultural feedstock, which underpins the country's thriving food-processing industry. Even so, a few Brazilian companies have made their mark through other means. Embraer, for example, has become the world's third-largest commercial aircraft manufacturer through a combination of a low-cost workforce and ingenious innovation.

Russia markets its rich energy resources either through direct exports of energy, such as natural gas, or indirectly through exports of aluminum. The challengers in the raw materials sector often generate significant cash flows that they can reinvest. Gazprom, for example, is a vertically integrated, government-controlled energy company based in Moscow that operates throughout the Russian Federation and countries in Europe. It is the largest natural gas company in the world, controlling 24 percent of global gas output and 23 percent of global gas reserves. It produces 85 percent of Russia's gas output and has complete control of the country's pipelines. In 2005, it increased its natural gas reserves by 54 percent, oil production by 44 percent, and trunk and branch pipelines by 38 percent.

Gazprom's access to abundant energy supplies provides the company with great pricing power that enables it to influence markets and deliver advantage to its home country and the companies based in it. Gazprom provides 25 percent of all natural gas to Europe. In 2004, for example, Gazprom priced liquid natural gas (LNG) to western Europeans at $160 per cubic meter and to Ukrainians at $138, while pricing it to Russians at $23.

Gazprom very clearly understands the leverage it has as a key supplier to Europe and Ukraine and is working to make sure that its role as a key supplier increases to guarantee growth and ensure attractive pricing. In Europe, Gazprom is building a new pipeline to Germany, which is already highly dependent on Russia for its energy supply. Gazprom signed a deal with the European Union to add 400 billion cubic meters of volume to its supply by 2036 (Europe is expected to be 70-percent dependent on foreign gas by 2020; it is 40-percent dependent now) and threatened to send more gas to Asia and the United States if Europe diversified its suppliers.

THE NEXT WAVES

As we've said, a tsunami is a series of rolling surges, unlike the single crest of a tidal wave, and it can keep on pounding against the shore for much longer than people expect. Often, the first crest is not the biggest one. Similarly, the tsunami of the challengers has hardly reached its peak.

This is partly because, for all the sense of optimism that the challengers throughout the rapidly developing economies feel, they also know that the advantages of their origins—low-cost manufacturing and services, proximity, and natural resources—will likely decline over time. They know they must avoid becoming simply low-cost commodity providers to the world's markets.

To do so they will continue to build on their existing sources of competitive advantage while creating new sources. They will increasingly take advantage of merger and acquisition opportunities, build their expertise in marketing and supply-chain management, and develop their management and human resources talent. They will continue to migrate their offerings upward in value, build world-class innovation capabilities, and take advantage of their own enormous economies as markets.

MOVING UP THE VALUE CHAIN

The challengers are steadily moving themselves up the value chain.

In the early days of the tsunami, incumbents outsourced the production of labor-intensive parts and components that were then shipped back to their developed-country operations to be finished and assembled. Typically, a challenger company would prove itself at these low-end tasks and then be awarded additional work, such as making the parts for entire products or doing the entire assembly of them. As it gained experience, it often sourced some parts from other rapidly developing economies—or from developed ones—rather than manufacture everything itself.

Next, the challenger company would become more sophisticated in its capabilities and take on functions of even greater value, such as design and development. China, for example, is increasingly favored by incumbents for such activities. GE Medical Systems started manufacturing medical imaging equipment in China in 1979. By 2002, one third of GE's global output of computerized tomography (CT) machines came from the company's industrial park in Beijing, which develops, produces, and exports the machines, in addition to supplying more than half of China's domestic CT market.

Johnson Electric, too, has steadily moved its products up the value chain. Faced with the aggressive pricing of Asian automakers, incumbent auto manufacturers have been squeezing costs out of their supply chain—demanding faster product-development cycles, more modularized manufacturing, just-in-time logistics integration—and ever-lower prices. Because of their market power over their suppliers, they've generally been able to get all those things, and Johnson Electric has seen the profit margins of its auto motors division suffer as a result.

Johnson Electric's response to these pressures has been to climb ever higher up the value pyramid. In the past, Johnson Electric sold its micromotors to auto-component assemblers for the final production of actuators, switches, fuel pumps, and the like. That made it a third- or fourth-tier player on the hierarchy of parts suppliers. Now the company is developing more modular products both in-house and in partnership with other parts suppliers to enable Johnson to provide more complete motor and motion-system solutions for the auto industry.[33]

In service businesses, a similar thing occurred. At first, low-end, back-office operations that feature repetitive tasks, such as accounting and report production, would be shifted to a company in a rapidly developing economy. Over time, where language was compatible, front-office functions like call centers and help desks were moved to the challenger as well. Then higher-value operations were transferred.

In India, many challengers are now moving beyond low-cost

transaction processing and offering increasingly sophisticated services. Instead of medical transcription, data entry, and minimal inbound call support, companies are now providing high-end research services.

At first, Wipro's value proposition focused primarily on cost. Now the company creates much of its value by completely redesigning its clients' business processes, which demands extensive process improvement skills. Moreover, its seventeen-thousand-strong engineering services group offers a complete range of R&D services—from product strategy to hardware and software design to quality consulting—to clients that sell electronics-based products. The group now accounts for 36 percent of Wipro's revenue.[34] Wipro has more than 500 professionals dedicated to innovation-led projects, and innovation contributes 8 percent of Wipro's revenues.

We have identified many U.S. and European companies that achieve significant cost benefits from the offshoring of high-value activities. One U.S.-based high-tech company achieved productivity improvements of more than 50 percent over six months, driven by higher-quality recruits, greater digitization, better domain and reengineering capabilities, and the continuous measurement of performance. The company had offshored a complex order-management process; those 50-percent gains showed up in about two thousand orders received every day from fifty offices speaking three languages. That's a far cry from the early days of the tsunami, when suppliers were entrusted only with simple production tasks and the most routine service jobs.

The Big Build-Out

The rapidly developing economies know perfectly well that their infrastructures need work and that their future depends on improving them, but it takes time and resources to create road systems, improve airports, and increase the capacity of ports. After all, the build-out of the U.S. Interstate Highway System, in which 45,000 miles of new roadway were created, took thirty-five years, from 1956 to 1991. It took sixteen years for Japan to build 664 miles of high-speed electric track for its New Trunk Line.

The big build-out of the rapidly developing economies has begun. And is likely to continue for decades.

China, thanks to its skill in manufacturing and driven by its need to export huge volumes of manufactured goods, has put much of its energy into building and expanding its ports. In 2003, China surpassed all other countries to become the world's largest handler of shipped goods and, by 2005, had more than twice the port-handling capacity of the United States—4.9 billion tons per year handled by its major ports, in comparison to 2.5 billion tons in the United States and 0.4 billion tons in India. In 2006, China's total port capacity (including river ports and smaller seaports) was 5.6 billion tons,[35] compared with India's 750 million tons.[36] China is expected to increase its port capacity to 8 billion tons by 2010.

Now China has turned its attention to other aspects of infrastructure, and the government is aggressively funding these activities. Beijing puts some 9 percent of its gross domestic product into public works. In 2005, China had a power generation capacity of 508 million kW.[37] In 2006, the country added 102 million kW of electricity generation capacity—an increase of more than 20 percent, an amount greater than the entire power generation capacity of the United Kingdom.[38] China's energy production is expected to increase by approximately 6 percent per year through 2020, hitting 690 million kW by 2010 and reaching 950 million kW by 2020.[39]

China is also investing heavily in increasing its road capacity to meet the rising demand for surface transport. In the early 1990s, China began a ten-year program to build high-quality expressways and spent some $25 billion a year to do so. But, according to the World Bank, the growth in the road system could not keep pace with the increase in both passenger vehicles (22 percent) and commercial traffic (10 percent) throughout the decade. In the past few years, however, China has made greater progress in developing a National Trunk Highway System (NTHS), which is scheduled for completion in 2015 and will total about 22,000 miles of toll highways and high-speed expressways. By 2006, China had about 83,000 miles of highways,[40] India had 41,000 miles,[41] and the United States had 162,000 miles.[42]

India has not put nearly as much resources (about 4 percent of its GDP) into power generation, roads, and ports as China has—and its sagging infrastructure has affected the ability of both challenger and incumbent companies to do business there.[43] Traffic creeps along at an average of 20 miles per hour on major roads.

In Maharashtra, which is India's second most populous state and home to Mumbai, major cities lose power one day a week in order to relieve pressure on the power generation grid.[44] Foreign companies working in India often tell infrastructure-related horror stories. One electronics manufacturer, for example, produces handsets in a factory in Chennai (formerly Madras) and delivers them in crates to an airfreight company at the local airport. One shipment, waiting to be loaded, was stored outside because the airport did not have sufficient warehouse space to hold it. It rained, and thousands of units were ruined. Such misadventures have a negative impact on India's ability to attract foreign investment—India captured only $8 billion in foreign investment in 2007 compared to China's $63 billion.[45]

The Indian government estimates that India will need to spend $150 billion over the next seven to eight years to bring the rest of its infrastructure up to par and knows that it needs to offer more help and support. A law enacted in 2005 enabled government officials to create public-private partnerships for infrastructure initiatives. A new airport for Bangalore was the first project to take advantage of the law; it was developed by the state government in partnership with Unique Ltd., a privately held Swiss company. The government contributed only 18 percent of the $430 million cost of the airport but will receive full ownership after sixty years.[46]

According to our research and analysis, the development of more and better roads, increased power-generation capacity, and more ports and airports could boost the growth rate of India's annual GDP from its current 7 to 8 percent to a sustainable 8 to 10 percent.

Even so, India's growth rate in 2005-2006 and 2006-2007 was more than 8 percent, despite all the infrastructural constraints.

Onward to Innovation

The global challengers started out as low-cost suppliers and have migrated to higher-value activities, but they are not content with either activity. They strive to move beyond their roles as brilliantly capable manufacturers and highly efficient service providers and become global leaders with world-class brands.

Incumbents have seen such a transformation before. In the 1960s, U.S.-based companies went to Japan to purchase low-cost electronics components and then low-cost transistor radios and televisions. The ability to supply the developed economies provides the challenger companies with the ability to learn and build scale positions. They grow in size, expand their presence, and improve their capabilities while increasing their capacity and improving the quality of their offerings. They begin to build R&D capabilities and create their own brands, which enables them to extend their distribution positions and gain the ability to source from other rapidly developing economies. Companies like Sony, Toyota, and Honda did this, displacing American and European consumer electronics and automobile companies from positions of dominance in the U.S. and European markets.

Similarly, the challengers that want to succeed over the long term are developing the capabilities they will need to transform themselves—world-class mergers and acquisitions, marketing, supply-chain management, and perhaps most important, innovation skills.

Currently, only a handful of challengers operate at the cutting edge of innovation. Their general weakness in intellectual property is reflected in the small number of patents they hold. From 1999 through 2003, all companies in the five largest rapidly developing economies obtained only 3,900 U.S. patents, compared to 166,000 and 54,000 for Japan and Germany, respectively. But that's changing. The challengers are fast developing R&D talent, and R&D

resources are still far less expensive in the rapidly developing economies than in developed countries. With about one-fifth the development costs of its Western competitors, a company such as Ranbaxy Pharmaceuticals can achieve much with its $87 million R&D budget. Little wonder, then, that incumbents are rushing to the rapidly developing economies to establish R&D centers. But the challengers may have an advantage when it comes to leveraging local talent effectively. China's Haier, for instance, claims to develop two new household appliances every day. So while few current challenger inventions are cutting edge, the most successful challengers will become true innovators over time.

China and India have both declared innovation to be a strategic national priority. In January 2006, China unveiled what it called its fifteen-year "Medium- to Long-Term Plan for the Development of Science and Technology." The plan calls on China to become an "innovation-oriented society" by the year 2020 and a global leader in science and technology by midcentury. It calls for steep increases in R&D expenditures over the next fifteen years, from 1.23 percent of GDP in 2004 to 2.5 percent of a significantly larger GDP by 2020. And it sets two far-reaching goals: first, for China to become one of the top five countries in the world in the number of new patents granted for inventions, and second, as noted by the American Institute of Physics, "for Chinese-authored scientific papers to become among the world's most cited." [47]

India's goals are no less ambitious and are nicely captured by the slogans used to promote the 2005 and 2006 national R&D expositions in New Delhi: "Think Innovation, Think India"; "Mind to Market"; and most telling of all, perhaps, "The World's Knowledge Hub of the Future." And in support of such ambitious goals, the sponsors of the annual meeting remind us that "India has 380 universities and 11,200 higher education institutions churning out around 6,000 Ph.D.s and 200,000 engineers, 300,000 science graduates and post graduates annually" and that R&D investment has been growing at a compounded annual growth rate of more than 40 percent. [48]

IMPLICATIONS: PREPARE TO STRUGGLE

No, this is not the first time we have experienced a wave of new challengers from developing economies sweeping onto the shores of developed markets. And it's hardly the first time that the enterprises of China and India and Russia and Brazil have figured prominently in world commerce, and that there have been extraordinary tensions among the players. Think of the spice trade, the tea trade, the cotton trade, the opium trade. Payment in silver and copper coins. The balance of trade shifting back and forth. Societies opening up, as Japan did in 1853. And closing down, as China did in the early 1900s.

The ability to supply more developed economies always provides the challengers with the opportunity to learn and grow. The smart ones seize the opportunity. They build on their national origins, take advantage of their access to the world's knowledge and resources, and allow their hunger for success to drive them forward.

That's what happened in the 1960s, when incumbents could not imagine that their Japanese suppliers would ever become competitors. But they did. Many of them became world leaders. Japan grew from the fourth-largest economy in 1960 to the second largest, after the United States, today.

It's happening again, right now.

For incumbents, it's easy to look at the challenger companies of China, India, Russia, Brazil, Turkey, and the other rapidly developing economies and be lulled into the same false sense of security.

A company with annual revenue of $1 billion—or even $100 million—could be a threat to my company? A factory without automation could match our volume? A company that started out making nameless widgets could create a world-class brand?

Yes.

It's happened before and it's happening again, right now. And this tsunami of the challengers will make all the previous waves look like ripples.

CHAPTER 3

Minding the Cost Gap

"The cost game determines our strategy, which is to be the biggest player in the world."
Anand Mahindra, M&M

A factory worker in the United States earns $25 an hour; in China it's $1. In Wenzhou, a construction worker carries cement in buckets for $0.40 an hour.

Need anything more be said?

There would have been no tsunami at all, no rising up of the challengers, no rapid development in these economies, without the fundamental advantage of low cost.

Although companies throughout the rapidly developing economies are now offering more complex services, becoming more innovative, and branding their own products, low-cost remains their bread-and-butter advantage.

However, achieving and maintaining that advantage is not as simple as it might seem. The challengers, as we'll see, have to struggle to manage their costs in order to keep prices low but also to grow and be competitive in worldwide markets.

For incumbents in many industries, for many years, choosing the low-cost capabilities and services of the rapidly developing economies has been virtually a no-brainer. Factory workers, manual laborers, unskilled service people—everybody who toils at the low end of the business food chain earns less, receives fewer benefits, and works longer hours in the rapidly developing economies than they do in the developed ones.

The U.S. factory worker who makes $25 an hour also works fewer hours, around seven a day. The Chinese worker who makes $1 an hour works ten to twelve hours. In Poland, a factory worker makes around $3 an hour.[1] In other parts of eastern Europe, a factory worker can earn as much as $10 to $12 per hour. A Mexican worker will sew together seventy pairs of loafers, by hand, for 120 pesos a day, or about $11. And that's a lot of money in comparison to the garment worker in Bangladesh, who takes home $20 a month.[2]

Service workers generally earn more than factory workers, but still much less than the wage for a roughly equivalent job in the United States or Europe. In the United States, a call-center rep earned about $13.22 an hour in 2005, while an operator based in Brazil made around $5.96 an hour. A process employee, like an accountant, earns $26 to $30 per hour in the United States, $15 to $18 per hour in eastern Europe, and $10 to $12 per hour in India.

Move up the corporate hierarchy a bit, to positions that require more education and entail greater responsibility, and the cost gap remains enormous. In China, a project manager will earn an average of about $23,309 per year, more than twice as much as the $9,995 that an Indian project manager earns, but still less than a third of the $90,000 a project manager in the United States can expect to take home annually.[3]

What about executives? Surely the general managers, directors, vice presidents, and presidents of Baosteel or Wipro or CVRD are closer in parity to executives in the United States and Europe? Well, that has not been true, but now the gap is closing. In fact, all things considered, senior managers stationed in some of the rapidly developing economies have more purchasing power (if not higher incomes) than their counterparts in the developed countries. According to a study by Hay Group, a human resources consultancy, managers in Turkey, Mexico, and Ukraine have more buying power than their

Western peers. But buying power isn't everything. It refers to buying power in the economy where you're living—where prices are lower, there is less variety, and there is often a lower quality of goods and services available.

Such low wages make entire companies cheaper to start and run. A hundred-person start-up company in the United States "might burn through $20 million a year," but a Chinese start-up of the same size might consume only $2.5 million. "That's why Chinese companies get very profitable very fast," said Richard Lim, managing director of GSR Ventures, the Chinese affiliate of Mayfield Fund, a China-focused venture capital firm.[4]

Independent service providers and professionals charge lower fees than similar companies in developed countries. When the Chinese office of a U.S.-based law firm proposed to a local manufacturer a fee of several hundred thousand dollars for a chunk of legal work, the potential client came back with a counteroffer of $15,000. (The law firm declined the work.) Some might find it surprising that Chinese attorneys don't command higher fees, when you consider that China has only about 115,000 full-time lawyers.[5]

Not only are wages and compensation low in the rapidly developing economies, capital assets, raw materials, and components are, too. Machines and tooling produced in the rapidly developing economies often carry price tags that are 30 to 50 percent less than the price on such machines in the West. (They often have different capabilities and life expectancies, however, so exact comparisons are hard to make.)

In Russia, Lukoil and Gazprom have built their companies—and virtually rebuilt the Russian economy—on ample supplies of natural gas and oil.[6] In Indonesia, food providers like Indofood have access to an abundance of palm oil, which gives them a big cost advantage. Add it all up, and the challengers can offer an extraordinary 30- to 40-percent cost advantage over incumbents in virtually every product they make or service they provide.

What's more, low cost goes even beyond wages and salaries, services and machine tools, products and palm oil—the challengers think low cost in everything they do: how they set up factories and offices, the ways in which they collaborate, how they design products, the expectations they place on their employees.

So the first struggle of globality—where you're competing with every company, everywhere, that has access, just as you do, to virtually everything—is to relentlessly drive toward the "global low cost" (no longer just the "China price") for your business or industry.

Incumbents are not always able to match or improve upon the global low cost, but what they can and must do is reduce their costs to the point that the price gap between their offerings and those of the challengers is small enough that it doesn't matter very much, if at all, to their customers.

Of course, there is an alternative strategy. Incumbents can also add so much value to the product or service—through innovation, branding, distribution, and other factors—that customers are willing to pay a little, or even a lot, more for the greater value they perceive. (More on innovation in the rapidly developing economies in chapter 8.)

There are four main actions that challengers have become expert at that help them keep their costs low and that incumbents can take to keep the gap small:

- *Optimizing with Labor*
- *Clustering*
- *Superscaling*
- *Simplifying*

OPTIMIZING WITH LABOR

Incumbents have a difficult time shaking out of their heads a bedrock, developed-country assumption: people are the most expensive resource. Over the past several decades, largely in response to the rise of the challengers, keeping the cost of the workforce down has become standard operating procedure for companies competing in the developed economies. The exhortations ring in their minds like cautionary voices in a B-movie nightmare:

Reduce headcount!

Run lean!

Flatten out!

Downsize!

Automate!

The challengers view the people issue very differently. They don't shy away from large workforces. Rather than reducing staff, cutting back on hiring, closing facilities, and automating wherever they can, the challengers are adding people, building new facilities for them to flow into, and even increasing wages to attract more people.

From the early days of the tsunami, when capital was hard for the locals to come by, they knew that the availability of an abundance of low-wage labor could be just as valuable as the money they didn't have to buy expensive machinery, complex systems, and production equipment. As a result, the challengers' workplaces are usually humming with human activity—very different from the automated, often sterile factories of the incumbents.

Visit ZTE, China's largest maker of equipment for wireless telecommunications networks, and you'll find 31,000 people at work. Ten thousand of them are engineers. They work in fourteen research and development centers, in China, the United States, India, France, and Sweden. The ZTE employees are young: the average age is thirty. And they're ambitious and work hard. "We're passionate, and that translates into diligence," Zhou Susu of ZTE told us. "Our local staff usually work twelve to fourteen hours a day. It sounds terrible to our competitors."[7] As one American manager in a U.S.-owned plant in Shenzhen told *Atlantic* editor James Fallows, "The people here work hard. They're young. They're quick. There's none of this 'I have to go pick up the kids' nonsense you get in the States."

Long-Term Low-Cost Wage Rates

Many observers argue that labor costs in the rapidly developing economies will increase much faster than in developed countries, and the wage differential will soon start to shrink.

In our view, the gap will persist over the next twenty years, if not longer. This is partly because there is an enormous reservoir of unemployed men and women in China and India who want to work, can work, and will work for wages far below workers in the developed economies. In China alone, more than 800 million people—some 12 percent of the world's population—live in the countryside, where incomes are just over $300 per year[8]—less than one-third of incomes of city dwellers in China[9] and a hundred times less than the $40,000 average annual income in the United States. When there are literally hundreds of millions of people looking for paying jobs, it is unlikely that wages for low-skilled positions will rise too sharply over the next few decades.

The same is true for positions that require greater education, training, or skills. India has a large pool of educated, English-speaking workers, and it is expanding by a million people every year. The demand for workers caused by the incredibly rapid growth of IT and business-process outsourcing (BPO) services in India has resulted in a rise in wage rates in those industries, but it has also provoked challenger companies to look farther afield for low-cost workers—they are now recruiting in the villages of India and are heading to China as well. India is one of the few countries in which the working-age population is projected to grow for the next forty years, which will further serve to keep wages low. Helping to fuel this supply of workers is the wide availability of high-speed Internet access in India, which enables companies to train and capitalize on the work skills of people throughout the country—even those living in rural areas.

The cost gap is still so enormous that even if labor costs in the rapidly developing economies were to increase at double-digit rates every year for the foreseeable future, the differential would shrink only slightly.

Do the math. Assume that a U.S.-based factory worker currently costs an employer $15 to $30 per hour and the Chinese factory worker costs about $1 per hour—for a gap of $14 to $29. Suppose factory wages in China increase at a rate of 8 percent annually, while in the United States they rise at an annual rate of 2.5 percent. In 2012, the average hourly wage would still be only $1.46 in China, but it would reach $24.55 in the United States. Do the math out to 2040 and, if the rates of increase remain the same, labor rates in China still will be only a quarter of what they are in the United States—$12.68 versus $50.82.

Labor costs in the smaller eastern European countries, Brazil, and Mexico might come under even greater downward pressure. The labor costs in these countries will remain low in comparison to those in the United States and western Europe, but they will likely find it harder to compete with China and India because their labor costs are already higher, and annual wage increases in those countries are generally higher as well. To continue to compete with everyone from everywhere, the eastern European challengers will have to keep a lid on their wages.

BYD: MORE PEOPLE, FEWER ROBOTS

It was not in class at a Western business school that Wang Chuanfu learned that low-cost labor could be optimized, but rather through experience. And it was that lesson that set him on the road to building what is now the world's largest manufacturer of nickel-cadmium (NiCd) batteries, with a 40-percent share of the market.

Wang Chuanfu, born in 1967, was educated at Central-South Industrial University, one of China's top research and education centers in metallurgical science and engineering. He graduated in 1987, then went on to the Beijing Shougang Metallurgical Research

Institute, where he earned his master's degree in 1990. He then was offered a research job at the institute and took it.

"My target was to be a very good engineer," recalled Wang Chuanfu. But the institute did not have much in the way of financial resources in the 1990s—many government-run R&D centers in China lacked funding in that period—and Wang got frustrated and itchy. "It was very difficult to do anything," he said.

At the time, mobile phones were arriving in China. Wang became interested in them and realized that, unless they could be offered at a significantly lower price, most Chinese people would never be able to afford one. After taking apart a phone or two, he concluded that the battery, which cost more than 1,000 yuan, was the big factor in the high selling price. Wang decided that it could not really be that difficult to produce a lower-priced battery. So in 1997, he quit his job at the institute to start his own enterprise.

The production of lithium batteries was then dominated by Sanyo, Toshiba, Matsushita, and Sony—Japanese manufacturers with abundant expertise in building world-class precision electronics on flexible and efficient assembly lines. Their battery divisions were no different, churning out products at world-leading combinations of speed, reliability, and cost.

Wang reasoned that he would simply go to Japan, buy the technology and equipment he needed to make lithium batteries back in China, and then cut costs through low labor rates and materials costs. However, he was stunned by the prices the Japanese companies were asking for robots and other automation equipment. A complete production line would cost more than 83 million yuan, or about $10 million (in 1998 dollars), an amount the former government researcher did not have.

Wang considered his options. Was there another way to compete in the battery-making business that did not involve a huge outlay of capital? Wang thought there was. He bought just one Japanese robot and shipped it back to China. There he studied how it worked and took it apart, piece by piece. He determined that it would be possible to design and build a similar robot, with the capabilities and performance that he needed, and build it in China for far less than the cost of a Japanese machine.

Then Wang had an even better idea. He studied the battery itself with great care. He realized that a cell phone battery is actually a pretty simple piece of technology, much less complex than, let's say, a printed circuit board or a printer engine. The battery is little more than a sandwich of several sheets of lithium cobalt oxide, stacked along with sheets of carbon, separated by still more thin sheets of plastic placed in between. There was no reason that people couldn't do the job of the robots, and do it just as well.

So Wang designed a production line that replaced the 83-million-yuan automated factory with six hundred people and a single robot. The people sat side by side in a long assembly line, passing the work from one person to the next, stacking sheets, bending bits of metal, wrapping film, building up the sandwich of layers until it was done. The whole line cost no more than 3 million yuan, or about $362,000 in 1998 dollars, less than 4 percent of the cost of the automated line from Japan.

BYD launched its battery at a price that was 40 percent below that of the Japanese competitors' products.[10] "Japanese firms did not believe we could do it," said BYD co-founder, Xia Zuoquan. "The key is to cut costs while keeping the level of quality," said Deng Guorui, a senior executive at BYD. "Our costs are 30 to 40 percent lower than those of Japanese companies and our function and quality similar—perhaps better."[11]

Wang did more than rely on labor rather than capital. He established a wholly different kind of factory, a facility that was incredibly labor-intensive and also extremely flexible. By replacing equipment with workers (or, more accurately, not buying equipment in the first place), BYD was able to do more than drive out cost—the company also cut the time it took to make its products and could do shorter production runs and produce a wider variety of products much more cheaply than if it had to retool and reprogram a room full of robots every time. The labor-based factory allowed BYD to move more quickly from design to prototype to commercial-scale production, which gave it an edge in the pace of innovation it could offer to its customers.

Optimizing with labor comes with its own challenges, of course— namely, the need for good workforce management. In rapidly developing economies, the demand for employees is intense, and competing job offers are plentiful, so the challengers are always struggling to keep compensation costs low, while also keeping worker retention high.[12]

CLUSTERING

Challengers are particularly expert at keeping their costs low by clustering—operating in concentrations of related, interdependent companies within an industry that use the same suppliers, specialized labor, and distribution channels.

As the tsunami gathered force, industry clusters emerged throughout the rapidly developing economies. There is an appliance cluster in Monterrey, Mexico, which serves the North American market. Cluster members include both incumbent and challenger companies, such as Whirlpool, Carrier, Criotec, Hussman, IMPCO Technologies, LG Electronics, Mabe, and York—along with some two hundred local suppliers.

There is a Mexican footwear cluster in Guadalajara, comprising 315 manufacturers of end products and 160 suppliers. About half of them interact directly with each other. Brazil has its own footwear cluster (this one focusing specifically on the production of shoe molds) in the Sinos Valley.

There is a large aerospace center based in São José dos Campos, which is about an hour's drive from São Paulo, where Embraer headquarters are located. The physical closeness and continuing engagement of aeronautical engineers in this cluster is one of the reasons for the company's success. In the 1960s, the Brazilian government provided support for the aviation industry and the local engineering talent that drives it. At that time, "Brazil had little in the way of industry," Satoshi Yokota, Embraer executive vice president, technology development and advanced design, told us. "Automobile manufacturing was only ten to fifteen years old, there was little electronics, very little more complex manufacturing. However, there was a nucleus of competent aeronautical engineers and a perception by the government that it should invest in that area."

Clustering is also getting big in Bulgaria, where furniture makers have centered around Razlog in the southwestern part of the country.

In India, there is an automotive cluster around the port city of Chennai, in the southern part of the country, where some 40 percent of India's automotive industry players have located.[13]

China is chock-full of clusters, and they account for a great percentage of the country's total production, so they're an important source of low-cost inputs, materials, and capital. Many of China's clusters have developed around growing urban areas. Educational institutions participate in them as well as companies by training people for the local manufacturing base, thus ensuring clusters a ready supply of engineers and other skilled employees. The city of Xiamen, for example, is home to an electronics cluster, a cluster of machine makers, and a chemical industry cluster.

The largest and most important of China's clusters is around the Pearl River Delta, in Guangdong Province, just north of Hong Kong. The principal city is Guangzhou, once known as Canton, which has been a trading city for centuries. Guangdong Province has a population of around ninety million people. According to one estimate, some eighteen million of those people hold manufacturing jobs.[14] That's more than the entire manufacturing workforce of the United States, which is about fourteen million. The Guangdong industrial area, according to one estimate, is responsible for 13 percent of all of China's industrial output.

James Fallows, of *The Atlantic*, has spent much time touring factories in the Pearl River Delta and describes a typical one this way: "One facility in Guangdong province, the famous Foxconn works, sits in the middle of a conurbation just outside Shenzhen, where it occupies roughly as much space as a major airport," Fallows writes. "Some 240,000 people (the number I heard most often; estimates range between 200,000 and 300,000) work on its assembly lines, sleep in its dormitories, and eat in its company cafeterias. I was told that Foxconn's caterers kill 3,000 pigs each day to feed its employees. The number would make sense—it's one pig per 80 people, in a country where pigs are relatively small and pork is a staple meat (I heard no estimate for chickens)."

Hundreds of companies and their suppliers have built up in the Pearl River Delta, where they take advantage of the many cost advantages that clustering delivers.

Sharing

Members of a cluster can effectively increase their capacity without bearing the capital cost of actually building new factories or facilities by sharing the capacity of other cluster members. A company can outsource orders, or parts of orders, that it can't handle itself to another company with similar production capabilities in the same geographical area. The company does not have to reject the order, or offer a later delivery date, and the customer is none the wiser.

This is exactly how the Mesta cluster—which is focused on furniture—got started around the business center of Razlog, Bulgaria. The cluster took shape when a Dutch entrepreneur wanted to place an order for a large quantity of furniture, and none of the local producers had the capacity to handle it. So the companies split up the production of the various parts and agreed to ship the final products under the brand of just one of the companies.

Cluster members can share the costs of building certain facilities that do require significant capital expenditure, such as the steam and sewage treatment plants required for the dyeing and printing industry. Companies in a cluster can also manage cost by jointly buying raw materials, components, final goods, labor, equipment, and support services from their suppliers—all without sacrificing their independence and flexibility.

Cluster members often save substantial amounts on transportation costs by collectively purchasing large volumes of goods and materials. About 60 percent of all the goods exported from China contain ingredients or components that had been imported from outside of China. When clusters purchase in bulk and aggregate their shipments so that there is a higher percentage of full container loads and full truckloads, all the companies in the clusters participate in the savings and, ultimately, the end customer does, too. And, within the cluster itself, shipping costs between suppliers and manufacturers are greatly reduced because the companies are close to each other.

Flextronics, a leading electronics manufacturing services provider, has established a massive industrial park in the Pearl River Delta town of Doumen, located about two and a half hours from Hong Kong. With a built-up area of 84 acres, and several factories employing 45,000 workers, Flextronics designs, builds, and ships a wide variety of products including mobile phones, game consoles, network infrastructure products, and various types of components. Flextronics is also able to provide low-cost, high-quality products to its customers by acquiring parts from suppliers located near its manufacturing campus and managing the entire supply chain, from the design phase through to final assembly and logistics. Within a two-hour drive of the Flextronics campus are thousands of suppliers that provide almost every service and production support required by Flextronics. This logistical setup alone results in component costs that are far lower than those of similar products manufactured in the United States.

Clustering also facilitates the exchange of information. Many companies in a cluster are of small or medium size, so they lack the means to build an effective information technology infrastructure. Although more and more challengers are using the Internet during the initial stages of business transactions, much information is still exchanged through face-to-face interactions. The physical proximity of firms in clusters is ideal for this kind of communication and for the cultivation of personal and community relationships so crucial to establishing trust. In turn, trust facilitates the sharing of extensive market, technical, and competitive information, which enables companies to create offerings that customers prize.

In the shoe cluster in Brazil's Sinos Valley, a group of manufacturers and their suppliers and other partners set up a technology-based innovation program that aimed to improve the production of footwear molds and shorten development times. The group included manufacturers, the local university, a training company, a private technology innovation firm, and a Brazilian *organização não governamental* (ONG), or nongovernmental organization.[15]

In the Pearl River Delta, Honda has a joint venture called China Honda Automobile Company (CHAC) that takes advantage of the production know-how and parts procurement network of its joint-venture partners—Guangzhou Honda Automobile Co., Ltd., and Dongfeng Honda Engine Co., Ltd. The company controls costs through the economies of scale it has achieved through its relationship with them. CHAC is the first passenger-car maker in China to begin full-scale exports to European markets.[16]

COLLABORATING

Beyond sharing facilities and costs, clustering also stimulates and facilitates collaboration.

China's great success with industrial clusters, especially in three of its largest ones—Yangtze River Delta, the Pearl River Delta in Guangdong, and Zhongguancun in Beijing, the largest R&D center in China—offers some important themes about how clusters can foster collaboration.

First, government policy can play an important role in stimulating cluster collaboration. The Chinese State Council's provisional rules regarding new-technology industrial development experimental zones in Beijing led to increased activity in the Zhongguancun region; similarly, the "Coordination & Development Plan of the Pearl River Delta city cluster 2004–2020" has helped development planning for the PRD cluster.[17] Government facilitation of preferential policies relating to finance, labor, land acquisition and usage, infrastructure, academics, and research has been the backbone of collaboration within clusters.

Second, cluster collaboration has taken the form of vertical linkages, that is, between suppliers and their customers. In the Pearl River Delta cluster in Guangzhou, automakers Honda, Toyota, and Nissan work in collaboration with a host of auto-component manufacturers. Cluster collaboration also takes the form of horizontal linkages—among multiple competitors or peer companies—as happens in the software parks in Jiangsu and Shanghai in the Yellow River Cluster.

Challengers have also used clusters as collaborative platforms to access, engage with, and train high-skilled talent. Many engineering and high-tech companies have set up R&D centers in India's Bangalore region in the last few years. General Electric maintains the John F. Welch Technical Center there, GE's first and largest integrated, multidisciplinary R&D center outside the United States, where it employs more than 2,200 scientists and engineers.[18]

Not only does Bangalore offer great weather and good pubs (both of which seem to be requirements for expats in these R&D centers), the region is also home to a great number of universities and research institutes, such as the Indian Institute of Science, one of India's premier basic research organizations. These make for good research partners and sources of ideas and talent.

SUPERSCALING

The third important cost lever that some challengers (and a few incumbents) have mastered is superscaling—developing the capability to create products on a massive, world-leading scale, with the ability to increase capacity still more with relative ease and at relatively low cost.

Hisense, the Chinese producer of consumer electronics, is without doubt a superscaler. The company has the capacity to produce 16 million color TVs, 9 million air conditioners, almost 5 million CDMA phones, 10 million refrigerators, 1 million computers, and digital equipment such as firewalls and servers each year, according to Guo Qingcun, a vice president of the company.[19] Hisense has already far exceeded its goal to produce 11 million TV sets annually by 2010, and is steadily increasing its global share.[20]

Goodbaby, the Chinese maker of children's goods, claims that it operates the world's largest stroller factory, car seat factory, bicycle factory, battery-operated toy car factory, sporting goods factory, wooden furniture factory, and diaper factory—all located on its 12,000-acre industrial campus in Kunshan.[21]

Likewise, Pearl River Piano, which is the world's largest manufacturer of pianos, has an annual production capacity of 100,000 vertical units and 20,000 grand pianos. The company claims to operate the largest piano factory in the world, with a staff of over four thousand musical experts at its site in the Pearl River Delta.

Juan Antonio Alvarez, of the Chilean shipping company CSAV, says, "We are in a business that is heavily influenced by economies of scale, and therefore size is a necessary step for profitability. I don't think it's necessary to be the largest to make good profits, but there's a minimum efficient size."

For incumbents, cutting costs through superscaling seems to come a little more naturally than the other cost-saving practices of the challengers.

GE Healthcare, the $15 billion unit of General Electric, is superscaling the production of some of its medical products. The company, headquartered in the United Kingdom, has built a scalable manufacturing facility in the manufacturing cluster around Shanghai that produces about five million X-ray and magnetic resonance imaging (MRI) products per year. GE Healthcare plans to invest $37.5 million to expand the facility over the next two years and increase production capacity to fifteen million units annually. The new facility will be designed so it can scale up to produce thirty million units annually.[22]

In 2005, Canon finished building a massive laser printer factory in Tien Son industrial park, located in the Bac Ninh province of North Vietnam. The 60,000-square-meter facility is valued at $70 million, employs some 3,500 people, and has the capacity to produce 700,000 ink-jet printers a month, or 8,400,000 per year. "We plan to make this the biggest laser printer factory in the world," said Yasuo Mitsuhashi, Canon's chief executive for printer products. Canon has become one of Vietnam's leading foreign investors, pouring some $236 million into operations there.[23]

JOHNSON ELECTRIC: MAJOR FORCE IN MICROMOTORS

Of all the challenger superscalers, Johnson Electric may be the champion. Johnson Electric is now the world's largest independent maker of micromotors—the tiny motors that make all kinds of products and components run, including hair dryers, power tools, and the adjustable side mirror on your car. Most of them are no larger than a spool of thread.

The company was founded by Wang Seng Liang as a manufacturer of textiles in mainland China, turning out products like towels and socks. In 1949, shortly after the Communist revolution in mainland China, Wang was dispossessed of his manufacturing assets by the Chinese Communist Party as part of its program of economic transformation. Virtually penniless, Wang decided to move his family to Hong Kong, where he soon opened the first of what became a chain of tailor shops. His company grew and prospered.

In the late 1950s, Hong Kong had become a center for the manufacturing of cheap, motorized toys for kids. Consumers throughout North America and Europe had discovered these products, and demand was soaring. One day, the head of a local trading company called on Wang. It seems that the trader had an idea for a new toy—a motorized boat that ran on a battery. He showed Wang a European model of the toy and, knowing that Wang had considerable manufacturing expertise from his textile days, asked if Wang could figure out how to make a cheaper version of the motorized craft. Wang considered the boat carefully. The product itself didn't interest him very much. He reasoned that toys were a fashion item, not unlike towels and socks. By the time the trader could be selling in volume, tastes would change, and kids would want a toy aircraft or figure, instead. But the motor interested Wang a great deal. As Wang's son Patrick put it, "His experience in Shanghai told him to build something that doesn't change. Toys are fashionable. Motors are not."[24] Wang told the trader he would develop the little motor.

The decision to make motors proved to be a shrewd one. Most of the toys being produced in Hong Kong at the time were powered by a little motor. So Wang was able to sell his product to not only the producers of boats but to all the other toy manufacturers in the area. Wang gradually gained experience and built the manufacturing scale to become the leading supplier of small motors to all of the industrial companies in Hong Kong, not just toy makers. (Even as his profits grew, Wang kept an eye on cost in all things. According to son Patrick, Wang bought cheap furniture for the factory and kept the factory lights dim to save electricity.[25])

Wang Seng Liang had six children, three sons and three daughters, all of whom he sent to be educated in the United States. When they returned to Hong Kong, three of them joined the management of the family business. They saw that the toy motors that had created such success for the company were fast becoming a low-value commodity product. They convinced their father that the company could not continue to focus solely on creating little motors for low-value products. There was a much more lucrative business to be built in creating more sophisticated motors for higher-value products— and for customers who were less price sensitive than the Hong Kong toy traders.

In 1972, Johnson Electric began to diversify, starting with motors for household appliances, and invested aggressively in research and development. By the mid-1970s, the company was producing motors for business machines. It also began to expand internationally, and by the late 1970s had become a supplier to the West German automobile industry.

In 1979, the Communist Party's economic modernization program opened up the opportunity for Hong Kong–based manufacturers like Johnson Electric to shift production to lower-cost locations across the border. Patrick Wang spent three years searching for an appropriate site in a town with local leadership that he believed the company could work with. It was in Shajing, an impoverished rural village in Guangdong province, where Wang finally met his man. "Here was this village leader saying his people were the most honest and hardworking in China," Patrick Wang remembers. "I wondered if he could be serious. Then I saw how he ran things. Chinese business is basically people and contacts. We struck up a very good relationship, and today he's still our partner."[26]

Johnson Electric was one of the first companies to move into the Pearl River Delta manufacturing area, then mostly farmland and villages. Johnson Electric set up its first assembly factory in a grain storage shed. Today on that site stands Johnson Electric's largest manufacturing facility, known as Johnson City.[27] The Johnson Electric Group employs approximately 45,000 people worldwide—of which around 30,000 work at Johnson City (though technically most of these workers are subcontracted labor rather than JE employees). The Group employs another four thousand people at other locations in China. Johnson City is virtually a cluster unto itself, with more than 80 suppliers located within or around the facility. Johnson Electric has created an operation that combines low-cost and superscale—with product quality—so as to make the company almost unbeatable in its micromotor niche. Today, the majority of auto micromotors are manufactured in China.[28]

Superscaling of the type that Johnson Electric does depends on low labor costs, but low-cost labor does not completely define the company's strategy or its success. Rather than swap labor for capital, the company invested heavily in modernization and automation throughout the early 1990s, so much so that, although JE's sales grew at double-digit rates during those years, its earnings remained flat. In the second half of the 1990s, earnings quadrupled as the company harvested the benefits of its capital investments.

Superscaling can be a good low-cost strategy for some companies, although it usually does require greater levels of capital investment than running a number of smaller-scale operations does. Even so, the cost of equipment, land, facilities, and services in rapidly developing economies is low enough that challengers can invest heavily in superscaling and still deliver a massive quantity of low-cost, high-quality products.

SIMPLIFYING

Challengers keep their costs low by approaching product design very differently than incumbents do—they simplify both the products and services they offer and the processes they use to create them.

In general, incumbents make a fundamental assumption about products and services: more is better. More features, more capabilities, more choice. (More opportunities, too, to charge higher prices.)

In the rapidly developing economies, the product and service development process rests on different assumptions. The challengers think about what their customers want and need and, above all, what they can afford. They seek to make simple products with just the right number of features that will sell at a price the greatest number of consumers can manage.

The $150 Washing Machine: Simple Product

In Brazil, for example, people want washing machines, but not the kind you can buy in the United States—as Whirlpool discovered when it introduced its first washing machine there. Brazilians want their washers small, because they launder their clothes often, in small loads. They want them to look nice, because owning a washing machine is a status symbol in Brazil, and status symbols should not be ugly. They also generally can't afford to spend more than $150 to buy one.

In most developed countries, more than 90 percent of households have an automatic washing machine, or easy access to one, but the majority of people in the rapidly developing economies do not. Only a quarter of all Brazilian households own one, 8 percent in China, and 4.5 percent in India.[29] Given those ownership numbers, Whirlpool, the U.S.-based maker of home appliances, decided that the potential market for an affordable washing machine was huge.

In 1998, Whirlpool launched its first "low-cost" washing machine in Brazil, a stripped-down version of a U.S.-designed model that retailed for $300. The average Brazilian earns about $200 a month. The average American earns about $3,300 a month. How many Americans would spend more than their entire monthly salary on a washing machine? Not many. In fact, the average cost of a machine in the United States is about $461. The same held true in Brazil. The product went nowhere.

Whirlpool still believed that the market could be developed. Although the company had been experiencing declining sales in Brazil for some years, there are some thirty million low-income households in Brazil, and they account for about a third of national consumption. According to some independent surveys, an automatic washing machine is the item that low-income consumers most want after a cell phone.

So Whirlpool decided to create a new low-cost model, but this time it would design it from scratch, especially for the consumer in Brazil—and, if all went well, for consumers in other rapidly developing economies. "It wasn't a matter of stripping down an existing model," says Marcelo Rodrigues, Whirlpool's top washing machine engineer in Latin America and the director of laundry technology at Multibras SA Electrodomesticos, the Brazilian unit of Whirlpool. "We had to innovate for that particular segment."

Whirlpool chose to develop the machine in Brazil, where the

company maintains a staff of skilled engineers and industrial designers and operates some of its most sophisticated factories. Marcelo Rodrigues's team dug deep into the basics of washing machine functioning to develop a low-cost design. Most washing machines work with a system of gears that shift the mechanism into its different functions—such as agitating and spinning—and the system has many parts and requires a fair amount of assembly in the factory. For the new low-cost model, the Brazilian team created a single-drive system that washes and spins clothes without involving gears. The simpler system does not spin as fast as the geared system, so the clothes come out of the washing machine a bit damper than they do from standard models. However, Whirlpool had conducted focus groups with target consumers and had been assured that the spin performance of the new system was good enough.

The team built the single-drive system into a machine with a small (4-kilogram) load capacity. And it added another feature that the curious Brazilian homemakers had requested—a transparent acrylic top that allowed the owner to look inside and watch the machine at work. Not only did the see-through top meet a consumer desire, it was also cheaper to produce than the standard top. The team also paid heed to the request for good washing machine looks. "We realized the washer should be aesthetically appealing; it's a status symbol for these consumers," says Emerson do Valle, vice president of Multibras.[30]

The Ideale washer was launched in Brazil in 2003 with a retail price of $150, certainly one of the world's least expensive washing machines. The Ideale essentially created a market for low-capacity, low-price, semi-automatic washing machines in Brazil, which gave low-income consumers an attractive choice they had not had before—most were making do with so-called "wash tanks," the most basic and unsophisticated electric washer available. The Ideale had strong sales and was essentially the only offering in this new category, so Whirlpool engineers upgraded the product—adding some new features and making it fully automatic—which enabled the company to charge a small premium to the initial entry product and improve profitability still more.

Two years later, seeing the success of the Ideale, Electrolux entered the low-capacity segment with a machine that offered six-kilogram capacity. Whirlpool, having demonstrated the viability of the segment, responded with its own six-kilogram machine, the Ciranda.

With the Ideale, Whirlpool proved that the company could compete at the low end and that even low-income Brazilian consumers would trade up when presented with product innovations that responded to their needs.

THE $5,000 CAR: SIMPLE PROCESS

When creating simple products for low-income consumers in the rapidly developing economies, companies have also found a variety of ways to take costs out of the process of designing, engineering, and manufacturing them.

The Logan, produced by Renault, the French carmaker, is a low-cost car, originally designed for new automotive markets like eastern and central Europe, and produced in Pitesti, Romania. In a second phase, it was introduced into the European market and then into several other countries around the world, including Russia, Colombia, and Brazil. It is now produced in seven countries and sold in more than fifty markets.

The Logan was tailored for India in a joint venture between Renault and Mahindra & Mahindra, the Indian conglomerate. "The purpose of the Renault Logan car," reads the company's Web site, "is to allow Renault to reach a new customer range with a product that packs the bare essentials without resorting to using a car that's been out of production for several years." It starts at about €6,400 in eastern Europe, although the selling price is significantly higher in India, due to the significant piling on of taxes.

The Logan had to be developed to keep the product basic, manufacturing simple, and the cost of everything low. Most carmakers build physical prototypes for their new models so that designers and executives can see how the car will look once produced. But this is an expensive process, usually requiring several iterations and consuming hours and hours of high-cost talent time. So Renault developed far fewer prototypes than it normally would and essentially modeled the car with a computer.

The Logan borrows as many parts and systems from other models as possible, to avoid the cost of custom designing new ones. It is developed on a platform derived from that of the Renault Nissan Alliance, which is the basis of the Renault Clio III, Renault Modus, Nissan March, and Nissan Note models. On close inspection, you'll notice that Logan's front axle, door handles, and steering wheel, among other parts, are identical to those of the Renault Clio.

The dashboard is created in a single molding rather than a more complicated, multifaceted design to save on tooling and reduce assembly time. The air vents, glove box door, and other parts are easily popped in. The body panels are stamped from standard sheets of steel and joined with conventional welding techniques. More expensive cars are sheathed in steel panels of varying thicknesses that are usually handled by laser-welding robots. The windshield and windows are as flat as possible, to reduce the cost of tooling.

The Logan is offered with few luxury features. No power windows or central locking. No radio controls mounted on the steering wheel in the base model. No complicated seating adjustments. Those features are all options. Alloy wheels are not available.

In India, 50 percent of the car's content comes from local sources, according to Rajesh Jejurikar, managing director of Mahindra Renault, and the power train is sourced from low-cost plants in Romania. Because Mahindra Renault sources so many parts in India from low-cost suppliers, the cost of producing the already low-cost Logan is even lower in India. "Our expense data shows the project cost is down substantially," Jejurikar said.

Carlos Ghosn, president and chief executive officer of Renault (as well as of Nissan), has built a worldwide reputation for squeezing the most out of a corporate penny. He maintains that it would have been impossible to adapt the Logan model for the Indian market without joining forces with a partner based in India. "Logan is the fruit of two years of collaboration of the two companies. The production started one month before schedule and at 15 percent less than the projected costs," Ghosn said. In India, the Logan has become the best-selling car in its class.

IMPLICATIONS: THINK OF COST AS THE CHALLENGERS DO

By skillfully working the levers of cost advantage—that are already so skillfully operated by the challengers—incumbents can narrow the cost gap so it approaches cost parity. This requires more than simply moving operations to a low-wage country. Doing so will not instantly solve the cost problem. This is because incumbents tend to operate in rapidly developing economies in ways that are very different from the way the challengers do—and that can have a significant effect on their ability to realize the cost savings they seek.

For example, incumbents tend to locate their operations in expensive cities, do not optimize their activities to take advantage of labor, ignore local work practices, invest heavily (and, yes, admirably) in environmental protection and worker safety, and work with their own global supplier networks rather than local ones. What's more, they often have to contend with other costs that the challengers do not—such as global overheads and allocations and the often considerable expense of expatriate personnel.

There are a number of actions that incumbents can take, and issues they can address, to help them with cost, beyond simple relocation.

RELOCATE MORE THAN JUST MANUFACTURING

Companies can cut the cost of product development by moving their research and development functions to India, China, or another of the rapidly developing economies, to take advantage of the cost differential for well-educated engineers and scientists. IBM, for example, will move its global procurement headquarters to Shen-zhen—the first time IBM has shifted the headquarters of a major corporate division to a location outside the United States. "In a glob-ally integrated enterprise, for the first time, a company's worldwide capability can be located wherever in the world it makes the most sense," says John Paterson, IBM's chief procurement officer.

The company wants to gain competitive advantages by positioning those in charge of procurement as close as possible to their clients and suppliers. Over the years, it has emphasized its aim of making supply-chain management a core business focus. This strategy enabled IBM to slash its logistics costs by some 20 percent from 1996 through 2003, despite a jump in the volume of goods transported.[31]

BMW, the German automaker, has announced plans to establish an international procurement center in India, most likely in Chen-nai, the most concentrated automotive area in the country.[32]

The challengers, too, are picking up on the message. Lenovo, the Chinese computer maker that bought the PC operations of IBM in 2005, plans to centralize its global advertising operations in Banga-lore, India. The move was made to tap into the skills of the low-cost creative talent and also to better create advertising for global prod-ucts. "The old model was you think it up in New York or London and send it around the world," Shelly Lazarus, chairman and chief executive of WPP Group PLC's Ogilvy & Mather Worldwide, told the *Wall Street Journal*. The company has created advertising for Lenovo for years and collaborated in developing the creative opera-tion in India. "Now we have to be able to think it up anywhere. As our clients are thinking about their brands more globally, we've had to adjust our model."

LEARN

"If I talk to my marketing manager who has not been there," said Dr. Amar Lulla, chief executive officer of Cipla, Ltd., the Indian drugmaker, "I will get an imaginary feedback." Too often, incumbents do not learn enough about the rapidly developing economies in which they are operating or intend to operate. They rely instead on the imaginary feedback gathered during a few cursory visits to their distant markets, or picked up from stays in those markets that consist mainly of meetings in five-star hotels and guided tours of gussied-up factories, or gleaned from reports written by partners or advisers who may have their own agendas to advance.

Procter & Gamble is one incumbent that has learned to focus closely and diligently on the needs and consumption capabilities of its customers. In Mexico, for example, P&G has focused on the needs of low-income consumers who frequent the tiny shops that P&G calls high-frequency stores.

In the rapidly developing economies, P&G estimates that 80 percent of the people buy the goods they want—mostly food, soda, and small household items—from the tiny high-frequency outlets that line busy streets in cities and towns. In Mexico, P&G says, there are some 620,000 such stores, and they show up every block or two. The high-frequency store shopper spends, on average, 23 pesos, or $2.14, a day at the little stores. But those pesos add up to annual sales of about $16 billion in Mexico, by P&G's calculations.

P&G is making a concerted effort to develop and market products to these consumers. This involves understanding not only what consumers want but how they think and how they operate on a daily basis. For example, in Mexico, workers are often paid at the end of a day's work and usually in 5- or 10-peso coins. So P&G has developed single-use packets of its products that don't require a lot of money changing. "If you want to sell to low-income consumers, you have to know what's in their pockets," said José Ramón Riestra, P&G's director of high-frequency stores in Latin America. "It doesn't make sense to have something cost 11 or 12 pesos." A single-use packet of Procter & Gamble's Head & Shoulders shampoo goes for two pesos, about 19 cents.[33]

Be There

There is no substitute for being there, and "there" means where the customers and your colleagues are—usually in lower-cost locations. Incumbents, however, generally set up operations in high-cost areas of the rapidly developing economies—typically in the large, cosmopolitan cities—and bring in high-cost senior management teams to run them. These expatriates are generally well paid and used to a certain standard of living that they're reluctant to give up. So incumbents install them (and their families) in large homes, often with household staff, help their children enroll in American schools, provide them with cars and drivers, pay for their travel back home, and provide a number of other perks that make living away from home easier and more comfortable.

Challengers take a different tack. In China, for instance, homegrown companies are willing and able to operate deep in the mainland to pursue the best cost position. While many incumbents set up their offices and operations in Shanghai and other industrial parks and urban clusters, Chinese companies are more likely to locate their factories in Dongguan or other areas with a less competitive labor market and more generous local government incentives. These far-flung areas have fewer of the international amenities and support networks that expat managers and their families expect. The linguistic and cultural barriers for foreigners are higher as well. And, of course, the costs are much lower.

Partner

Incumbents are at a disadvantage when it comes to understanding and navigating local practices and procedures—even when they have local employees. Chinese companies know how to leverage the local clusters of industry suppliers that provide low-cost components and fast design services. And they're also more likely to have insider relationships with government officials and state-owned enterprises. Thanks to these connections, they're aware of and can take full advantage of the incentives given out by local and regional governments competing for investments.

By entering into joint ventures and other forms of collaboration with challengers, incumbents can learn from—and leverage—their low-cost advantage.

California-based Palm, Inc., forged an alliance with Taiwan's HTC on the Treo 650 Smartphone. Palm designers determined the product's look and feel, picked such key components as the display and core chips, and specified performance requirements. But HTC did much of the mechanical and electrical design. "Without a doubt, they've become a part of the innovation process," says Angel L. Mendez, senior global operations vice president at Palm. "It's less about outsourcing and more about the collaborative way in which design comes together." The result: Palm has cut months off development times, reduced product defects by 50 percent, and boosted gross margins on the Treo by around 20 percent.[34]

When Carlos Ghosn, president and chief executive officer of Renault, talked about his company's alliance with Mahindra & Mahindra to produce and sell the low-cost Logan, he said, "There is a fundamental difference in attitude to cost savings between Western companies and Indian companies. And this is what we want to capture with this partnership."

MAKE IT A MANTRA

Minding the cost gap is, above all, a matter of mind-set.
Repeat the following mantra at least once a day:

- *High headcount isn't always bad.*
- *Automation isn't always best.*

- *Sharing cuts costs.*
- *When going big, go superbig.*
- *Simplicity sells.*
- *High-value, low-cost.*
- *Mind the gap.*

CHAPTER 4

GROWING PEOPLE

"Growing people, that is the fun part."
Amar Lulla, Cipla

Whenn the Silicon Valley entrepreneur Thomas Perkins decided it was time to build a megayacht, he knew the best place to get the work done: Tuzla, Turkey. Twenty years ago, he would have taken his design for the 88-meter, $80 million clipper—named Maltese Falcon—to one of the venerable shipbuilders in Europe, most likely Italy, the Netherlands, or Germany. The idea of building such a craft in Turkey would have seemed like "building a Ferrari in Afghanistan," according to Baki Gökbayrak, the Turkish naval architect who managed the Perkins project and is one of the entrepreneurs who sparked the rise of shipbuilding in Turkey.

Gökbayrak got started in the late 1980s by producing low-cost aluminum "naked hulls" for European firms. Since there were not enough skilled workers in Tuzla, Gökbayrak hired woodcutters from the countryside and trained them in the marine crafts. Just like the Indian outsourcing firms that quickly enhanced their skills, the Turkish companies took on ever more complex tasks. The Maltese Falcon—made entirely in Turkey—is an advanced design that sports three carbon-fiber masts, which required the construction of custom furnaces, and a touchpad console that controls the rotating masts into which the sails retract.

In just the past decade, the town of Tuzla has been transformed from a fishing town of 50,000 people into an industrial capital with 150,000 residents. Some 30,000 of them are employed in the ship-building industry, and many come from Turkey's heartland, where megayachts rarely venture. Not only are construction costs lower in Turkey than they are in the European countries, the workmanship is of equal or higher quality. According to Perkins, if he had built the Maltese Falcon in Italy, "the cost would have been a lot higher, and it wouldn't be as perfect."[1]

The Turkish boatbuilders—like the Indian outsourcers and Chinese manufacturers and other challengers throughout the rapidly developing economies—have found that the best (sometimes the only) way to get the people they need to do the work they want to perform is not to find them, but to grow them.

In India, Wipro has built its considerable success on its ability to recognize and realize the potential of human talent—enabling people to grow so a company could grow along with them. In the mid-1960s, Azim Premji, now Wipro's chief executive officer and managing director but then its fledgling leader, sat around the dining table in his home with a handful of colleagues, talking about the future. According to Pratik Kumar, Wipro's executive vice president of human resources, the leaders "started articulating how they would like to build this company. How would they like to professionalize? How would they like to bring in talent? And most importantly, what values—what elements of our behavior—would they like the organization and its employees to demonstrate?"

In addition to the company's fundamental values, Wipro's value proposition to their employees would be built around three "pillars," as Kumar called them, upon which they would build their human resources activities: early opportunities for growth, investment in learning and development, and a world of opportunities in the spectrum of work available to do.

"There is also a softer element," Kumar added, "which is the role that culture plays in making people believe that they have come to the right place and would like to invest their years in a career here."

Regarding Wipro's rise from a distance, it's easy to imagine that the company's success has come relatively easily. Isn't India brimming over with well-educated, English-speaking people who are young, available, and eager to work?

Not exactly. In fact, throughout the rapidly developing economies, there is a talent problem, a misalignment of the quantity and quality of people and the quantity and quality of jobs that need to be done. In some places, there is an abundance of workers and in others, a serious shortage. Elsewhere, there can be a yawning gap between the number of people who are available to work and those who are actually employable.

For both incumbents and challengers, the issue of talent is no longer an operational one ("We'll need to hire X people at such and such a location and pay X per hour"); it has become a matter of strategy. "Which products can we create where, given the availability of and constraints on labor and talent?" So, when competing in the era of globality, it's necessary to pay attention to the main actions involved in growing people:

- *Recruiting for Rapid Growth*
- *Developing for Depth*
- *Deploying for Early Results*
- *Letting Leaders Build*

RECRUITING FOR RAPID GROWTH

The tremendous demand for people comes about largely as the result of the blistering rate of growth that challengers have experienced in the past several years. Demand for laborers in China is so great that there are some 140 to 150 million migrant workers constantly on the move from province to province, crowding into cities where there is the most work. In the southern metropolis of Guangzhou, for example, there are about 7.5 million registered residents and 3.7 million migrant workers living in temporary housing all around them.[2] In 2007, the city banned the use of motorbikes, the migrant workers' primary means of transport, to cut down on street crime committed by biker-muggers.

Demand is also high for educated and skilled workers, especially English-speaking managers, in China. According to some estimates, more than 99 percent of the country's university graduates are employed, versus 96.5 percent for the thirty countries of the Organization for Economic Co-operation and Development (OECD).[3]

In India, there will be a million new jobs added in 2007. The IT and business-process outsourcing industries need to make 20,000 new hires every month. The organized retail sector is expected to add 2.2 million jobs by 2010. IBM alone plans to add over 50,000 new employees in India between 2007 and 2010. The big growth centers, like Bangalore and Pune, face severe shortages compared to many other parts of the country. As a result, senior managers there have enjoyed annual wage hikes of 20 to 25 percent over the past four years.

In eastern Europe, workers are pouring out of their countries to take jobs in developed countries. In "Detroit East," the huge carmaking cluster near Bratislava, Slovakia—where Volkswagen, PSA Peugeot Citroën, and Kia run factories—the demand for workers is so intense that Peugeot Citroën provided more than 1,000 housing units to entice people in from the eastern part of Slovakia. Skoda, which operates factories in neighboring Czech Republic, raised wages by 12.7 percent for some 25,000 of its workers.

In Romania, more than 10 percent of the country's population of 22.3 million, about 2.5 million people, worked abroad after 1989, the numbers increasing particularly after 2002.[4] Romania's population woes are worsened by the country's low fertility rate of 1.3 lifetime births per woman, which is significantly lower than the 2.1 rate needed to ensure replacement of the population (a problem that is common throughout Europe). A study by the National Institute of Economic Research (INCE) predicts that Romania will rely on immigrants to satisfy the demand for labor for at least the next five years. The study also says that the number of university students will drop by as much as 40 percent by 2013.[5]

In Poland, the exodus of workers to the developed countries for higher-paying jobs is so massive (as many as two million Poles have left the country since 2004), President Lech Kaczyński had trouble finding anyone to paint his apartment in Warsaw.

Joke heard in a bar in Gdansk:

Pole 1: Statistics show that four out of ten young Poles live in stress.
Pole 2: And the rest?
Pole 1: They live in London.[6]

THE EDUCATION MYTH

In any high-growth economy an intense demand for human resources might not seem unusual, but in the rapidly developing economies, it does. This is not only because the populations are so vast, but also because the educational level seems so high.

In fact, India and China both have difficulties in educating their people, and the employability of those who are educated is lower than one might expect.

The problem is most acute in India. There are some 80,000 institutions of higher learning in India, including three hundred to four hundred universities, in comparison to about 4,000 in the United States. The number of education institutions has been rising over the past three years—although this total includes a very wide variety of colleges, universities, trade schools, training facilities, and other types of learning establishments. An educational accreditation system has been in place for only ten years, and in many states, accreditation is voluntary. It's certain, however, that a great percentage of these institutions would not be classified as colleges in the United States or other developed economies. One study suggests that only a fifth of them can be considered up to world standards.

A 2006 survey by the *London Times Higher Education Supplement* put only two Indian universities on a list of the world's two hundred best universities—the Indian Institute of Technology at #56 and the Indian Institute of Management at #68. China got three into the top hundred: Peking University at #14, Tsinghua University at #28, and Hong Kong University of Science and Technology at #58. Mexico's single entry, Universidad Nacional Autónoma de México, ranks #74. Russia also has one university, Lomonosov Moscow State University, on the list, at #93. By contrast, thirty-three of the world's best universities, according to the *Times* survey, are located in the United States, including seven of the top ten. (Guess which one came first? Yes, Harvard.) Fourteen are located in the United Kingdom, and all the rest are in developed countries.

Three to four million students graduate from Indian colleges and universities each year. Sixty-five percent of them earn non-technical degrees, including BAs and BSs. According to Hewitt Associates, the human resources consulting firm, only about one-fourth of all graduates are directly hirable without extensive in-house training.[7] Other estimates put employability at 15 percent. Some analysts predict a shortfall of some 500,000 workers in the IT and BPO industries in India as early as 2010.[8]

James Surowiecki, writing in *The New Yorker*, cites a study led by Vivek Wadhwa, of Duke University, that concludes that the standards for the job "engineer" are very different in the United States than they are in India and that, by U.S. criteria, India produces about 170,000 engineers a year rather than the 400,000 that are often cited.[9] Even so, the number of graduates keeps rising. By 2010, India is expected to graduate 600,000 engineers, mathematicians, technicians, and scientists.[10]

In China, the Cultural Revolution—which took place from 1966 to 1976—severely disrupted or ended the education of millions·of people who would now be members of the management ranks, but are instead working at lower-paying jobs that require less education.

Today, many of those people who lost their educations are parents or grandparents, and they have become so concerned about getting their kids into the best universities that they put tremendous resources and energy into education. According to the Chinese Academy of Social Sciences, households spend more on education than anything else, even though town and city dwellers are allowed to have only one child. Chinese public schools generally have large classes and poor equipment, so parents often bribe officials to get their kids into the best schools. They also spend liberally on private tutors and independent programs like FasTracKids, which calls itself a "junior M.B.A. program" and accepts children as young as four.[11]

There has been an explosion in the number of colleges and universities throughout China—up from 1,041 in 2001 to 1,800 in 2006, an increase of more than 70 percent. What's more, China's big public universities—such as Renmin University of China (formerly People's University), Beijing Normal University, and China Medical University—have expanded considerably in the past decade and opened satellite campuses in fast-growing cities like Zhuhai. In the United States, by contrast, the number of institutions of higher education has declined a little in the past few years. In 2001, there were 4,197; in 2006, the number was 4,162.

As a result of the proliferation and expansion of China's colleges and universities, many more places were made available. In the past, only the top 4 percent or so of China's college-age students could gain admission, but now there are places for about 17 percent. In 2007, a record ten million Chinese students took the gaokao, an exam that lasts two to four days and determines whether the test taker will receive one of the five million undergraduate slots available.[12] The number of university graduates has skyrocketed from 1.5 million in 2002 to 2.8 million in 2004 and about 3.4 million in 2005.[13] By 2010, it is expected that about 800,000 of those who graduate from Chinese colleges and universities will receive degrees in engineering, math, science, or other technical subjects.[14]

Taken together, then, India and China will graduate nearly 1.5 million science and engineering students by the year 2010, twelve times the output of the U.S. university system in the same disciplines. If these trends continue (and they are more likely to accelerate than slow), by 2020 or sooner, the bulk of product development and research resources will be in China and India rather than in the West.

The question remains: how many of them can do the job?

DEVELOPING FOR DEPTH

Because the demand for talent is so high and the supply so frustratingly available yet unavailable, the challengers put a great deal of effort into the second aspect of the talent struggle—training, educating, and developing potential hires and new recruits so they have the depth of skills they need, as well as a deeper sense of commitment to the company.

ICICI Bank, India's second largest bank, first faced the "employability" problem in 2003, when its demand for workers began to seriously exceed the supply. At the time, ICICI Bank was a small institutional lender. Today, it is a leading retail bank with assets of $79 billion, a network of 950 branches, 3,300 ATMs, and—most important for this discussion—an employee base of 42,000 people. It brings on board 15,000 to 20,000 new employees each year and achieves an attrition rate much lower than its banking rivals.

To find and secure the people it needed to fuel its growth, ICICI Bank made a key strategic decision: to develop talent rather than try to find it fully developed. As K. Ramkumar, group chief human resources officer for ICICI Bank, explained to us, the process meant—and still means—identifying people who have "undeployed, nascent potential" and then training and developing them to become high-performing ICICI Bank employees. "There is no talent shortage in India," he told us. "There is a shortage of skills, but not of talent."

To provide the people with the knowledge and basic skills they will need in their jobs, ICICI Bank has essentially created its own institution of higher education, a state-of-the-art training engine. It includes extensive e-learning capabilities, nine management institutes located throughout the country, and some 2,500 "content providers," aka teachers. A typical course of study lasts about a month—with another two weeks of functional training some time during the first year—and the recent recruit emerges with the ability to be productive almost immediately.

ICICI Bank is onto an important concept, one that many other companies in the rapidly developing economies are embracing in their struggles with talent: an employee's "learnability"—the person's inherent ability to learn, rather than just the applicant's academic credentials or knowledge of technical or other business content.

Many Indian companies in the information technology and business-process outsourcing industries have come to the same conclusion, and the success of such initiatives suggests that the concept of "nascent potential" is an intriguing one. Indeed, the initial results of a study conducted by a highly successful challenger have shown that there was not a strong correlation between the quality of an employee's education (defined by the quality of the school the employee had attended) and his or her success within the company.

Wipro developed the Wipro Academy of Software Excellence (WASE) to recruit and train non-IT graduates in IT and software engineering skills, in conjunction with Birla Institute of Technology and Science, an engineering institute in Pilani, India. Wipro pays all admissions and school fees and selected candidates work on company projects during weekdays while attending classes at the academy on the weekends. The program has been a runaway success—this year, Wipro will be employing as many as five thousand of its academy graduates.

Similarly, Tata Consultancy Services (TCS) is grooming science graduates for an IT career through TCS Ignite—a program in which new hires receive seven months of training but are on the payroll and work on real company projects throughout that period. The company's Tata Academic Interface Program works with local colleges to create various types of academic engagement while enabling the company to gain exposure to local talent.

In China, Hisense, the producer of consumer electronics, has entered into a relationship with the Beijing University of Aeronautics and Astronautics to set up an engineering postgraduate program approved by the Ministry of Education and with Peking University to set up an MBA remote-education training program. "These measures turn out a large number of recruits for Hisense," said Guo Qingcun, vice president of Hisense, and help to guarantee the company a "supply of talent."[15]

In India, many challengers are looking beyond the educated talent pool from the top colleges and universities of the major cities, to graduates of schools in smaller cities and towns. But because the quality of education at these institutions is so inconsistent, companies have to develop intimate knowledge of local educational standards. When necessary, the challengers provide course material and even teachers to local colleges. They may also create assessment tools to help them evaluate both the knowledge and learnability of applicants. S. Ramadorai, chief executive officer of Tata Consultancy Services, says that such activities enable them to "normalize different skill levels" better than competitors and effectively tap into the talent that exists in abundance through much of small-town India.

Several IT companies in India are betting even further on the idea of nascent potential by piloting a program to hire good students from exceptionally poor backgrounds who do not have the means to afford an education at a top university. The companies have designed a special training program for these recruits, who go on to take positions in the company.

Challengers from China, India, and other rapidly developing economies are making an end run around their own educational systems by sponsoring some of their brightest people to pursue graduate studies at the best universities in the United States and spend some time working there for incumbent firms. Then the challengers draw these people back to their home countries, on the theory that their companies will benefit from this combination of Western education and home country experience and understanding. Between

2001 and 2004, an estimated 25,000 IT professionals returned to India from developed countries.[16] Not only are the challengers pulling talent from the developed countries to fill leadership positions, some 68 percent of the Indian executives now working in the United States are actively looking for employment opportunities that will take them home.[17] These West-educated returnees are helping to fuel the challengers' drive to build their innovation capabilities. Many of the major challengers' R&D functions are headed by leaders who have worked for leading incumbents at some point in their careers.

Developing special recruitment programs, creating academies, scouring the remote countryside for talent, paying employees to learn at home, and sending them abroad may sound expensive, but challengers like Wipro and TCS say that such processes do not add cost. Although it takes Wipro about six months to train a graduate with a nonengineering degree, in comparison to three months for a graduate with an engineering degree, the difference in compensation is enough to offset the cost of the longer training program. To train a nonengineer "actually costs us about 50 percent of what an engineering grad would, from a salary point of view," said Pratik Kumar of Wipro.

If these recruiting programs continue to achieve results, they could open up new, untapped applicant pools throughout the rapidly developing economies while providing opportunities for young people that were previously unavailable.

REALIZING NASCENT POTENTIAL

Recruitment, however, is only the first part of the struggle. Next, the challengers must work hard to identify their top performers, continue to educate them, and engage them enough that they do not want to jump ship at the first attractive offer they receive from a competitor—all very difficult to do when a workforce is growing by as much as 30 to 35 percent a year.

At ICICI Bank, once the new hires join the workforce, senior leaders devote a great deal of time (hundreds of hours each year) to reviewing talent at all levels of the organization. To succeed there, Ramkumar says, "You need strategic agility, not strategic thinking."

Similar training and shared learning can be seen in the Tata Group in India. The Tata Management Training Center (TMTC), which is supported by the Group Corporate Center (GCC), is used to "develop and share knowledge relating to globalization, innovation, and company-specific experiences," as Alan Rosling, an executive director of Tata Group, explained to us. Senior and junior managers from all Tata Group companies attend the TMTC to learn from one another and reaffirm the Tata Group values—trust, integrity, and social commitment—that underpin the company's globalization efforts. The Tata Quality Management System (TQMS)—again supported by the GCC—ensures that all Tata's companies are evaluated by a team of more than 400 assessors who, as Rosling says, "share knowledge, best practices, and international learnings."

Tata Consultancy Services (TCS), part of Tata Group, has opened a training center in Montevideo, Uruguay, to supply trained manpower for Latin America's developing IT and BPO industry. This marks the first such investment in the area of training and development by any Indian firm in Latin America. "We intend to train over 3,000 employees in the next four years in a wide range of technologies, methodologies, language skills and cultural sensitivity in serving clients from offshore," Mario Tucci, vice president of TCS Iberoamerica, said in a statement.[18]

"Each step of growth throws a new set of challenges—in recruiting, training, deploying, retraining, or remanning. We are in an industry where getting people from training to deployment, without any wastage, is a key measure of utilization," said Ramadorai of TCS.

In China, Johnson Electric's Session C program (named after a similar program at General Electric) is a process designed to identify and develop top talent in the company and is the direct responsibility of the company's chief executive officer. A regular audit identifies top talent, who are referred to inside the company as the "JE Jenes." In 2005, Johnson Electric launched a senior management development seminar to bring together Johnson Electric's international cohort of senior managers for one week each year to learn and network with each other. This is a senior-level supplement to JE's flagship JEN-ESIS residential leadership-development program. JE also operates the in-house Johnson University, which each year provides the company with an essential supply of highly qualified motor engineers.

One of the strategies adopted by Wipro to help develop its people is to facilitate role switching by creating an in-house labor market. At Wipro, every job posted externally is made available internally through a program called Wings Within. If an existing Wipro employee is selected for a new position, the employee has the liberty to move, and his current manager does not have authority to block the new assignment, provided that no current work would suffer from the proposed reassignment. The scale of this internal labor market is impressive; of seven thousand people taking on new roles at Wipro every quarter, five thousand are new hires and two thousand come from inside the company.

Not only do these efforts attract and engage people, they help the challengers retain their talent once they have them. Because there is so much growth, such high demand for talent, and such a shortage of well-educated employees—and because companies often increase compensation rates to attract the people they need—there is an astonishingly high level of attrition and very little employee loyalty in many of the rapidly developing economies. Twenty years ago, before the tsunami began, there was an unspoken social contract between employees and employers. Today, it has been jettisoned in favor of individual career opportunism.

In China, it is not uncommon for an employee to land a highly desirable role with a well-known incumbent, only to leave after six months on the job for a pay increase of $5,000. Attrition rates for executives in China are 25 percent greater than the global average.[19] A survey by the Corporate Executive Board shows that in China and India, employees are besieged by offers from other companies through headhunters, employment agencies, and direct inquiries— more than 50 percent of employees are contacted. In developed countries, some 20 to 25 percent of employed workers are scouted by other firms.

The high attrition rates are not just the result of employee-snatching by competitive firms nearby or in the same country. In India, just as in eastern Europe, workers are being enticed to work in other countries around the world. "It is a huge crisis. Huge!" said A. M. Naik, chairman and managing director of Larsen & Toubro. "Insurmountable, nearly. All the engineers are leaving. My welding engineers, metallurgical engineers, construction managers, project managers. All going. In 2050, almost 15 to 17 percent of the work-force around the world will be Indians."

THE BENEFITS OF TRAINING YOUR OWN AT EMBRAER

Aircraft manufacturer Embraer decided to confront its need for spe-cialized engineers by taking on the task of training them itself, with an eighteen-month course of academic and practical studies for its own engineers, culminating in a master's degree for those whose final work is submitted and approved. The company pays all the bills for expenses, a laptop per student, and for the courses. By training the students using the company's own software and equipment, Embraer can produce between 100 and 150 new and "extremely capable" engi-neers each year, while maintaining a staff of about 4,500.

Students apply the skills they have learned to design—with the guidance of supervisors, mentors, and other engineers—an original product, over the last six months of the course. This system helps to ensure the ultimate quality of Embraer service, as the company finds itself with a pleasing talent pyramid rather than a bottleneck. It also allows for a significant retention rate, as students are motivated to further their professional and personal growth.

Since the university was founded in 2001, the company has invested more than $100 million in engineer training and has lost fewer than 10 percent of graduates from the program. This strategy is not only improving the company's retention and sustainability rates, it is also helping it to grow, as the program gains increasing attention and praise from insiders and outsiders alike. The training program is an attractive feature for many Brazilians who lack any education beyond high school and is an important step in professional development. The competitiveness in turn allows the company to select only the best candidates for employment.

Training your own engineers becomes still more attractive when the cultural implications of globalization are considered. As Satoshi Yokota pointed out, Embraer at first tried to hire foreign employees to fill its need for engineers, including more than three hundred Russians, Canadians, Americans, Indians, and others. Yet this solution was inadequate, he said, because many of the recruits were little more than "mercenaries" to the cause. Thus the university emerged as the perfect solution for creating skilled local labor for a locally based company.

Gaining popularity by providing training services is a strategy picked up by other South American companies as well, for example the Brazilian mining company CVRD. Tito Martins, director of corporate affairs at the company, pointed out how useful business experience in Brazil becomes when applied to doing business in other developing countries. In his view, local perspectives on the company's investment in social programs, employee support, and training can have a substantial impact on CVRD's growth and success abroad.

DEPLOYING FOR EARLY RESULTS

In addition to their activities in recruiting and developing, challengers also deploy and utilize talent very differently from incumbents—they have perfected the science and art of rapid deployment and productive utilization of their talent.

In China, Hisense established the Hisense Research Institute of Shandong University, which cooperates with higher-education institutions to develop new knowledge of various kinds. The center enjoys "special zone" status from the Chinese government, and the chance to be one of the 140 people who work and study there is very attractive to potential recruits. "The basis of technology innovation is the gathering and cultivation of talents," said Guo Qingcun, vice president of Hisense. The company believes in a "talent-oriented operation," he says, and has "formulated a human resources exploration system" that is expert in all the aspects of managing talent—"hunting, utilization, cultivation, promotion, and holding," as he calls them.

Wipro believes that it has a competitive advantage over its incumbent competitors thanks to its deployment capabilities. These include its speed in training and integrating its new hires and its practice of moving people between projects so they are as fully utilized as possible. Wipro also breaks down complex processes into smaller and simpler elements, so that employees with an average of four to five years of experience can accomplish tasks that would formerly have required an employee with eight to ten years of experience to do. The result is that the average age of the team is often lowered, with no decrease in productivity. All of this is particularly important for Wipro, because its workforce of nearly eighty thousand people continues to grow at 30 to 35 percent per year, and 50 percent of its hires are "freshers"—recent college graduates—so the average age of the Wipro employees is just twenty-seven.

These efforts to recruit, develop, and deploy engineering and science employees are very important because the challengers that are able to build engineering operations of very large size can gain significant competitive advantage. In China, for example, Huawei Technologies has built a leadership position in the telecommunications equipment market—not just in China but in many overseas markets—by leveraging its enormous bench strength of engineering talent. Huawei employs thirty thousand engineers (nearly half its total workforce) and locates them in twelve R&D centers, five of which are outside China, and is constantly working to build its capabilities. Huawei bids aggressively on new orders, knowing that it can bring to bear its vast engineering resource to design and install products and systems faster than competitors.

In India, Tata Motors and Bajaj Auto have taken a similar approach and created very large engineering groups. Not only can they create new products at a fraction of what it costs the incumbents, they are also developing new forms of advantage. For example, using their engineers in key functions like process and production engineering can lead to a reduction in capital costs for new plants and equipment of 20 to 30 percent. An in-house team of engineers generally goes into far more detail about how to optimize plant layouts and equipment specifications than do similar teams in incumbent companies, which often outsource this function due to the high cost of talent and depend more on expensive external specialists and equipment suppliers, who prefer to sell standard solutions.

LETTING LEADERS BUILD

The rapidly developing economies are growing so fast that companies can catch a glimpse of an opportunity, jump on it, and ride it up quickly. However, leaders who are accustomed to five-year plans, unwavering strategy, and well-defined success factors may be unable to recognize such fleeting opportunities or, if they can see them, may not have the ability or authority to grab them fast enough and build on them immediately.

The successful challengers are led by strong individuals who are empowered by their organizations (and by themselves) to get the job done—people who are, above all else, builders. Builders are part entrepreneur—a person who constantly looks for new opportunities and takes make-or-break personal risks to win them. They are also part team captain—constantly recruiting, developing, and inspiring their people and looking for partners to augment capabilities.

Builders are quite different from operators, whose strength lies in maintaining and making incremental improvements to established operations. Operators tend to be more effective in relatively mature environments. Builders often make it up as they go along and demand that their managers and employees do the same. They're more willing to act fast and to base decisions on intuition as well as due diligence (which, given scant market information, may be unavailable anyway).

To build a company that can succeed in the rapidly developing economies, builders are needed in leadership positions throughout the company. The environment is a tangibly more opportunistic business space than the one that incumbents—especially those with operators in charge—are accustomed to. There are interventionist governments that actively seek to protect certain industries, openly favor domestic manufacturers, mandate the transfer of overseas expertise to local firms—all of which opens new opportunities for local enterprise. There are relatively young industries, companies, and markets in which no company can yet claim a decisive competitive edge (the way, say, Wal-Mart can in lowest-cost retailing). There are compelling social development objectives (employment, poverty alleviation, education) alongside profit objectives, meaning that sometimes instead of doing what is commercially expedient (laying off people), the leaders have to work to find another solution that is personally and socially acceptable. And there are better funded, more sophisticated incumbents planting flags all over the domestic market space.

When companies come up against big, established global firms in these environments, they need to find a competitive edge somewhere, and often that means grasping at maybes, taking risks in search of some new advantage.

Cheung Yan is an unlikely entrepreneur who built her company, Nine Dragons, from nothing. From humble origins, and without a formal education, Cheung started working at a young age in a textile plant, before getting a job in a small paper company. While there, she became aware of the growing demand for waste paper to be recycled into packaging material, so she started a company in Hong Kong in 1985, but soon moved to the United Sates, where more waste paper was available. Surfing the wave of globalization, Cheung's company was collecting the packaging of Chinese goods imported into the United States, to export it back to China. In just five years the company became the largest exporter in the United States of waste paper.

In 1995, Cheung returned to Hong Kong and founded Nine Dragons. It took her three years to set up the first papermaking machine, with a production capacity of 200,000 tons per year. She continued to increase capacity by adding more machines and, by 2007, had a capacity of 5.4 million tons. She plans to double that by constructing a third production site in China, which she says will make Nine Dragons the world's largest paper producer. While gaining scale to reduce cost per unit, Nine Dragons has also managed to maintain prices and enjoys a 20-percent margin, one of the highest in the industry. Cheung has become one of the richest self-made women in the world.

In the rapidly developing economies, successful companies recognize their builder-leaders and give them plenty of room to operate.

IMPLICATIONS: OVERINVEST IN PEOPLE

The worldwide talent situation is in turmoil.

Low-skilled laborers are wandering the globe, drawn away from one low-wage situation by another one slightly higher up the pay scale. Indians head to the Gulf. Mexicans cross the border to the United States. Chinese leave the farm for Changsha and Guangzhou. Slovakians migrate to Poland. The Polish decamp for England.

Educated, highly skilled workers are in high demand everywhere. "If you want to retain them, you'd better have different geographies for them to work in within your company," said L&T's A. M. Naik. "This is all about being multinational. A GE employee can get transferred from anywhere to anywhere. If you want to work in Africa, you can go."

Of all the resources that everyone from everywhere will be competing for, talent is the most precious and hard to come by. Many challengers, as we've seen, are working to grow their own talent. The rest, you can be sure, will be looking to poach.

Plan for Global Talent Requirements

Understanding the competencies required to achieve strategic growth plans requires more than just forecasting headcount targets. Incumbents have to plan talent needs on a global basis if they truly want to exploit worldwide talent pools. This is easier said than done, given the entrenched geographical, functional, and mental boundaries that exist in many incumbent companies.

In order to effectively place their activities around the world and tap into the global talent pools, incumbents must consider each individual country and region in their approach to planning, sourcing, and deploying talent. This strategy calls for collaboration between the global executive committee (which should include functional and business representatives) and country executives from high-growth markets. By accurately forecasting the global talent requirements and optimally best-shoring their talent planning, companies can get the best people for the right jobs anywhere in the world. This may mean opportunistically tapping into the engineering talent in India or the programming talent in China, or exporting Brazilian business leaders to head up Venezuelan operations.

Global talent planning to effectively capture growth and talent pools in the rapidly developing economies requires a shift in corporate thinking.

Shane Tedjarati, head of Honeywell China, speaks of the paradigm shift that is necessary to fully capitalize on the potential of China. He believes that many incumbents approach China and India with a "West-to-East" mind-set, but that this attitude will not get them very far. Global strategic direction, product design and innovation, and policies and procedures are often developed in the West and transplanted to the East with little or no local tailoring. To fully unleash the potential of local talent, incumbents must allow their local organizations to innovate and develop products (for consumption both in that market and abroad) and create local operating policies and strategies that are not only better suited to their local markets but can also be exported to other rapidly developing economies and even, in some cases, back to the West with great success.

It may seem like a risky move for an incumbent to abandon the policies and products that have brought it success, and riskier still to give free rein to new talent in comparatively uncharted territory. Yet this approach is the most effective way to gain an edge in a local market, and with careful planning and collaboration, it is also the best way to build trust and familiarity with the new talent and the new branch of the company.

The small Silicon Valley Internet start-up WebEx offers an example of utilizing a local talent pool. WebEx offers online collaboration tools for the global Internet user. In the company's early days, it realized that to compete effectively, it would need to tap into a lower-cost global talent pool for skilled engineers than it had access to in the United States.

One of the founders of WebEx is a Chinese national who had moved to the United States in his thirties and had a deep knowledge of the Chinese market. Out of financial necessity, he and his partner, who was born in India and educated in the United States, were able to successfully launch development and programming centers in three second-tier cities outside Shanghai. They hired an exceptionally capable human resources person who was able to recruit highly skilled engineers. They have eight hundred Chinese employees (a large number of whom were born and raised in China) and have developed an effective U.S.-China team structure to offer complex and highly valuable work to both Chinese and U.S. programmers. The company was acquired in 2007 by Cisco Systems, which had been watching WebEx's strategy.

Cisco, too, has managed a mind-set shift. The company is planning to create a second headquarters in India to capitalize on the opportunity in the rapidly developing economies, and more than 20 percent of its leadership team is based there.

BUILD LOCAL LEADERSHIP

Incumbents have to become (or at least appear to become) more like locals to take on the challengers in the challengers' home markets. This means that they must put together a strong local leadership team to guide the company's progress. A local leadership team is able to understand the subtle cultural nuances; is inherently aware of and able to navigate the complex market, regulatory, and political dynamics; and can communicate with local partners (suppliers, distributors, retailers, etc.) in their own language.

Building a successful local leadership team is a multifaceted challenge. First, to attract and retain top local talent at all levels of the organization, there must be a clear and viable path to leadership. There cannot be a real or perceived glass ceiling for locals, or they will look elsewhere for a career that will allow them to realize their potential. Second, it is often a costly endeavor to pay expat compensation packages to the majority of a leadership team on a sustained basis. Finally, many incumbents are finding it increasingly difficult to have a large enough pool of senior executives within the company who are willing and able to relocate to all the growth markets. Many incumbents are struggling to overcome these hurdles and build a visionary, entrepreneurial, and people-focused leadership team using local talent.

To combat this problem, successful incumbents systematically build a program to fast-track the path to leadership for local employees. A career track that would normally take ten to fifteen years in the United States or Europe can be shortened to five years in China if high-potential junior talent is given the right experiences. Requirements like extensive skill sets, assignments in multiple locations, and operational and strategic experience are not that difficult to meet as long as you know well in advance that you will have to strategically orchestrate these opportunities among the locals. Similarly, providing the appropriate networking opportunities for high-potential local talent to gain the trust of a U.S. or European executive is not impossible—it just takes planning.

BALANCE LOCAL NEEDS WITH GLOBAL STANDARDS

Effectively balancing local human resources customization with global standards spans all talent-management capabilities. From recruiting to training and development to succession planning and performance measurement, companies must effectively leverage global programs and approaches while bolstering or tailoring them to meet the local demands and complexities.

For recruiting, this means tailoring the employment value proposition for the local markets to offer top talent the packages and opportunities that are most important to them. P&G does this by offering mortgage financing support to employees in Russia—a perk that would not be as highly valued in the United States, where low-cost mortgages have been so readily available. For training, this requires that companies understand the skills, experience, and knowledge gaps that may be present in one market, but not another, and adjusting their activities accordingly.

As we saw, challengers have developed their unique solutions in the form of in-house universities to bridge the gap between the inherent talents of their people and their academic credentials. Most incumbents have been trying to hire away these trained professionals from challengers to meet their own hiring needs. This increases wages and also creates retention issues all around.

We spoke with one senior manager of an Indian IT company about how challengers can deliver a "sucker punch" (said partly tongue-in-cheek, but partly seriously) to incumbent competitors.

In the big metropolitan cities, there is low availability of talent, and the people are relatively high cost, in comparison to other parts of the local economy. In the second-, third-, and fourth-tier cities and towns, the opposite is true—there is a high availability of people (the majority of the workforce, after all, lives outside the big cities), and they will work at low cost because of the low level of development and industrialization in these areas, and thus the low demand for their talents.

The incumbents generally base their operations in the tier-one cities and seek their talent from the pool available there. The challengers can move their operations to the outlying cities and towns, because they need to lower their costs and because they know how to operate in those areas.

So, according to this manager, the incumbents get sucker punched—they find themselves locked into a position where talent availability is dwindling and costs are going up, while the local firms quietly exit the cities and reduce their costs by taking advantage of large, low-cost talent pools away from the big downtowns. This manager may have been exaggerating the problem that incumbents face, but incumbents can draw a lesson from his interpretation about localizing their recruitment and training activities in the rapidly developing economies.

Schindler Group, the Swiss elevator manufacturer, is an incumbent that is experimenting with recruiting people from second- and third-tier cities. Although experience at incumbents is highly valued by top Chinese talent, these people prefer to work for well-known brand names. In addition, the sexier the industry or company and the higher the starting salaries, the easier it is to recruit top talent in first-tier cities. Schindler, although well respected in its industry, is hardly an iconic, global brand name. Nor is elevator manufacturing looked upon as a glamour industry. And Schindler did not wish to upset its entire compensation structure by overpaying talent in order to attract it. So the company has begun to focus its recruiting efforts on a pool of applicants outside the big cities that it is more likely to succeed in hiring and retaining. This approach, although still a work in progress, has great potential for Schindler. They believe that it will contribute to a higher retention rate and even stronger employee loyalty.

Once talent is hired, incumbents like Unilever have integrated their local leadership teams into their global succession planning and performance-measurement process to effectively bubble up top talent from around the world. Among these incumbents, all talent is reviewed against the same global performance and potential metrics at a local level. Once top talent is identified, regional and functional committees review the talent in light of positions available globally. They then develop global plans for rotations, career opportunities, and individual development needs.

Balancing the benefits of lower costs with the need for a baseline quality of talent is a challenging proposition. A well-known U.S. industrial goods company has experienced great difficulty in attracting and retaining quality talent in one area of China. In an effort to lower operating costs, it established a satellite office in a city about a ninety-minute drive away from Shanghai. The company is discovering that it cannot attract the type of talent it requires at the salaries it is comfortable offering in this second-tier city. Rather than move operations to a more expensive, metropolitan location, it is currently reevaluating its compensation offering.

So incumbents must keep a finger on the ever-changing pulse of the talent market when it comes to employee needs (prioritization of compensation, best job locations, and the like). And, when calculating the cost benefit of low-cost locations, it is essential to evaluate the impact on recruitment and retention of talent.

THINK WHO, NOT HOW

How many world-class automotive designers are there in the world? How many automotive companies want to hire them? Which comes first, the application or the software engineer?

Companies that want to succeed in the age of globality think just as carefully about *who* will accomplish what needs to be done as they do about *how* they'll do it.

CHAPTER 5

REACHING DEEP INTO MARKETS

"We listened to the market."
Luís Carlos Affonso, Embraer

In the poorer neighborhoods of Mexico, when do-it-yourself home-owners buy a bag or two of cement, they have more on their minds than pouring a new floor or building a patio wall. For them, cement is a matter of *patrimonio*—family legacy. The cement floor speaks directly to the children and grandchildren of their forebears, who cared enough to add value to the place. When Cemex made the connection between cement and family heritage, the company began marketing its products in easy-to-heft bags and supporting them with aspirational advertising.[1]

Consumers in the rapidly developing economies—especially those who live beyond the city lights and high-income districts—sometimes behave in ways that surprise not only incumbents but the challengers themselves. In rural China, for example, repair-men for Haier—the world's largest maker of refrigerators and the fourth-largest maker of appliances—found they were making a lot of service calls to consumers whose clothes washers had clogged drainpipes. The repairmen discovered that, in addition to washing their clothes in the machines, the customers were also washing vegetables in them. Sweet potatoes, in particular, were getting the machine-clean treatment. Haier pondered the situation, made a few modifications to the product—including larger drainpipes—and provided instructions on how to use the machines to do the vegetable wash.

In the earliest days of the tsunami, only a small percentage of incumbents could see the vast populations of the rapidly developing economies as the enormous markets they were or could become. This was primarily because the incumbents just didn't understand the needs and wants of the mass-market consumer—or of the business customer, for that matter—in China or India or Mexico or Poland. Even if they did understand what the market might accept, or thought they understood, they were easily and understandably daunted by the countries' distribution systems. How do you deliver a product through this maze of warehouses and country depositories, middlemen, tiny shops and street kiosks, rickety trucks, three-wheelers, bicycles, donkey carts, and men with baskets on their backs? So most incumbents stayed away from the rapidly developing economies as markets altogether or focused on high-end customers whom they could better understand and urban markets they could manage more easily.

Now, however, the markets of the rapidly developing economies are becoming extremely attractive to incumbents in a wide variety of industries because of their huge size, increasing prosperity, and greater business friendliness. Those economics are experiencing an average of 4 to 5 percent higher annual growth than that of developed markets, and by 2010, those economies will account for 45 percent of the world's gross domestic product and 60 percent of GDP growth, according to the Economist Intelligence Unit.

China, for example, is already the largest consumer of mobile handsets. In India, the market for consumer durables is expected to double in five years, growing from $4.8 billion in 2005 to more than $9.7 billion by 2010. The retail market, worth more than $230 billion in 2005 and growing at 6 percent per year, is projected to reach $310 billion by 2010. And the growth will not be restricted to China and India. Russia is predicted to experience a 22-percent compound annual growth rate (CAGR) for retail sales. Brazil will see a CAGR of 12 percent for clothing. Turkey has already been on a tear. Its gross domestic product has grown by an average of 7 percent, its exports have more than doubled, and foreign direct investment has jumped from $1 billion to a whopping $18 billion.

So there is no longer much doubt that the rapidly developing economies are on their way to becoming the most important growth markets of the future. There is uncertainty, however, about how the markets will develop, which segments will take off, and which companies will be successful in them. Growth will be achieved through a handful of key actions in the struggle involved in reaching deep into these markets:

- *Creating New Categories*
- *Finding the Sweet Spot*
- *Localizing*
- *Distributing Amid Chaos*
- *Doing Business with Business*
- *Stepping into New Markets*

CREATING NEW CATEGORIES

In the developed economies, the categories of consumer and industrial goods are well defined and well known, and it's pretty rare for a company to disrupt the business environment with a product or service that breaks new ground. In the rapidly developing economies, however, consumers (and businesses) have been so limited in their consumption for so long that it's easier for a challenger to find new territory to explore and develop.

HUIYUAN: LET THE CHINESE PEOPLE DRINK PURE JUICE!

If you are offered a glass of orange juice or kiwi nectar when visiting China, it is largely thanks to the efforts of Zhu Xin Li, a former government official who helped to create a fruit juice industry where none had existed before. In the early 1980s, Zhu was the official overseer of Shandong, the second most populous province in China. One fall, as Zhu tells the story, he received a decree from the central government in Beijing, saying that all available land throughout the country should be planted with rice. But the area around Zibo, the city in which Zhu lived and worked, was rugged and mountainous, and therefore completely unsuited to the cultivation of rice. He decided to ignore the dictate and planted apple trees instead. The orchard thrived and produced such a harvest that Zhu found himself with a surplus. He scraped up some cash to buy an old juice-making machine, set it up, and began squeezing apples.

At that time, Chinese families did not think of juice as an important drink in their lives, or even as a particularly healthy one. There was no glass of orange juice at the morning meal. Mothers did not tuck juice boxes into their children's lunches. Milk was a popular drink for children. Adults drank tea or water or beer. If people drank juice at all, it was a "juice drink," a sugary, pulpless blend that was 90 percent water and other ingredients, and only 10 percent mixed juices.

But Zhu was not thinking much about the market, or lack of a market, as he made his apple juice. He was just converting his harvest into a product. In 1992, while still a government official, Zhu set up a little company called Shandong Zibo Huiyuan, known as Huiyuan. One year later, he abandoned his old juice squeezer and installed a proper fruit-processing line. With little demand for juice products at home, Huiyuan's apple concentrate became a Chinese export. The company prospered from its exports, and its success gave Zhu an idea. What if he could produce real juice, 100 percent juice, juice nectars—not the insipid and tasteless stuff that local Chinese consumers were used to—and get people to see how delicious and healthful juice could be?

In 1994, Zhu moved Huiyuan's headquarters some 500 kilometers north, to a location just outside of Beijing, and built a new juice-processing plant. Shortly thereafter, Huiyuan introduced its first all-juice product and distributed it to local retailers in Shandong Province—and was surprised when demand was almost overwhelming. The company stepped up its manufacturing capacity and expanded its line of products, adding different juices in a variety of packs.

By 1997, to the delight of its ever-confident founder, Huiyuan had become a household name throughout China, especially in households with children. The company began advertising and positioned itself as a brand of natural and healthy drinks, good for children and the entire family. The marketing line read: "Let 100 Percent of Chinese People Enjoy 100 Percent Juice!"

Huiyuan went public in early 2007, in an initial public offering that raised $308 million. Institutional buying was one hundred times oversubscribed; individual investors were 938 times oversubscribed.[2]

FINDING THE SWEET SPOT

Although Chinese consumers have embraced Huiyuan's fruit juices (as well as the products of local competitors that have flooded the market since Huiyuan opened the category), the company's products are still priced well below those of incumbent brands. So even though consumers in China, India, and elsewhere are beginning to notice and care about differentiations of product features and brand values, the single characteristic that the overwhelming majority of them seek is value for their money.

The struggle, for both challengers and incumbents, is to find the sweet spot, and it's usually at a price point lower than incumbents are used to or would expect—for the obvious reason that the great majority of the people in the rapidly developing economies are still poor in comparison to the consumers in developed economies. Only a small segment of the people have enough income or wealth to be considered consumers in the sense that incumbents understand the term.

When the tsunami began, consumers in the rapidly developing economies had little exposure to the consuming ways of the West. Most people bought (or traded for) their staples from local merchants and had little if any extra money to buy discretionary items. But as the tsunami gained strength—and as the challengers had success and created value and as people became more sophisticated—a great number of people were able to leave behind a subsistence existence and improve their standard of living.

The Rise of the Consuming Class

Just what percentage of the populations of the rapidly developing economies can be considered the "consuming class" or a "middle class" is very difficult to estimate, but it has certainly grown in size, wealth, and buying power.

In China, consumers born after the mid-1970s have embraced a consumption-oriented lifestyle, are more willing to spend money, are eager to experiment, are much more style-conscious, and are more sensitive to advertising than those of their parents' generation. Similar consumer trends are evident in India, Brazil, and other rapidly developing economies. Rapid change plus abundant opportunity pushes rapid product and business-model innovation.

In India, per capita income is around $600, while in developed economies, per capita income is above $20,000. As the average per capita income has risen, India's consumer market has grown tremendously. From magazines and fashion to vehicles and cricket equipment, India's increasingly consumption-oriented middle class is spending more on the things they want. As of 2007, India's middle and lower classes account for 75 percent of the country's total spending.[3] India is currently the world's twelfth-largest consumer economy, and all signs point to its rank rising in the years to come.

In China, per capita income is at least twice what it is in India. Research and analysis by the Boston Consulting Group concluded that, in general, wealth in China is increasing and is spreading from the largest cities to those of the second and third tiers. By 2008, more than half of China's affluent households (urban households earning more than $4,300 per year) will be located outside the forty-five biggest metropolitan areas. Some sixty million households in China will be considered middle class.

Even as incomes increase, however, the money that consumers in the rapidly developing economies have is not particularly flexible in terms of use. In the developed countries, the great majority of people have bank accounts—around 90 percent of consumers in the fifteen countries of the European Union have accounts, as do about 91 percent of Americans. Financial institutions and financial regulators do not collect much data (or, more likely, find it very difficult to collect data) in the rapidly developing economies about bank account usage. National surveys show that 43 percent of people in urban Brazil have bank accounts, and 21 percent in Mexico City do, and that the numbers are lower in less-affluent localities.

There is more data available on credit card usage, and it reveals just how reliant Western consumer society is on credit and debit cards and how little saturation of these cards there is in the rapidly developing economies. In the United States, there were 2,249,780,000 (that's two *billion* plus) financial cards in circulation in 2006, or 7.5 per capita, and the average annual retail transactions on these cards, per capita, was $11,041. In western Europe, there were some 837,143,000 cards in circulation in 2006, or 1.8 per capita, with an average of $7,730 in annual transactions per capita. In Brazil, the number of financial cards per capita was 2.25 in 2006, in China there were 0.93 per capita, and 0.08 in India. Russians don't carry a lot of cards—just 0.56 per capita—but those who do make heftier transactions, with a value of $2,304 per capita per year, than do cardholders in the other RDEs. China's per capita financial card transactions amount to $138 per year; in India it's $25.

Message to tourists: when traveling to towns and villages in India, China, Mexico, the Czech Republic, or most of the other rapidly developing economies, bring cash!

The disparity in incomes in economies is accentuated by the enormous diversity of their populations. In India, fifteen major languages are spoken, with more than 1,600 dialects. In China, eight major languages, seven dialects, and several other minority languages are spoken. Mandarin is the dominant language in the main cities of northern China, while Cantonese is the dominant language in the south, particularly in Hong Kong. And behind each language is a unique regional history, culture, and economy that gives rise to radical differences in tastes, activities, and aspirations. In the United States, Japan, and most of the countries of Europe, there is a single, dominant language.

Such differences present a major challenge for companies in the most fundamental of go-to-market activities: segmenting the population to understand motivations, expectations, and aspirations—and estimating how much spending power each segment has. It makes the term "mass market" almost meaningless. Yes, there is a mass of consumers in the rapidly developing economies, but they can hardly be addressed en masse, at least not through one set of product propositions or one campaign of spoken or written communications.

TLI (Too Little Information)

A large part of the problem for any company marketing its products and services in the rapidly developing economies is that there is far less demographic and market data available than there is in the developed economies.

In the United States, there is a wealth of consumer data available through multiple sources, both public and private. Governments spend millions (in the United States, billions) compiling detailed census information, producing extensive formatting and analysis of it, and making it available through a variety of channels, including the Internet, absolutely free. (If you haven't yet visited www.census. gov, you're in for a statistical treat.) For a fee, private research firms and commercial services will provide much more information about consumers and their characteristics and behaviors.

What's more, companies can find out most things they need to know about their competitors, thanks to the wide range of laws, regulations, standards, practices, and procedures that companies must adhere to and report about, as well as to a relatively unfettered press. Plus, most companies are eager to let you know who they are and how they're doing with press releases, Web sites, and all the rest. The developed world is, as all Western readers know too well, awash with 24/7 data and too much information.

In the rapidly developing economies, market data beyond basic demographics is often not available, which makes it difficult, if not impossible, to do detailed behavior- or needs-based customer segmentation of the kind that incumbents are accustomed to using when developing or fine-tuning their product portfolios.

In the developed markets, even mom-and-pop shops have electronic cash registers and bar-code readers, so their suppliers can get a good idea of what's going on in small towns and remote villages. But once you get out of the larger cities in the rapidly developing economies, there is very limited point-of-sale data available. Producers are almost completely unable to track what is selling, when, at what price, or to whom, except by doing it the old-fashioned way—field visits. The lack of data makes it hard to assess product performance and apply the knowledge to future product and pricing decisions. Even basic company and product performance metrics, such as return on investment (ROI) or rough order of magnitude estimates (ROME), are difficult to generate.

LOCALIZING

The challengers intuitively understand the need to customize their offerings to specific consumer segments in order to succeed. Hui-yuan did not sell its 100-percent fruit and vegetable juices as "juice" to its first Chinese customers but rather as pure "nectar" to differentiate its products from the fruit drinks then available on the market. It built its brand around the platform of family and health—very important to Chinese customers. It extended its brand very rapidly to connect with children, which is perhaps the best way to appeal to the Chinese family. It then started to segment its customers more finely and entered other niches.

If one asks Zhu what his go-to-market strategy was when he started out in Shandong, he would be at a loss, except to say that it was to survive in whatever way he could. While his success can be ascribed to a certain nimbleness in his moves to exploit opportunities, more important was perhaps his inherent deep understanding of his Chinese customers and ways to connect with them.

In some categories in some of the rapidly developing economies, however, local knowledge has appeared to be unimportant, and so big multinationals have been successful at selling their global products with little, if any, adaptation to local conditions. In Brazil, this was the case with the cosmetics and beauty business—until a local challenger rose up and showed that beauty, too, has local meaning.

Natura: Brazilian Beauty

The Brazilian obsession with beauty is legendary. The number of registered plastic surgeons in Brazil is second only to that in the United States. The country is renowned for producing a disproportionate number of fashion models, including the likes of Gisele Bündchen, a top model who has achieved spectacular international success—so much so that her prominence on the world stage has caused a surge in the number of Brazilian girls who enroll in modeling schools and enter beauty competitions.[4]

The national obsession is clearly seen in the enormous growth in the consumption of cosmetics and toiletry products, which in 2005 grew 34 percent from the year before, to $13.8 billion. That's far above domestic GDP growth and four times the international industry average. By 2007, Brazil will become the third-largest cosmetics market in the world, after the United States and Japan. The growth is unlikely to abate, as key demographic trends—the relatively young population, the strengthening middle class, and the growing share of working women—will support further increases.

For years, giant global companies like Unilever, Avon, and L'Oréal held strong positions in the Brazilian beauty market. Then, in the 1990s, Natura Cosméticos (founded in 1969), based in São Paulo, began to shake up the market. Ten years later, Natura has become the market leader in cosmetics, fragrances, and toiletries, with 2006 sales of about $1.8 billion and a total market share of around 13 percent, slightly higher than that of Unilever. Natura has a range of offerings for men, women, and children, including products for face and body, hair care, bath, sun protection, and oral hygiene, as well as makeup and fragrances.[5]

Natura has built its brand and its success on emotional and functional attributes (such as pleasure, naturalness, Brazilian soul, biodiversity, innovation, and quality) and on the company's philosophical commitment to sustainable development and to nurturing quality relationships with all its stakeholders. "We have a concept called *bem estar bem*, which means 'well being well,'" Rodolfo Guttila, director of corporate affairs and government relations at Natura, explained. "Well-being is the harmonious, pleasant relationship of a person with oneself, with one's body. Being well is the empathetic, successful, and gratifying relationship of a person with others, with nature and with the whole."[6]

So rather than use animal fat in its formulations, Natura whips up its lotions and creams with special types of palm oil. Many of the plant and vegetable ingredients used in the company's products—such as açaí, andiroba, breu branco, castanha, copaíba, cumaru, cupuaçu, murumuru, and priprioca—are harvested in the Amazon rain forest, where the company works with small local growers and encourages them to plant their crops using sustainable forest management and cultivation processes. Natura uses biodegradable formulations and recycled and recyclable packaging, and is a pioneer among Brazilian manufacturers of continuous use goods in the sale of refill products. The company also engages in a variety of initiatives that support sustainability, such as the Rainforest Education and Recovery Project.

As a result, Natura has a decidedly Brazilian image, in sharp contrast to the global brands offered by the incumbents, many of which have European or American origins. This has likely been a factor in Natura's success, as the traditional concept of Brazilian female beauty—which has favored more well rounded curves and more generous hips and bottoms than the Twiggy style of the international fashion runway—has been challenged by models like Bündchen. "Hers is a globalized beauty that has nothing to do with the Brazilian biotype," Joana de Vilhena Novaes, a psychologist and author of "The Intolerable Weight of Ugliness: On Women and Their Bodies," told *The New York Times*. "She has very little in the way of hips, thighs or fanny. She's a Barbie."[7]

Natura's understanding of its consumers is not limited, however, to its concerns about naturalness and sustainability.

The company sells its products through a direct sales network of more than 600,000 self-employed "consultants" in Brazil and another 70,000 elsewhere in Latin America, mostly women who work part-time and are paid on a commission basis. This approach works well because employment opportunities in Brazil can be scarce, wages are low, and retail networks are immature. It enables Natura to reach deep into the middle market of consumers who live in its sprawling cities as well as in the smaller communities throughout its vast countryside. (Brazil is the fifth-largest country in the world by area, just behind the United States.)

Consumers like direct distribution, too, because of the personal service and close interaction. First-time buyers, in particular, feel more comfortable dealing with friends and acquaintances, rather than with sales clerks or beauty professionals. In addition, the direct sales model provides Natura with a built-in word-of-mouth channel, which enables the company to spread its corporate vision of sustainability with high effectiveness and at very low cost.

As a result, the productivity of Natura's sales force is considerably above the industry average, thanks to the company's extensive training program, strong sales leadership, and—as the company claims—the "convincing and unifying vision of the company."[8]

Natura has recently been ranked among the global top 20 companies for leaders by *Fortune* magazine, Hewitt Associates, and RBL Group, in a study of the ways that companies around the world develop their leaders. According to 2,000 executives who responded to a survey by *Carta Capital* magazine and the Interscience Institute, Natura is the most admired brand in Brazil.

And despite its expansion at a breakneck speed which increased its share in its key market segments (skin care, sunscreen, make-up, fragrances, hair care, shaving products, and deodorants) from 12 percent to 22.8 percent in four years—2002 to 2006[9]—Natura's profitability has consistently been above that of its peers. Catering to customers in the intermediate price segment, Natura is good at things that matter in fast-moving consumer goods. Its Cajamar plant is one of the most efficient in the industry, and with an impressive average of more than two hundred new product launches per year, Natura fulfills customer demands for change and improvement.

Natura's leaders are now doing what so many other challengers do once they have achieved solid success in their home markets—they're setting their sights on international expansion. "We think there is a lot of space in the cosmetics industry to grow, and we think we have good products that will appeal to consumers in other countries," says Alessandro Carlucci, Natura's chief executive officer.[10]

In a typical first step for challengers, Natura first entered markets closest to home, then quickly expanded its reach so that now it has a presence in all the important markets of Latin America. In 2007, Natura made an even bolder move by opening its first flagship store,

Casa Natura, and did so—not in São Paulo or Rio de Janeiro, but rather at 2 Carrefour de la Croix Rouge, in the posh Saint-Germain district of Paris, capital of the most demanding cosmetics market in the world. Casa Natura is an "experience space," not a shop, according to the company. Consumers can take advantage of a free massage and coffee, and then familiarize themselves with the brand and what it stands for.

Carlucci considers this an experiment to gain a foothold in Europe and to kick-start brand building in markets where Natura is unknown. He says he is "very happy" with initial sales in Paris and, in addition to the inauguration of operations in the United States in 2008, is now eyeing both Russia and the United Kingdom for future expansion. By 2017, Natura intends that a much greater percentage of its annual revenue will be generated by operations outside Brazil. But, adds Luiz Seabra, founder and co-chairman of the board, "Wherever we go, it is important to remain true to our values. This is our passion. This is who we are."[11]

DISTRIBUTING AMID CHAOS

In 2007, The Transport Corporation of India, a publicly held "multimodal integrated supply chain solutions provider," as the company describes itself, released a study that chronicled how a typical cargo moves by truck between two of India's major cities, Kolkata and Mumbai—a journey of 1,340 miles. The study found that a person could travel the distance in two days by train and four days by car, but that the cargo vehicle took eight days to travel the same distance, due to all kinds of official holdups and other snags.

The following excerpt from *The Economist* provides a taste of the travails of the two truck drivers during that seemingly endless journey:

> The lorry is loaded at 2 P.M. in central Kolkata. But it cannot leave until after 10 P.M., because heavy vehicles can use the city streets only at certain times. By then, there is a jam and it is 4 A.M. before

the lorry hits the National Highway 6. It takes a good 14 hours to travel the 180km to the border of this state, West Bengal, with Jharkhand. By then the border is closed for the night.

At 5 A.M. the following morning, the lorry joins the border queue. It takes two hours for the documents to be cleared, and the same time again to cross a sliver of Jharkhand. After another two-hour queue, it enters Orissa and enjoys a relatively uneventful 200km. But then it has to stop for the night, because the road is closed to avoid the danger of attacks by bandits or Maoist insurgents.

Day four begins again at 5 A.M., and after 12 hours on the road the lorry reaches the next border, with Chhattisgarh. Here it queues for four hours, but at least it can cross at night, making a creditable 350km in one day. So by day five, the lorry is in Maharashtra, the state of which Mumbai is the capital.

However, the lorry still has to pass a further 12 tollbooths and inspection points after the 14 it has already negotiated, so it takes another two days to get to Mumbai itself. The driver then has to telephone the octroi agent and get this tax processed, which takes all night. It is the morning of day eight before he reaches his customer in Mumbai, having achieved an average speed of 11 km per hour and spent 32 hours waiting at tollbooths and checkpoints.

The challenges of distribution begin with the large geographic areas of the countries of the rapidly developing economies—China, India, Brazil, Argentina, South Africa, and Russia account for about 31 percent of the world's landmass. The challenges are exacerbated by the relatively primitive road systems. Although China is pushing hard to build a world-class infrastructure, it currently has only 0.15 kilometers of paved road per square kilometer of area, compared to 1.62 in the United Kingdom and 2.43 in Japan. And many developing countries are much worse off than China.

Large areas and poor roads make distribution tough enough; now add to that the wildly uneven population dispersion across these areas. At one end of the scale are the fast-growing megacities with highly concentrated populations. China has more than 660 cities, eleven of which have populations of over two million people. In India, thirty cities have populations of more than a million. (The United States has twenty cities with populations of 500,000 or more, and four with more than two million people.) However, cities in these economies tend to be defined quite differently than they are in the developed world. The large ones sprawl across large areas, and there may be no dense, concentrated area that Westerners would consider a city center. Sometimes the city limits are generous enough that they contain farmland and farmers, who are technically city dwellers but are hardly urbanites.

The majority of the populations in the rapidly developing economies still reside in small towns and villages. In India, there are some 600,000 villages in which nearly 70 percent of the population resides. In China, there are 680,000 villages and towns. These markets, as dispersed as they are, contain so many people they cannot be ignored.

Retailing in these markets is just as fragmented as the populations are. Most retail outlets are mom-and-pop shops; in India, more than 10 million small stores account for 95 percent of sales across most product categories. Only 4 percent of India's retail outlets can be classified as "modern" or "organized," meaning supermarkets, hypermarkets, malls, department stores, or chains. China has some 23 million retail outlets, of which about 78 percent are mom-and-pop shops. In the United States, there are fewer than 40,000 cities and towns, and 85 percent of retailing is modern.

Over the decades and even centuries, distribution networks have been developed (or simply emerged) to serve these incredibly fragmented populations and the maze of shops that serve them, and they include a variety of different types of intermediaries. There are a number of large, powerful wholesalers that buy products from manufacturers and then sell them to retailers, many of which are also financed by the wholesalers.

The manufacturers have little or no control over these wholesale channels and no contact with the retailers in the networks, but the wholesale channels do provide them with great reach. Manufacturers can also choose to work with a distributor that functions like an extension of the company—it does not handle products of other manufacturers—and operates exclusively within a territory.

There are also dealers who operate both as wholesalers and retailers and receive products directly from the manufacturer. Some manufacturers also work through stockists and substockists, who collect goods from the manufacturer and deliver them directly to retail outlets. Intermediaries often wear two hats at once. A distributor selling to retailers in one territory might also have a retail presence of its own in the same or a different territory. For an outsider, it can be very difficult to determine the best way to get products into different markets and very confusing to determine who is who and what is what.

To the incumbent, there are islands of familiarity in this forbidding landscape. Large-scale retail has begun to emerge and is starting to impose more familiar disciplines into supply channels. In India, the big retail segment is still nascent, with only 3 to 4 percent of the market. Yet the environments are changing, particularly in China, where big multinational retail chains are proliferating, with global players such as Carrefour and Wal-Mart opening new stores at an aggressive pace. Best Buy, The Home Depot, Walgreens, and many luxury-goods retailers are also entering the market, albeit in different ways (some with acquisitions or joint-ventures) and at varying rates of speed.

Domestic retailers are also on the move. Leveraging funds raised from capital markets, companies like the grocer Wumart and others are expanding to take advantage of a steadily growing market. Lianhua, a local Chinese retailer, operates some two thousand outlets in sixteen provinces, and the regional chain Hongqi has more than two hundred supermarkets in Sichuan province alone. During the past few years, sales in these modern retail formats have grown more than 50 percent a year but still account for less than 30 percent of all retail sales in China and serve only one-quarter of the 500 million consumers who live in or near China's thousands of cities and towns.

At this stage of the market development, players, both challengers and incumbents, must serve both the organized retailers and the mom-and-pop stores to reach deep into the populations.

GOODBABY GETS TO EVERYONE

Goodbaby, one of the world's largest makers of baby goods, first built its success in China by overcoming the distribution challenge to get its products out to parents. Goodbaby's chairman and CEO, Song Zenghuan, told us, "We gained our success by directly dealing with the problems and conflicts in China's commercial development and learning from those tribulations."

In China, Goodbaby is the most recognized baby and child equipment brand, with a product portfolio of more than 1,600 items in fifteen categories, including strollers, beds, clothing, car seats, toys, and diapers. It dominates the mid- and upper-end segments in the Chinese market for strollers and baby carriers and controls about 80-percent market share in its primary product categories.

Goodbaby also has a presence in over eighty countries in developed and developing markets. In these markets, the company offers a variety of products that range in price and quality from midlevel to upper-tier offerings, but it is best known for strollers, which can sell for more than 700 euros in Europe. Goodbaby ships about four thousand strollers to the United States every day—the majority of them branded as Geoby—and has captured a 25 percent share of the U.S. stroller market.[12] In Europe, its share is 20 percent.[13] Goodbaby also makes about half of the children's bicycles purchased in the United States each year.[14]

Goodbaby, based in the industrial city of Kunshan, has built the most extensive sales and marketing organization in its industry. The network consists of thirty-five branch companies, each of which operates within its province or city to establish agreements with the large local distribution network to open new points of presence. Across the country, Goodbaby operates over 1,600 stand-alone specialty stores and large-size department-store counters. Including smaller stores and sales representatives, the company boasts 10,000 sales points and 4,000 marketing and sales personnel, as well as another 300 independent distributors.[15] A further 230 or more centers nationwide provide service on Goodbaby products, many of which are sold with a lifetime guarantee.

With its distribution network established, Goodbaby expanded its domestic presence through an aggressive build-out of stand-alone retail outlets. In August 2006, in Shanghai, Goodbaby opened the first in a series of domestic "flagship" stores. Goodbaby Mother and Babies Boutique is China's first one-stop shopping store for mothers and their infants. The store offers products and appliances—both Goodbaby brands and foreign brands with which Goodbaby has sales agency agreements—as well as professional consulting. The first opening was followed that year with stores in Beijing and Shenzhen. Goodbaby says it will open an additional five hundred stores in China by 2010, using funds from the hugely successful initial public offering on Hong Kong's Hang Seng, completed early in 2006.[16]

The strength of Goodbaby's domestic distribution network has enabled the company to sign exclusive distribution agreements with many of its original equipment manufacturer clients, who hope to leverage Goodbaby's well-developed distribution network to gain a share of the world's largest potential market for themselves.

ICICI Bank: The Self-Help Group Model

Some challengers have followed the model of the self-help group (SHG) to establish themselves in a small community. These SHGs are village-level circles of ten to twenty people, usually women, who undertake projects and investments for personal and community economic development. The groups depend on local knowledge, private information, and moral contracts among their members to build the right structures and incentives.

The SHG model has been applied most famously in the financial services sector. The nonprofit Grameen Bank in Bangladesh, founded by Nobel laureate Muhammad Yunus, developed the template for microlending projects around the developing world. In India, ICICI Bank, a leading commercial and retail bank, has found that the template can be adapted for profit-making companies.

In India, banking for the poor has traditionally been viewed as a social obligation. Commercial banks are required to extend some credit to poor farmers and provide a certain level of rural branch coverage—break-even operations at best. More recently, those requirements have broadened to include giving grants and loans to microfinance institutions.

In 2001, ICICI Bank merged with the Bank of Madura, a pioneer in the commercialization of the SHG model. At the time of the merger, 1,200 Bank of Madura SHGs were already formed under the bank's Rural Development Initiative. Within each circle, women followed an agreed meeting schedule and savings program and participated in a training calendar structured and financed by the Bank of Madura. When groups reached certain savings and training milestones, they were entitled to jointly apply for a small, unsecured loan of about $5,000. If the group paid off the loan successfully, it could renew it again and again, steadily increasing credit limits. "Savings First, Credit Later" was the motto for each SHG. Saving money, members learned, could reduce their vulnerability to variations in income and health. The program was a considerable social success: participants felt empowered and found more confidence to manage their own lives and speak up on community issues. Microbusinesses and vital village investments were enabled. Federations of SHGs were forming, representing thousands of members.

Financially, however, the initiative had yet to prove that it could be sustainable. When it took over the reins, ICICI Bank realized that, to achieve profitability, the SHG program would need vastly more members for the same overhead cost. The solution ICICI Bank conceived was a talent-development model that trained and incentivized SHG members to promote new SHGs in neighboring villages and ultimately rise to become regional coordinators of a handful of SHG promoters. This tiered incentive program—reminiscent of Mary

Kay in the United States—swelled the ranks of SHGs dramatically. Up from twelve hundred in 2001, by early 2003, more than eight thousand SHGs had been set up.

The initiative remains a challenge for ICICI Bank. It's an ongoing task to drive down overhead costs through new technologies and distribution models, while at the same time improving rural access and convenience. But the program is profitable, and ICICI Bank believes it is sustainable.

DOING BUSINESS WITH BUSINESS

When journalists write about the rapidly developing economies, they tend to focus on consumers and consumer products to which their readers can easily relate, and so the impression one gets from the media is that the consumer markets are the only markets that really matter in the rapidly developing economies. However, there is also a tremendous set of opportunities for businesses selling goods to other businesses (B2B).

Combined, the five largest RDEs—China, India, Brazil, Mexico, and Russia—in 2006 accounted for 43 percent of the world's registered commercial vehicles, 39 percent of its mobile telecommunication equipment sales, 32 percent of global electricity consumption, 19 percent of refined products sales, and 15 percent of revenues from construction and engineering activities.[17] China alone consumes nearly half of the world's cement output and a third of the world's steel output.[18] Needless to say, all forecasters expect demand for business-to-business products in the rapidly developing economies to grow much faster than demand in developed economies.

Going to market with business-to-business products presents challenges that are in some ways even more daunting and less understood than the challenges faced by providers of consumer goods. Not the least of these challenges is the strength of the challengers that serve their business customers. In fact, only about a quarter of the BCG Challenger 100 companies can be considered pure business-to-consumer operations. Another quarter have significant parts of their businesses in both business-to-consumer and business-to-business, and about half of them sell mostly to other businesses.

Why are so many of the challengers business-to-business companies? The most obvious answer is that that's where a great percentage of them started out—as vendors supplying goods and services to other businesses. It's also because the incumbents have not penetrated the middle of the business-to-business market and, therefore, have left lots of room for the challengers to operate. In most business-to-business categories, incumbents have operated just as they have in consumer markets—by attacking the top end of the market, where they can leverage global products, command a price premium, sidestep the complicated distribution systems, and avoid the severe cost competition from local competitors. This has left huge markets open to local competitors, who have risen to fill the voids.

Business-to-business markets are well suited to challengers' strengths and do not expose their most obvious weaknesses. Industrial companies supplying products to other businesses compete primarily on their low-cost manufacturing and distribution capabilities, which have been fine-tuned through years of competing domestically and, in many cases, through competition in export markets as well. Low cost and high quality are of paramount importance. Branding and marketing are less so.

GOVERNMENT AID FOR PILLAR INDUSTRIES

Many business-to-business companies that are state owned (or were at one time) have also gotten a leg up from their government connections. It is common knowledge that state-led industrialization in many parts of the world was biased toward business-to-business industries. What is less known is that the state still plays a major role in these industries in such countries as China and Russia. The Chinese government, for example, defines so-called "pillar" industries, which are given preferential treatment and are restricted with regard to foreign participation.

These include power generation and distribution, oil and petrochemicals, telecommunications, coal, aviation and shipping, machinery and engineering, automotive, metals and mining, and construction.

State intervention takes different forms. In some cases, it is outright ownership. Since 2003, China's largest enterprises have been controlled by the State-Owned Assets Supervision and Administration Commission (SASAC), a megashareholder that oversees a portfolio of more than 150 companies (14 of which are in the *Fortune* Global 500) with combined revenues approaching the $1 trillion mark. More indirect means of control include the entire arsenal of industrial policy: licensing, import controls, fiscal subsidies, preferential access to bank credit, government-sponsored mergers and acquisitions, and the appointment of cronies to senior management positions.

The main objective of such policies is to transform bureaucratic and loss-making state-owned enterprises into viable businesses—and, in some cases, to create global champions. Exactly for this reason, however, things are changing. Knowing that openness ultimately will ensure competitiveness, Chinese policy makers are gradually easing state controls.

THE BATTLE FOR THE B2B MIDMARKET

There is an assumption that is appealing to make about the business-to-business market in the rapidly developing economies: that the high-end segment of the markets will grow as businesses become more successful, accumulate assets, and offer more and more product differentiations with greater brand distinctions.

Won't incumbents be in the best position to serve these high-margin, steadily growing customers?

The answer is probably no, at least for many industries. The important battle—where future challenger fortunes will be won or lost—will be for the midmarket. A big chunk of the value is here, one-third to one-half of the market. The midmarket is also the fastest growing, driven by demand and supply factors.

ZTE: TELECOM MIDMARKETER

In China, the midmarket battle has been particularly dramatic in telecommunications. What happened in this industry in China, beginning in the 1990s, is unprecedented in the history of the industry. The China market grew from virtually nothing to become the single largest fixed-line and mobile telecom market in the world, measured by the number of customers. The country now boasts close to 500 million mobile subscribers, adding another 5 million every month.[19] Each year, more than 300 billion text messages are passed back and forth, and the number of broadband Internet users soared past 80 million in 2007, passing the United States to become the world's largest broadband market.[20]

When looking at which equipment makers—from network gear to base stations to mobile handsets—benefited from the gigantic network build-out that enabled this growth, one finds, of course, the global giants: Ericsson, Nokia, Alcatel, Siemens, and Motorola.

But local Chinese companies, such as ZTE, have also prospered. Founded in 1985 as Zhongxing Semiconductor under the Ministry of Aerospace Industry, ZTE has grown by 37 percent per annum since 1995 and recorded revenues of $2.7 billion in 2005. It is the only Chinese IT and telecommunications manufacturer listed in the *BusinessWeek* Top 100 information technology companies. A coming-of-age milestone for both China's telecom sector and ZTE was marked in 2001, when ZTE beat its foreign equipment-making peers in a bid to provide a major contract for China Unicom's CDMA mobile network.

To some extent, the ZTE success story is built on cost. ZTE typically offers its products for prices that are 30 percent lower than those of the incumbents.[21] Yet ZTE has also succeeded on its ability to understand its customers and compete for the midmarket.

In China, ZTE made investments in large rural markets, where competition was relatively weak, consumers were relatively unsophisticated, and where ZTE could customize its offerings—which were based on technological offerings from foreign partners—to meet the needs of local customers. The products were very similar to those of the incumbents but were not exactly knockoffs. According to Zhou Susu, senior vice president of ZTE, the company had to go through a period of imitation and adaptation. "The Chinese telecom industry is only about 20 years old—globally the industry has a much longer history. It is going to take us time to go through the phases: from processing, to manufacturing, to R&D, and finally participating in global standard setting. So what the public says about us being an imitator is only partly right."[22]

ZTE is outgrowing the imitation stage. It now invests heavily in research and development, with an impressive rate of 12 percent of sales, operates fourteen R&D centers around the world, and as of September 2006, had applied for five thousand national and international patents.[23] And although most of ZTE's products are not yet cutting-edge by international standards, they match the requirements of many customers—at a much lower price.

STEPPING INTO NEW MARKETS

When a product or service hits the value-for-money sweet spot in one developing market, it is quite likely it will be just as appealing to customers in other rapidly developing economies. What's more, it may prove attractive to customers in developed economies, even when no equivalent segment currently exists there. Small wonder, then, that many challengers are venturing overseas to sell both to other businesses and to consumers. Some use other developing markets as stepping-stones, while others attack mature markets directly.

Bajaj Auto: Bikes for Buyers

Bajaj Auto, once a producer of older-design two-wheel and three-wheel vehicles for the Indian market, has built both share and brand by reaching deeper into its own market and then stepping carefully into other developing economies.

In India, where the dominant vehicles are two- and three-wheelers—and a four-wheeler is aspirational for most people—there are many more variations of the device that incumbents think of as a motorcycle. Bajaj Auto has become one of India's leading players in two-wheelers—with $2.5 billion in revenue in 2007 and a 34-percent market share—thanks to a keen understanding of what Indians want in their scooters and motorcycles.

To a Westerner, it doesn't sound like there is much difference between a motorbike with a sub-100-cc engine and one with a 125-cc engine—even a basic Vespa has a 150 cc engine, and it's tough to find a Harley with one below 500-cc. But in India, the customer segments are sliced much more finely. The sub-100-cc buyers are entry-level and first-time buyers who typically are switching from a scooter for the first time, and price is all important to them. The buyers of 125-cc bikes are value buyers, willing to pay a little more to get a few more features, such as better styling and digital twin-spark technology (DTS), which boosts performance. The value buyer is usually a seasoned biker and has long since grown beyond the basic sub-100-cc bike.

Bajaj uses an extensive dealer network that extends deeply in the rural areas, where the next generation of entry-level bikers is to be found.[24] "Twice or thrice a year, we go out and do a customer satisfaction audit with our products and with competitors' products," said Sanjiv Bajaj, executive director of Bajaj Auto. "We try to understand whether customers are still achieving the kind of satisfaction level that we hope our products provide. We also are able to pick up how the customers are evolving."[25]

One of the main reasons that Bajaj sends its people into the countryside to observe and talk with consumers is because there is virtually no other way to gather information about the people who use their products: there just isn't much data available. This is a problem for challenger companies in their home countries that gets more difficult as they seek to penetrate other RDE markets.

Bajaj continued the practice as it approached other markets outside India. In small markets, where fewer than a hundred thousand units a year are sold, Bajaj worked entirely through existing distributors. "Our role in the market became a role of auditor," said Bajaj. "Which meant that, in addition to providing a good-quality product and assuring that spare parts were being supplied, we'd make sure that quality to the customer was assured. Our fundamental purpose was that the customer must still get the same service whether Bajaj is directly there or not. That meant training local people for everything from sales service to availability of parts."

In the Philippines, Bajaj created a relationship with Kawasaki, the Japanese motorcycle maker. Kawasaki had long designed small-engine bikes for Bajaj for sale in India under the Bajaj brand. But Bajaj had improved its small bikes to the point that its quality was as good as Kawasaki's. In the Philippines, Kawasaki had a strong presence and needed a wider portfolio of products to sell, so it agreed to import kits for 100-cc bikes from Bajaj. Kawasaki assembles them and sells them through its sales and distribution network—branded as Bajaj. In 2005, five thousand bikes were sold. In 2006, the number leapt to twenty thousand. In 2007, Bajaj sold 30,000 and, in 2008, the company projects sales of sixty-five thousand.

In Colombia, Bajaj found that consumers particularly liked the Bajaj 100-cc product called the Boxer. It is a fuel-efficient bike that can get up to 200 miles per gallon. When fuel prices began to rise in 2005, the Boxer really took off, and Bajaj became the largest supplier of motorcycles in Colombia, surpassing the Japanese makers.

By gathering feedback from its distributors and through information gained in customer audits of both sales and service, Bajaj picked up on how consumer needs and tastes were evolving in these small markets. Sometimes the company would modify the product to satisfy local preferences. In Nigeria, for example, customers were satisfied with the performance and reliability of Bajaj bikes but said they needed a longer seat, because as many as three or four people ride on the bike at one time. They also wanted a carrier for small loads, and brighter colors.

Bajaj also did competitive mapping to see which companies were present in the market and which of their products were moving. From this information, Bajaj considered the key questions that must be answered to penetrate deeper into unfamiliar markets: Are our products positioned right? Do we have the right price point? Are they slotted into the right customer perception?

Gradually, Bajaj built share and leadership in many smaller markets. Sri Lanka: number one, with a 50-percent market share in two-wheelers. Bangladesh: number one, with a 25-percent market share. Number one in motorcycles in Colombia, and number two in Central America. "We were able to prove in many of these markets that we are able to succeed," said Sanjiv Bajaj. "If you screw up in that size market, you will certainly lose out in the big ones. Now we had the guts to go to the big market."

Bajaj turned its attention to markets that had the potential to reach volumes of up to half a million two-wheelers a year, within three to five years. "In these markets, we believed that we would have to play a greater role. In addition to the customer audits, we decided to put in a small marketing and service team, to be sure we were getting the reach in the market."

As of 2007, Bajaj had a distribution network that extended into fifty countries, with exports of 440,000 units, an increase of 77 percent over the previous year. "Given the nature of our existing product range, we do not have the luxury of entering western Europe, the United States, and Japan," said Bajaj, "where the political risk and country risk are significantly lower. In addition, the developing countries account for over 90 percent of worldwide two-wheeler sales, or around 40 million units annually."

But, as fuel prices continue to rise, it may not be long before America's city dwellers become accustomed to the sight of Bajaj three-wheelers on their streets.

THE NEXT BILLION

Beyond the midmarket and the members of the rising consumer class, there is yet another large group of potential consumers—across all of the rapidly developing economies—that is poorly defined and hard to categorize and is often referred to as the "next billion." This is a segment of the population that lies between the emerging middle class (which is also fairly fuzzy in definition) and the group of extremely poor people who exist at the bottom of the economic pyramid.

This group has been virtually invisible, and so almost completely neglected, by challengers and incumbents alike. Companies have not created offerings especially for these customers, who have been served through an informal retail network of independent shops and street dealers, where they put up with limited choice, poor service, and usurious rates. This retail environment runs on local information, private relationships, and informal—even illegal—means to conduct business. Sellers often manage to extract high prices even from these consumers.

The informal retail network is thriving enough to demonstrate that the consumption potential of the next billion is significant. If these populations were a nation, its GDP would be larger than that of Brazil, South Korea, India, Mexico, and Russia combined. The condition of the next billion people is quite like that of the rapidly developing economies as a whole, before they started on their rapid development path. It is a group that is on the cusp of high growth and increased consumption.

That's why some challengers—having achieved a good degree of penetration in both the affluent and middle-class markets—are beginning to look at this neglected section of the population as a new source of profits.

However, converting the next billion into customers poses a unique challenge for businesses. Although the demand is there in aggregate, the purchasing power of the individuals of the next billion is such that they cannot be served profitably by conventional business models and the distribution systems currently in place. The informal retail network, by its very nature, is difficult to scale.

The problem is not just one of distribution, it's about the needs and aspirations of the consumers themselves. Next-billion customers are not looking only for the lowest-price, stripped-down version of a product designed originally for higher-end markets. They value convenience, flexibility, and timeliness and are willing to pay a price for them.

Next-billion customers, entering the market for the first time, do not recognize or respect traditional industry boundaries. For example, when they need a provider of payment and transaction services, they don't particularly care if they deal with a bank, a telephone company, or a retailer. In the Philippines and Zambia, customers in urban areas have figured out an ingenious way to transfer cash to family members who live in remote areas. The customer buys a card that has prepaid minutes for mobile telephone usage, then transfers the minutes to the family member. The family member sells back the minutes to the local telecom operator for cash. In this way, the customers can completely bypass the banks, which usually charge people without accounts high fees to make remittances and whose procedures tend to be cumbersome, annoying, and time-consuming.

The challengers, many of which were spawned from this very population segment, understand that such behaviors will not be revealed through standard market-research techniques. Even talking with such consumers may not be particularly informative. They may not be able to articulate their basic needs and problems and may be completely unaware that there are goods and services available to help them meet those needs and solve those problems. You can't describe the different features you'd like in a washing machine if you are completely unaware that such a machine exists at all. This is why people in rural China had no compunction about throwing sweet potatoes into their Haier clothes washers. Why not?

The only way for companies to find out what the next billion are doing and what they want is to immerse themselves in the lives of their target consumers. Bharati, an Indian mobile phone operator, found an ingenious way to distribute SIM chips and prepaid cards to its customers in the city of Mumbai. The company created a delivery system by tapping into the existing network of some five thousand *dabbawallas*, men who pick up homemade lunches prepared in the suburbs and deliver them to consumers in offices in the downtown area. The *dabbawallas* have been performing this service for 125 years in Mumbai with what might be called six-sigma accuracy. Now, along with curries and naan, they deliver phone cards and chips.

IMPLICATIONS: REACH AS DEEP AS YOU CAN

While the size of the prize is compelling, going to market in the rapidly developing economies involves a struggle to define, reach, and understand your customers. It is a struggle to meet their needs and price points. And it is a struggle to get the product to them.

While some global players, such as Unilever, Siemens, Citi, and HSBC, have had a significant presence in many of these markets since the early twentieth century, most incumbents have increased their focus and investments in these markets only in recent years. Many have encountered very strong challengers and have learned some hard lessons during their forays into these markets.

Any company with global leadership aspirations must confront a scary question: how fast do you want to lose global market share? Every day, a global company's sales represent a smaller slice of an expanding worldwide market pie. Capturing a share of market growth in the rapidly developing economies is a necessity. The question is how.

KNOW THE CONSUMER

First and foremost, it's about developing a deep understanding of the real needs of customers.

In the very early days of globalization, stories were rampant about incumbents taking their products abroad and making all manner of faux pas as a result of misunderstanding the local language or culture. (One unconfirmed legend has it that when Coke entered China in the 1920s, the name Coca-Cola was represented on shop signs by a variety of Chinese characters that often meant weird or indecipherable things, including "bite the wax tadpole."[26])

The need for consumer understanding had not changed when Campbell Soup Company, another producer of iconic consumer brands, sought to market its products in rapidly developing economies in the early 1990s. When Campbell introduced its soups into Russia and China, it offered the same varieties it did everywhere else. But both countries are highly soup conscious and huge consumers of soup in comparison to the United States. The Chinese consumer downs about 200 bowls of soup per year, Russians about 225 bowls, and Americans only 46. They take great pride in their soup-making skills and love rich flavors and textures, and so had little interest in buying factory-made soups with unfamiliar flavors in little cans.

"Russians consider themselves the foremost experts on soup in the world, and they have words they only use for soup, which tells you how ingrained it is in the culture," Larry McWilliams, president of Campbell's international division told the *Wall Street Journal*.[27]

In 2007, Campbell made a concerted effort to align its soups with the people it hopes will consume them by creating a new line of soups that Russian cooks can use as a base for their own homemade creations.

Never assume that you understand the role that cement or a washing machine or soup plays in the lives of local consumers and their national culture.

LEARN THE DISTRIBUTION SYSTEM

Distribution in the rapidly developing markets is difficult, and that is probably the single most important realization that should govern your approach.

Accept complexity. In most developing markets, you need to plan to have more than one distribution model and a host of channel partners to reach different market segments or geographic regions. One model is rarely sufficient for them all. A consumer goods company in India could easily find itself with a thousand distributors and stockists to cover mom-and-pop retail outlets in major urban centers, an in-house corporate sales team to serve larger retail chains, and partnerships with wholesalers and local purchasing agents to service rural areas.

Exercise patience, and invest in your channel partners. Companies that provide their channel partners with training (classes and trips), equipment (trucks and personal computers), sales support (subsidized sales reps, merchandisers, and promoters), and coaching programs stand out from the crowded field of goods manufacturers, enjoy more stable relations with distributors and attract the good ones, and ultimately earn higher returns.

How do you know the good ones from the bad? Measure performance. One leading packaged-goods company in India records its products' availability at the retail counters of nearly a million outlets every week, and it links each distributor's payments to the results. PepsiCo has sales reps in the rapidly developing economies whose sole responsibility is to monitor the movements of prices in wholesale markets and track down wholesalers who undercut the agreed prices.

Take a Long-Term View

Take a long-term view, but establish short-term milestones. In our experience, executives consistently underestimate the difficulty of going to market in the rapidly developing economies. It will be more expensive than you think. Your strategies will be less effective than you think.

Think three to five years out. Focus on getting a few basics right: build the right team, get the right channel partners. Set your organization on a path of continual, incremental improvement. Without these in place, aggressive sales targets aren't worth the slides they're printed on.

With the team and goals in place, concentrate on execution. Don't be surprised when tasks that should be straightforward become bizarrely difficult. Standardize and simplify what you can. Accept complexity where you must.

Keep your eyes on the customer and what's actually happening in the market, but don't forget to take a peek at the horizon now and again, to remind yourself of the huge opportunity that awaits.

"It took Microsoft 15 years and billions of dollars of lost revenue to learn how to do business in China," says Sigurd Leung, an analyst at Analysys International in Beijing. "We were a naive American company," said Bill Gates. "You've got to just keep trying and trying and trying. Now we have a wonderful position in China, and we're going to see great growth every year for the next five years."

According to a spokesperson, Gates says he's certain that China will eventually be Microsoft's biggest market, although it may take another ten years.

CHAPTER 6

PINPOINTING

"The physical limitations of the past are gone."
Patrick Wang, Johnson Electric

Early in the sixteenth century, a cod-fishing industry began to develop along the coast of what is now Newfoundland. Early each spring, vessels from England, Ireland, France, Portugal, and Spain embarked on a voyage that could last three months or more.

The early fishing industry depended on a key resource, salt, as a preservative. The continental European fishermen had access to large resources of cheap salt in their home countries, so they would typically sail to the banks well off the coast of Newfoundland, catch as many cod as the ship would hold, salt them heavily, and take them home for curing—without setting foot ashore. The English merchants, however, had to import their salt at great cost, because the cool and damp English climate was not suited to making it by seawater evaporation. So they developed a "dry" method of preserving their catch, which involved very lightly salting and then sun-drying the fish on wooden frames, a process that could take several weeks.

This method required the establishment of an onshore operation. Every harbor and inlet had its own particular characteristics, and the cod ran differently each year into every one, so the fish-drying plant had to be sited in a location that was near the best fishing grounds, accessible to the fleet of shallops that fished from the main vessel, and had a ready supply of trees and brush, from which the onshore crew could build a wharf, fish-drying frames, and small dwellings.

Over the years, the English built their knowledge and experience of cod-fishing in the New World and became expert at siting their operations, improving the process, and refining the product. Gradually, people settled in Newfoundland, and permanent operations were established there. Saint John's became the center of the industry. The ships arriving from Europe now were carrying traders, not fishermen themselves.

It was an early, basic exercise in pinpointing—establishing certain operations of a business enterprise in distant locations in order to achieve the most effective use of resources and create the most profitable value chain.

Within India's Tata Group, people still talk about the seminal meeting when Ratan Tata challenged his senior management team to think differently about the company's value chain. "I wonder why we have always regarded India as our market," the chairman had said to them. "Can the rest of the world not do something for us?"

What could the rest of the world do for Tata? For India? The question was intriguing but puzzling, remembers R. Gopalakrishnan, one of Tata's directors, who was there. "When the chairman makes a statement like that," he told us, "people cannot leave it alone. This idea wafted round and round; it never would go away. We all kept thinking, 'We are to become global and look at the world as our market? But how?'"

The question provoked a good deal of discussion. "At last we came to the idea," recalls Gopalakrishnan, "that globalization is not just about getting market share in other countries. Don't think of them only as markets. Think of them as members of the supply chain. One member could be at the front end. Another at the back end. One in the middle."

If other countries were not only markets but also members of the supply chain, what would that mean for Tata's operations? "It's really about unbundling the supply chain and relocating pieces where it matters most," said Gopalakrishnan. "It means asking: 'Have we broken up our whole business process? Where is it that we can do each thing with most efficiency?'"

The early form of this activity was known as offshoring and, for the incumbents, it was fundamentally a cost-cutting exercise—the original force behind the tsunami. Offshoring typically involved shutting down manufacturing facilities in high-cost countries like the United States and Europe and moving the work to low-cost countries, including China, India, South America, Mexico, and eastern Europe. Offshoring extended the incumbents' value chain geographically, and could sometimes change ownership of parts of the chain if outsourcing was also involved, but it didn't fundamentally change the manner in which the value chain was managed or where the center of gravity was located. Control (and the center of gravity) remained at a central headquarters in a developed market. High-value activities, like design and engineering, were usually carried out at the central location as well, or at business-unit headquarters, also in developed markets. Offshore centers often seemed like far-flung outposts of the empire, or like a child reporting to a parent. Offshored employees were either low-skill workers or managers who reported to an executive from the developed economy, who was sometimes resident in the offshored location, sometimes not.

Many challengers started their lives as offshore centers of the incumbents. As they grew, they too began looking beyond their home countries for customers and took steps to offshore parts of their own growing operations.

The challengers' goals in offshoring, however, were quite different from those of the incumbents. First and foremost, they needed to get close to customers outside their home countries. They also needed access to the new pools of skilled, specialized, and experienced talent that existed in other markets, especially the developed economies. But, most important, they wanted to continue to leverage their own home-country advantage of low-cost labor and materials, so they knew they couldn't move all aspects of their operations out of their original bases.

The challengers had an important edge over incumbents when it came to locating operations offshore: they didn't have to worry much about shutting down plants, laying off workers, paying off long-term financial commitments, selling assets, or dealing with those other legacy issues that were so troublesome for the incumbents who were looking to move overseas. The challengers just didn't have that much in the way of assets to be disrupted or displaced. They were free to move and build.

So they gradually developed a business model that went further than offshoring. They already had the cost advantage of their home country (as we saw in chapter 3). They wanted to exploit the advantages of customer proximity and access to talent so that for the customer, the delivery of the product or service was optimized and seamless—and the locations of these capabilities were irrelevant. This involved disaggregating their value chains into discrete elements and locating them based on considerations of cost, customer need, talent, and other resources—a process we call pinpointing.

Pinpointing involves deconstructing the value chain and performing activities wherever they are best done. Some focus on low cost, some focus on where the right talent can be found, and some are located in a place close to the customer because that is what's most valuable. The value chain needs to be reconstructed seamlessly so all the parts work best together. Pinpointing is dynamic—conditions change, customers change, and costs change, so pinpointing locations will change over time.

It is not just the core manufacturing (or its equivalent for services firms) that is disaggregated and located optimally. Other value-added activities like R&D and sales and service are also aligned with this approach so that the whole business model is internally consistent and globally advantaged. And not being bogged down by legacy assets, the challengers made this business model dynamic by accessing new centers of capabilities even as the competitiveness of old centers eroded.

In China, Johnson Electric (JE), the world's largest manufacturer of micromotors, began acquiring companies outside its home country in 1999. Through these acquisitions, JE developed customer proximity and accessed new capabilities. It closed some production sites, including facilities in Thailand and Mexico, and relocated some of the work to its low-cost, large-scale manufacturing platform in China. But JE still operates some thirty manufacturing and assembly plants in eleven countries worldwide. In fact, around half of its revenue is derived from production plants outside of China. JE also retained and expanded its sales and product-development functions close to customers in the Americas and Europe and linked them to R&D centers in Asia. As a result, in 2007, JE's business model looks very different than the sum of all its acquisitions.

In India, Wipro, the IT services leader, had built its software and application development business with almost all of its operations in India and virtually none of its customers there. In its early days, Wipro, like other IT services companies in India, used to send large squads of employees to client sites to carry out the programming work—a practice often called bodyshopping. As Wipro won more clients around the world and began offering more complex and value-added services, it realized that certain aspects of its operations could not be completely done at customer sites or accomplished remotely from India. The company also saw that as its contracts grew larger and its offerings more sophisticated, it needed more highly skilled people than were available at home. So Wipro built a network of development centers around the world (forty-six in early 2007) that exploited the cost advantages of the rapidly developing economies, near-shore advantages of customer intimacy, and the regional advantages of skills, capabilities, cultural awareness, and language fluency—such as native language speakers in eastern Europe and Mexico. Over a period of time, Wipro began to call this pinpointed value chain its "global delivery model."

Wipro and other challengers continue to add new centers to evolve and refine their global delivery system and maintain an edge over their incumbent competitors. "It's not about labor arbitrage and cost," Sudip Nandy, Wipro's chief strategy officer, told us. "That is a sweetener. Offshoring is a process of being able to break down a complex process and disaggregate the skills required. Today we can have many different combinations of highly skilled people and less-skilled people, more than was possible in the past."

Companies throughout the developing economies and in industries of all types—not just high technology—have begun to struggle toward a better configuration of their value chains. "It's a question of finding out exactly where the production chain can be," says Gabriel Stoliar, executive director of planning and business development at Brazil's diversified mining firm Companhia Vale do Rio Doce (CVRD). "At CVRD we strongly believe in planning, positioning, focusing, concentrating efforts, and integrating along the production chain—independently of geography."

An important consideration in pinpointing is to keep costs low, which usually means retaining important parts of a company's operations in the home country. But, unlike the incumbents' offshoring operations, cost is rarely the primary issue for the challengers. Pinpointing for them involves three main actions that can deliver significant advantage:

- *Connecting with Customers*
- *Distributing Complexity*
- *Reinventing the Business Model*

CONNECTING WITH CUSTOMERS

One of the earliest and most compelling reasons that the challengers began pinpointing was to overcome the gulf that often existed between them and their overseas customers, especially those based in the developed economies.

The challengers saw that the incumbents had an advantage in their ability to be close to and connect with customers in the developed countries. "The incumbents are ahead of us in customer intimacy," said Sudip Nandy. "They have the access to the boardrooms and the relationships that we don't have yet. I think we are significantly ahead of them in operational excellence, and we are probably better at innovation. Now we are investing in customer intimacy, and it's just a question of who gets the combination right first."

Johnson Electric provides "end-to-end" (concept-to-production) capabilities for new products by having a truly global design-to-manufacture process. High-cost designers in Europe and the United States, located near JE's customers, work closely with clients to understand their needs and develop high-level concepts. In China, lower-cost employees carry out the detailed design, tooling, prototyping, and testing. The customer, however, sees only a seamless delivery of high-quality, affordable design and manufacturing.

Bharat Forge and Dual-Shoring

Bharat Forge, based in Pune, India, has developed its own distinct approach to pinpointing that it calls dual-shoring—a strategy that enables the company to deliver low-cost, high-quality products and services to customers throughout the world from at least two of its manufacturing facilities.

Founded in 1961, Bharat Forge initially served the Indian automotive industry by forging a variety of components such as crankshafts, connecting rods, and axles. Through the early 1990s, the company focused mainly on the industry in India and produced few exports. In 1997, just after it had made a large investment in increasing capacity in India, Bharat Forge faced a crisis when a sudden and extreme downturn in the Indian economy hit the automotive industry. As Baba Kalyani, chairman of Bharat Forge, says, "It was at this time that we decided to aggressively grow exports to reduce dependence on the Indian market." By 2001, Bharat Forge's exports from its only plant in Pune were over 25 percent of its sales as it expanded its customer base to companies in the United States, the United Kingdom, Germany, and Japan.

It was in 2001 that Bharat Forge set its next goal: to become one of the top global players in the automotive forging industry within five years. This meant expanding its presence into other types of parts and segments (particularly passenger cars) and geographies. To achieve its goal, Bharat Forge made a series of acquisitions of forging companies in the United States, Germany, Sweden, and Scotland. In 2005, Bharat Forge formed a joint venture with FAW Group Corporation, the largest automotive group in China, to handle forging. This joint venture will cater not only to the fastest-growing automotive market in the world but will also add another low-cost manufacturing site to the group's global network.

Bharat Forge did not close down the operations of the high-cost plants it had acquired and shift the activities to India. Instead it used this global network of plants to implement its dual-shore manufacturing approach—establishing more than one production location for all the core components it makes. Typically, one location is close to the customer for jobs that require intensive collaboration or very fast turnaround, and the second is in a low-cost but technologically competitive destination such as India, for jobs that need to be produced at the lowest possible cost and that have reasonably predictable demand.

This enables Bharat Forge to pinpoint its operations so that its tasks are geographically dispersed, which enables the company to provide a full range of design, forging, and machining services to its customers around the world in a cost-effective manner. For example, Bharat Forge India has a large capacity for the production of engine and chassis components for passenger vehicles, commercial vehicles, and light trucks and can provide design and engineering services, as well. Its operations in Germany can do all of this, although with smaller capacity, and offer customers a close and responsive interface.

The next stage of this business model was to align the R&D and sales processes with this dual-shored manufacturing footprint. Maintaining plants in high-cost locations would reduce the company's margins—unless Bharat Forge could replace some of its lower-margin products with new ones that had higher margins. To win more of the new orders for more complex parts, Bharat Forge provided an integrated offering of R&D and manufacturing to its global customers. Unlike the manufacturing plants—which operated fairly independently within the network—Bharat Forge integrated the design centers across the globe. That enabled the company to cut the cost and reduce the cycle time for new products significantly by having 70 percent of the design done in its center in India.

The final stage was to make the business model dynamic by periodically evaluating the profit margins of each order and migrating orders with lower margins to the lower-cost plants and replacing them with higher-margin products.

It is no wonder that Bharat Forge boasts an EBITDA margin of 20 percent, while its most profitable incumbent competitors struggle to get past 10 to 15 percent. Pinpointing makes Bharat's customers feel that every capability is within reach and that the company is delivering the highest possible value. The actual location of the work is irrelevant.

DISTRIBUTING COMPLEXITY

Offshoring generally involved simple activities and basic manufacturing. The incumbents usually kept the really difficult stuff—the jobs that required the brightest talent and heftiest brainpower—at home. But the challengers demonstrated they could handle virtually any job, no matter how complex. However, as they moved into more value-added services, they became increasingly constrained by the amount of talent available in their home countries. So an important part of pinpointing has been to locate elements of these complex processes in places where the necessary talent already is— or where they wouldn't mind moving to (or, at least, staying for a while).

That's why many challengers have established research and development operations in such developed countries as Germany, Austria, Sweden, and increasingly, the United States, as well as metropolitan centers in other rapidly developing countries such as the Czech Republic and Romania.

However, when the challengers compete in less-developed economies, such as Indonesia and Africa, pinpointing operations and activities can get tricky. "We put a small team in Indonesia because it's the third-largest market for two-wheelers in the world," Sanjiv Bajaj, executive director of Bajaj Auto, said. "We may also set up an assembly and manufacturing plant in Brazil because that is the largest market in South America. For West Africa, we will have a small base out of Nigeria. You have to go to Indonesia, you have to go to Nigeria, you have to go to Iran, you have to go to Brazil, Argentina, and Colombia—but these are not necessarily the safest places of the world to enter, both from the point of view of setting up a business and from the point of view of building teams."

WIPRO: DISTRIBUTING THE UNDISTRIBUTABLE

In 2007, Wipro Technologies—"the number one provider of integrated business, technology, and process solutions on a global delivery platform" as the company describes itself—purchased Infocrossing, a provider of outsourced IT services, based in Leonia, New Jersey. At $600 million, it was one of the largest overseas purchases ever made by an Indian software company.

"Infocrossing is a perfect fit in our remote infrastructure-services offering," said Suresh Senapaty, Wipro's chief financial officer. "We expect to achieve an industry-leading role with this acquisition."[1] Infocrossing was the latest in a series of acquisitions made by Wipro to gain capabilities and customers it did not have in the developed markets. Wipro knew these acquisitions would have a high cost structure and would dilute the company's margins. What's more, the acquired companies offered a set of services that appeared to be so complex that it would be difficult to move them from their original locations and make them part of Wipro's global network of delivery centers. Through pinpointing, however, Wipro has managed to make these acquisitions, offer the complex services to customers worldwide, and maintain margins that are among the highest in the software industry.

Wipro did so by distributing its complex and advanced IT processes within its global development centers through concepts such as usability design, agile software development, and the implementation of the factory model of software development.

Usability design involves the creation of software and other features involved with the human-computer interface. "In designing usability, it is almost unheard of that you can do the work remotely," said Sudip Nandy, Wipro's chief of strategy. "People say it is not possible to do it offshore. Well, we said, 'Okay, let's see. We are talking to some experts who are in this very, very interesting area.' What we are looking at is deconstructing the whole usability process and seeing what parts of it can be done from India with the right skill people—and how to get the right people to do it."

Agile development, which enables incremental change during the engineering process, is another approach that has been considered unsuitable for offshoring because it typically is accomplished by small teams working in real time, with much face-to-face collaboration, and involves less written documentation and defined process than other types of development. The goal is to produce very high quality software quickly enough to meet the constantly evolving needs of the customer and do so cost-effectively enough not to break the bank.

"We are now pushing the frontier on agile," Nandy said to us. "We are trying to find out how we can do part of the agile process sitting here in India, and part of the agile process sitting with the customer. How can we do it, first in two locations, and then really make it distributed. While we have successful projects already in the distributed agile mode, it may be another year before we find the real answers and internalize those processes on all our support systems, but these are some of the things we are bringing to bear on how we make our services unique."

Wipro pioneered the industrialization of software development by following the factory model—specifically that of the Toyota Production System and lean manufacturing. "That is a unique thing that we have," says Nandy. "We are bringing that factory model, with specialization and reuse of complex process, to bear on all the new areas we're entering, where we are pushing the boundary and definition of IT services. We will try to make each one equally scalable, equally measurable, and equally offshorable." (Wipro's application of the factory model and lean principles to software services became the subject of a Harvard Business School case study.)

To address these new challenges, Wipro has pinpointed aspects of its operations that most incumbents have only begun to think about. "We are trying to stay ahead by not just doing the same work we did in India but trying to use Latin America, the Middle East, and China in the same way as we did India," said Divakaran Mangalath, chief technology officer at Wipro. "We are not using India the way Accenture and IBM use India. We are trying to use China and the Middle East as a base for development of exports to other countries."

The limiting factor of pinpointing such operations outside of India is scale. "I can't visualize any center which potentially can scale up to the size of any of the development centers in India," said Pratik Kumar, executive vice president of human resources at Wipro. "I have lost count of the number of centers we have across the globe, but you have to take a view that it can scale up to a point, and beyond that it can't. The India piece is still going to be a very strong part of our growth story. But the workforce will begin to become more diverse. The nature of the engagement with the customers will change with all these centers."

And now, with acquisitions like Infocrossing, Wipro is leveraging the United States for its globally advantaged operations. "Even as we speak, we're talking about setting up near-shore and client proximity centers in America," Kumar told us, before the Infocrossing purchase. "The employees of those centers will be local Americans and not Indians on assignments going there. That's a trend that will

increase." So is Wipro an offshore company? Perhaps yes, offshoring
to the United States!

TATA TECHNOLOGIES: ENABLING THE
ENGINEERING CONVERSATION

Like Wipro, Tata Technologies (TT) has implemented a pinpointed
business model in one of the most complex processes in business and
industry: the engineering and design (E&D) of new products for the
automotive and aerospace industries. In a 2007 report, DataQuest
named Tata Technologies India's leader in automotive engineering
design services and the second largest in revenue across all E&D
industry sectors, accounting for 16.1-percent market share.

Tata Technologies, a subsidiary of Tata Motors, is based in Mumbai but is led by an international team headquartered in Singapore.
The organization comprises two subsidiaries, INCAT and Tata
Technologies iKS. INCAT is an engineering services outsourcing
(ESO) and product development IT services firm, based in metropolitan Detroit, with operations in thirteen countries. Tata Technologies iKS, based in Denver, is a provider of engineering knowledge
to a growing community of engineers in twenty-five countries
through its software as a service (SaaS) site myigetit.com. This site
helps address the challenge caused by many engineering graduates
not being employable. It offers an affordable means to provide practical engineering education to engineers, regardless of where they live.
The engineers can also get certified in certain practical domains,
such as automotive engineering disciplines that are not taught in
school. Also, iKS provides corporate solutions that allow some of the
world's largest automotive and aerospace companies to manage the
capture and dissemination of knowledge to their engineers.

Tata Technologies has facilities in twelve countries—including
in the rapidly developing economies of India, China (through a
partner), Thailand, and Mexico, as well as developed economies,
including the United States, the United Kingdom, Ireland, France,

Singapore, Japan, Germany, and Canada. The company employs more than three thousand engineers. Eighty percent of its employees are citizens of the countries in which they work; 20 percent are Indians—"India's first truly global E&D services provider," claims the company on its Web site.

Patrick McGoldrick, the company's chief executive officer, has set a goal for Tata Technologies to become the largest independent provider of engineering and design and product life cycle management (PLM) services to the global automotive and aerospace industries, with revenue of $500 million, by the year 2010. What makes McGoldrick confident that he can reach his 2010 growth target? He claims that it's because of the combination of the customer intimacy and knowledge that the company's onshore operations deliver and the low-cost, high-skill offshore engineering activities that take place mostly in India and Thailand. Thanks to these advantages, TT can assign different activities to whichever locations enable it to best satisfy each customer while also meeting the company's performance goals.

This is particularly tricky to accomplish—and very unusual in the automotive and aerospace industries—because of the nature of the E&D process in these businesses. "Most companies treat product development as a conversation, an art rather than a science," says Warren Harris, chief executive officer of INCAT. "We add structure to the process that, in the past, has not been well defined," McGoldrick maintains. "IT has become a modular architecture, where you can easily shift things around. In product design, it is extremely creative. But we have tremendous strength in mechanical engineering, in component design, and in how you improve the whole process of engineering. It is a very unique area. It is a really hard business to do correctly."

Tata Technologies delivers end-to-end product development services for some of the world's most complex products and projects. Engineers at its product development center in Pune have helped design complex exterior surfaces for a major North American truck manufacturer and vehicle doors for a U.S. fire truck manufacturer.

Conceptual detailing was done with the client's team on-site, while design and development were handled offshore.

"We took weight out of the door, reduced the thickness and the complexity of the mechanisms inside of the door. Some of the work was done onshore, and some of the work was done here in Pune," said Harris. "That approach couldn't be done if we were purely an offshore company, and it couldn't be done at the same cost and as swiftly as we were able to do it if we had been purely an onshore company."

Managing such complexity long-distance and accomplishing the job with no loss of quality is no mean task. When you walk into a BPO center in India, you see quality and customer satisfaction metrics for each process being performed for a customer in the United States tracked in real time and displayed on digital boards—something that used to happen mostly in automotive plants. With their revenues directly linked to performance on these metrics, it's no wonder that offshore BPO vendors are obsessed with getting the job done right the first time.

Challengers like Wipro have taken this obsession with the quality of their global delivery model to a higher level by shifting their focus from low-cost efficiency to process improvement through initiatives such as lean IT services. Adapted from the vaunted Toyota Production System, the lean philosophy stresses process improvement through incremental enhancements in quality and innovation, accompanied by organizational change. By January 2006, Wipro had more than 235 lean projects completed or in the pipeline.[2] Its goal? To achieve at least a 10-percent improvement in such project metrics as delivery, effort, and quality. Azim Premji's strong belief in delivering value to the customer through innovation and quality processes has culminated in the system the company calls the "Wipro Way."

As they reconfigure their value chains to manage more complex processes and enhance their quality of service, challengers like Wipro and Tata Technologies strive to make their customer offerings ever more compelling. Sudip Nandy, the head of strategy at Wipro, told us, "We are moving beyond being people who take orders from customers and do them very efficiently in a low-cost manner. Now we are making effectiveness a part of our story and proactiveness a part of our offering."

REINVENTING THE BUSINESS MODEL

Many challengers are driving the transformation of industry value chains through pinpointing by fundamentally rethinking and radically redefining their business models and creating new value propositions and business architectures. Johnson Electric, Wipro, and Bharat Forge all have done it. Such incumbents as IBM, American Power Conversion, and Standard Chartered are beginning to.

VSNL is India's leading international long-distance telecommunications operator, with $1 billion in sales and $14 million in profits in 2006. To strengthen its global position, VSNL acquired the undersea network of Tyco (based in the United States) and the operations of Teleglobe Communications Corporation, a Canadian company. With global bandwidth and customers in place, VSNL created a low-cost offshore center for the noncore operations of the combined entities. With its operations pinpointed (and it was one of the first providers of commoditized bandwidth to do so), VSNL moved to transform its business by offering highly competitive, value-added services such as network management, for its global customers.

As N. Srinath, chief executive officer of VSNL, told us, "Bandwidth gives margins, but we also need a portfolio of businesses that are sticky." The "sticky" businesses he refers to include network-based solutions for customers—such as infrastructure management, network management (including managed security and other applications), IT services, and content management. As Mr. Srinath remarked, a "plumber can never outperform an architect." That is, a basic telecommunications provider cannot beat a company that combines telecommunications and information technology services.

Major IT service providers have also remade their business models through pinpointing—moving beyond application development and maintenance to providing broader business solutions for companies around the world. Wipro, for example, has made several acquisitions to gain access to new domain knowledge and customers in developed markets. And it is combining these capabilities with its low-cost engineering capability to create compelling engineering value propositions for customers. "Eighty-five percent of the value added to R&D activities is added in India," says Wipro chairman and chief executive officer Premji.

As Wipro's chief strategy officer Nandy explains, "We are trying to change the landscape by integrating relevant service lines to offer a unique solution to each customer. Sometimes that could mean taking ownership of a process—which includes the underlying infrastructure, the application that runs on the infrastructure, and the business process." Wipro sees growth in the provision of services to healthcare organizations and anticipates more involvement with the travel industry.

These self-reinventing challengers have several characteristics in common. They have the ability to visualize the industry's and their own offerings and value chain not in terms of "what is" but "what can be." They don't just leverage the low-cost advantage of their home market, they also build capabilities close to their customers. They don't remain satisfied with what they have, they find ways to add new capabilities. And in doing all of this, not only do they transform themselves, they drive the transformation of their industries.

Cipla: Transforming Itself and an Industry

Cipla, one of the world's leading manufacturers of generic drugs, saw immense opportunity in transforming the value chain of the global pharmaceutical industry and making India the shore of choice for generic drug manufacturing.

Cipla develops a highly specific category of product: generic antiretroviral (ARV) drugs. It was the first firm to get approval for

Triomune, which became the largest-selling ARV used in the treatment of AIDS. It was also the first to launch Viraday, an advanced ARV, in India. Its single-minded focus on becoming the best in this narrow market has enabled Cipla to build scale large enough to produce generic drugs at a fraction of the cost of its U.S. competitors.

Like other Indian pharmaceutical companies, Cipla benefited from process patents that allowed firms to introduce molecules already released in Western markets by multinational pharma companies, so long as their manufacturing process was different. Process patents made it possible for companies to manufacture vital drugs locally and at prices affordable to local populations. Today, under India's new multilateral obligations, product patents—which stipulate that a previously released molecule cannot be copied even if it's produced using a different manufacturing process—are the norm.

Cipla's chief executive officer, Amar Lulla, tells his company's story with a strong nationalistic tone. "In 1935, during the war, there was a shortage of medicines, and that's when Cipla came into being. The pharmaceutical industry was dominated by the multinationals, and up to 1970, they had about 75- to 80-percent market share. The Indian pharmaceutical companies, which had very little share, got together under the leadership of Dr. K. A. Hamied and began the debate about whether India could afford to have product patents." In 1972, the government recommended that product patents be abolished and process patents instituted. That was the turning point for the pharmaceutical industry in India.

"So, we were free to manufacture any molecules as long as it did not infringe the process that was patented," says Lulla. "As a result, over the last thirty years, India has become the medicine chest of the world. All the molecules were manufactured in this country, all the processes were done, the pharmaceutical industry came into being—the pharmaceutical machinery manufacturers, the software, the infrastructure, everything. It immensely threatened the multinationals."

In 1985, incumbents began to feel the pinch from the pharmaceutical industry in India and lobbied successfully to bring back product patent laws. "Until that time, the pharmaceutical industry was very inward-looking; it was a very controlled market and a very difficult time," Lulla explains. "But, when product patents were reinstated, free trade and the free economy began to operate. The shackles were removed, and you began to see performance by the better companies."

In India, the industry developed a complete drug-making infrastructure and has taken its place on the world stage as the shore of choice for global pharma companies that have high cost structures or that cannot bring out new products as fast as Cipla and the other Indian generic manufacturers can. In addition to its revenue from acting as partner, the company exports raw materials, intermediaries, prescription drugs, and over-the-counter products to markets in Europe, the United States, Africa, Asia, Latin America, and the Middle East.

Cipla is ranked first in terms of domestic retail sales, with 2006 revenues of $644 million (compound annual growth rate 2001 to 2006 of 25 percent) and operating profit of $179 million (CAGR 2001 to 2006 of 26 percent). The company has manufacturing facilities in Kurkumbh, Bangalore, Patalganga, and Vikhroli, a suburb of Mumbai. Its product portfolio includes antibiotic, antibacterial, antiasthmatic, anti-inflammatory, anthelminthic, anticancer, and cardiovascular drugs.

Cipla's version of pinpointing did not involve building a network of facilities around the world. Nor did it make acquisitions to get closer to its global customers or access new talent pools. Rather, Cipla chose to pinpoint its activities throughout India, and leveraged its scale and process-engineering capabilities to achieve one of the lowest costs of manufacture in the industry. In doing so, Cipla has not only become a partner of choice for other players in the global pharma value chain, it is forcing competitors to create their own versions of a pinpointed business model.

"The growth opportunities are tremendous," Lulla notes. "Big pharma needs us to give them cost-effective development technology and cost-effective products quickly. Their operations are very slow and sluggish, at very high cost. They realize this, and every day we have quality-control people who are coming to India, wanting to invest to build manufacturing infrastructure here."

IMPLICATIONS: RETHINK, RECONFIGURE, REINVENT

Offshoring began as an exercise in cost reduction by incumbents, and their business models are still rooted in their high-cost home countries. Only a few of the incumbents have gone beyond offshoring and begun to realize the benefits of creating products and managing services in the rapidly developing economies. While most of the incumbents were focusing on cost, the challengers were taking their version of offshoring to best shoring to dual shoring and finally pinpointing their operations by siting facilities and processes beyond their borders to gain the advantages of customer intimacy, talent, and other capabilities—and now the incumbents must take similar actions.

Pinpointing requires that a company completely rethink its processes, reconfigure its value chain, and even reinvent its business model. No company can expect to get its pinpointing exactly right— at least not for very long. The best it can do is get close and be flexible enough to adjust and refine as quickly as possible.

FACE UP TO LEGACY

The process of pinpointing can be extremely difficult for incumbents—primarily because their value chains are so large and well established that it takes a great deal of willpower, energy, and resource to make changes.

Many of the challengers have had the advantage of building their value chains from nothing: No factories to be closed. No workers to be laid off. No territories to be abandoned. No rules to break. No egos to bruise.

The onerous legacy issues are largely why global automakers have been slow to pinpoint their activities. Although they started over a decade ago and despite all the hype from the leadership, the percentage of parts sourced from low-cost countries still remains in the single digits. Fewer than 5 percent of all their R&D engineering is carried out in the rapidly developing economies—even though China and India are known to have large pools of engineers. And of the plants that incumbent vehicle manufacturers and their major suppliers have set up in a low-cost country like China, many of them do not achieve a lower cost than their home-market operations because they have been set up as replicas of the high-cost plants in home markets.

To improve their track record, incumbents must learn how to uncouple the links in the value chain, and move them to the most advantageous locations globally. These links should not function as replicas of their high-cost operations at home, but rather should take advantage of local conditions and capabilities, and then seamlessly reconnect with the home-country links to provide a product or service. This could involve working with partners in various parts of the world and giving up on the desire to "own" the entire value chain. It will also require a strong project management mind-set and powerful tools (including technology) and appropriate metrics to handle the increased complexity involved (for example, coordinating far-flung project teams).

Some incumbents are getting good at the game. Consider American Power Conversion (APC), based in West Kingston, Rhode Island.[3] APC makes cooling and surge-protection devices and offers services such as project management and training that relate to power management. The bulk of APC's customers are in the United States and Europe; more than 85 percent of the company's global supply of products is manufactured in the Philippines and India, the rest in final-assembly units close to the customers. The company has design centers throughout Europe and the United States to be close to customers, and in Asia to take advantage of low-cost capabilities and be close to manufacturing plants. It created a global sourcing organization that is centered in India and China and an online supplier database that is transparent to managers anywhere in the world. It took many years and a lot of sweat and angst for APC to achieve this footprint. But the effort has paid off in significantly increased profitability.

IBM, too, is pinpointing its activities. "Work flows to the places where it will be done best," says Sam Palmisano, chairman and chief executive officer.[4] The company's goal is to drive down costs and exploit talent for research and development. IBM has more than fifty thousand employees in India, the company's second-largest operation after North America. The firm invested $2 billion to build the local sales and marketing organization and global development centers in India over the past three years, and it plans to invest another $6 billion from 2008 to 2011 and more than double the headcount.

Practice Seamlessness

Pinpointing is not just about disaggregating and siting a set of activities in the best locations; it requires fluidity—the ability to allocate work to any of the best-shored locations by treating global capacity as fungible.

No player—incumbent or challenger—has fully mastered the art of seamlessness. Service firms such as Wipro and Tata Technologies are among the best at it, but even manufacturing companies such as Bharat Forge are moving toward it. They evaluate each new order or IT or R&D project and allocate it to different centers based on capabilities and available capacity.

Achieving seamlessness requires three capabilities. The first is the ability to modularize the components of the process, which means that the company must break down a process into separate, discrete parts that do not necessarily have to be collocated. The second capability is to manage work while it is happening, across locations around the world. This usually requires that different locations work with the same project, management tools, conduct weekly review meetings, follow the same problem-resolution and decision-making process, and designate one project manager to be responsible for the various modules, wherever they may be located around the world. Third is the ability to bring the different modules together into a unified end product and to test it for quality and performance.

Simple offshoring does not lead to seamlessness. R&D centers operated by incumbents in rapidly developing economies that work seamlessly with their parent R&D centers in Europe and the United States are able to grow, develop capabilities, and retain talent. Those that do not end up carrying out low-end work, find it difficult to recruit talented engineers, and become stunted. Similarly, pinpointed sourcing requires a high degree of seamless collaboration between the sourcing centers in low-cost countries and home markets, between buyers and designers and manufacturing engineers. Our research shows that the most successful firms not only source parts from low-cost countries but also integrate the local sourcing organization with their global product development and local manufacturing teams. This gives the companies both a scope and scale advantage and makes the most of what the rapidly developing economies have to offer. Those that don't collaborate seamlessly have been unable to achieve their goals, despite tall claims from their leaders.

Most challengers, often starting from a position of weakness in their low-cost economies, seem to be more eager to do business smoothly across geographies and across links in their firms' value chain. As Subramaniam Ramadorai, managing director of TCS, told us, "It is not about the size of the operations in Brazil, the United States, the United Kingdom, or Japan, because parts of the work will get done in Japan, India, Korea, China, or Latin America. The question is how do you connect these locations, how do you partition the pieces of the world, when all of these are changing. We need to create these mechanisms, which means mobility of a different order, communication of a different order, collaboration of a different order, delivery of a different order, measurements of a different order, performance of a different order—and all of these in an integrated fashion. We must create a global consistency, a global commitment that a service delivered in Brazil will be no different from a service delivered in India, service delivered in America, and service delivered in China. That's the challenge."

PLAY THE ENTIRE FIELD

As with all the other globality struggles, the most important change that incumbents will need to make in order to pinpoint their operations is a major shift in mind-set. If you're an incumbent, you'll need to think holistically. When you're pinpointing, the entire world is your playing field. There are no "U.S." or "European" firms.

But you'll have to balance this holistic perspective with a granular one. Look at your industry's entire value chain in detail. How could it be disaggregated? Which business processes or value-chain links could be performed elsewhere more efficiently, effectively, and profitably? What regions of the world would make the most suitable locations for handling each of the disaggregated pieces? What will you do with your legacy assets—physical, informational, and human?

And never ignore the possibility of reinventing your business model. Who are your customers? What do you really sell? What's the best way for you to make money? Should you focus all your resources on a single, well-defined offering and build scale in it and partner with others? Or should you have a presence at some or all of the links in your value chain?

Also consider ways to use acquisitions, collaborations, and mergers to enhance your value chain. Should you operate alone? Partner with other companies? If you partner, who will make the best candidates?

Yes, these questions can prove difficult enough to answer that you may be tempted to put off the whole business. The chief operating officer of one large U.S.-based chemical company told us, "We are a high-value, patent-based company and have got a long time to figure this out."

That's music to the challengers' ears.

CHAPTER 7

THINKING BIG, ACTING FAST, GOING OUTSIDE

"We live in an ecosystem of opportunity."
S. Ramadorai, Tata Consultancy Services

Song Zhenghuan, a mathematics teacher and principal of a middle school in the Shanghai suburb of Kunshan, had never been formally involved in business, but he felt he had talent for it. So when the teachers in his school collectively decided that they wanted to start a business to serve the needs of parents, Song was ready to take the helm. They pooled their meager savings and founded a company called Goodbaby. They struggled. There wasn't enough cash flow to pay full wages, and the teachers got worried and wanted to pull out of the enterprise. Goodbaby came to the edge of bankruptcy.

At that time, in the early 1980s, the production of baby products was overseen by the government, and manufacturing took place in facilities run by the Chinese military. One of the factories, located near the middle school, found itself short of capacity for producing its latest state assignment: making strollers. The military managers asked Song if the fledgling Goodbaby could handle the production of some of the parts, as well as final assembly.

Song agreed and committed Goodbaby's entire production capacity to its new customer. The decision saved the company from extinction but was wholly unsatisfying to the inventive Song. He was thoroughly unimpressed by the state's design and longed to create his own stroller from scratch and return to independent operation. Song began tinkering with ideas for new features and better designs and soon hit upon a modification that he thought had merit. Unfortunately, Goodbaby didn't have enough capital to buy raw materials or the production equipment for forming metal parts and molding plastic components. So Song decided to patent his innovation and sell it, to raise cash.

To his delight, the patent sold for 40,000 RMB, a few thousand dollars. Song used some of the money to pay the teachers the salaries they were owed. Some of it he put into the operating budget. With the rest, he built a factory gate. "A real factory has a gate," Song told us. "And I wanted our workers to feel like they worked at a real factory. Somehow in that first year, a gate felt more important than new equipment."

Song was thinking big. Within a year, he had come up with another innovation—a stroller that could be converted into a car seat. This time, he was able to secure a loan from a local bank and went into full production. The product was a hit. Within a decade, Goodbaby had become the premier provider of children's goods in all of China.

Many challengers, like Goodbaby, are young companies that started from nothing; others were small local players for decades before the tsunami struck. A few were national or industry leaders—big fish in economic backwaters. But they all share something in common: in their early days, none of them had the office parks, modern factories, state-of-the-art technologies, R&D operations, hundreds of patents, high-powered talent, extensive capabilities, mature management systems, portfolios of products, and big brand names that the incumbents had.

Before the tsunami, the challengers were way behind. They knew they could never catch up through incremental organic improvement alone. But there was another way. They could collaborate and form joint ventures with the best people and partners in the world. They could merge with or acquire companies that had the capabilities and knowledge and positioning they lacked. They could buy established global brands and then use them as platforms for building new ones or bolstering their own home-country brands.

But it has only been in the past few years that challengers have amassed sufficient capital and clout to make the acquisitions and form the partnerships and joint ventures they needed to transform themselves. In 2000, the BCG Challenger 100 companies had completed a scanty twenty-one publicly recorded acquisitions. That number grew by about 28 percent per year to reach seventy-two merger and acquisition deals involving foreign companies in 2006. The magnitude of the deals increased, too—from an average of $156 million in 2001 to $981 million in 2006. Eight deals over $1 billion were publicly disclosed in 2006, versus just two in 2000.

As Tito Martins, director of corporate affairs at CVRD, the Brazilian iron ore company, put it, "Being Brazilian is very complicated. We needed to improve our grade, our rating. The best way to do so was by acquiring companies." In 2006, CVRD made its largest acquisition to date—and the largest ever made by a Latin American company—buying Canadian-based nickel miner Inco for $19 billion. "We got lucky," said Martins. "Soon after the acquisition, the price of nickel went up."

This fever for acquisition and joint venturing has struck all the rapidly developing economies and every industry. Tata Tea, through its international acquisitions, went from a local Indian plantation and packaged-tea producer to a company with a global footprint and a reputation as a provider of health solutions.

Suzlon Energy, the Indian wind-energy company, made a series of acquisitions to create a global value chain with R&D and manufacturing presence in Australia, Belgium, China, Denmark, Germany, India, the Netherlands, and the United States. Twenty percent of its 8,600 employees are based outside India.

América Móvil, a Mexican mobile network operator, spent more than $5 billion on fourteen acquisitions between 2001 and 2005 to build its presence in Latin America.

In 2006, Moscow-based Vneshtorgbank spent $1 billion for a 5 percent stake in European aerospace concern EADS, makers of Airbus. Russian steelmaker Evraz paid $2.3 billion in cash for Oregon Steel Mills Inc., in Russia's biggest overseas deal ever. In total, Russian companies spent $13 billion in 2006 on overseas acquisitions, up from $1 billion in 2002.[1]

Tata Steel's acquisition of the Anglo-Dutch steelmaker Corus—for $13.1 billion—made headlines around the world. Here was a large, established, Old World incumbent being hunted by two small, New World challengers, Tata of India and CSN of Brazil. Why couldn't Corus attract a white knight from among the many steel companies in the United States and Europe? Why were these challengers willing to pay a premium for a company saddled with high-cost plants?

To achieve such feats, these companies have had to think big about what they acquire and how. They've had to act fast. And they've had to be willing to go outside their geographical and industry boundaries. They have done so with these important actions:

- *Scaling Up*
- *Building Brands*
- *Filling Capability Gaps*
- *Bartering*

SCALING UP

For Tata, the rationale behind its purchase of Corus was clear: the company needed to build scale in an industry that was starting to consolidate. Without scale, it would soon have become an acquisition target itself. Challengers have found that acquisition is one of the quickest ways—if not *the* quickest—to build scale, especially across geographies.

For example, after Cemex, the Mexican cement company, bought RMC Group of the United Kingdom in 2005 for $5.8 billion, it became the world's second-largest cement producer. In 2007, Hindalco, an Indian producer of various materials, bought the U.S. aluminum maker Novelis for $6 billion and—overnight—became the world's largest aluminum-rolling company.

Challengers in high-technology businesses like telecommunications have also seized the opportunity to build scale through acquisition. For instance, VSNL, the telecommunications provider, pursued acquisitions to scale up its infrastructure so it could increase its bandwidth and lower costs. Armed with greater capacity and healthier profits, it moved up the value chain to offer network management services, where it could really put on heft. To this end, VSNL purchased the cable network and traffic infrastructure (for voice, data, and IP) Tyco and Teleglobe, at fire-sale prices.

Sometimes a challenger targets particular companies for acquisition because the would-be acquirer has home-market experience with business conditions similar to those of the target company's market. In other cases, targets have technological and operational know-how that will enable the acquirer to build scale quickly in the target company's market. In other situations, however, a partnership—often with a larger company or one with particular expertise in a product segment—may be a more effective way to increase scale.

MAHINDRA & MAHINDRA: BIG DREAMS REALIZED

On a balmy day in April 2007, Anand Mahindra, chief executive officer of Mahindra & Mahindra (M&M), glanced out the window of his office on the sixth floor of the Mahindra Towers in Central Mumbai during a conversation with us about his company's past and future.

Today, M&M is one of India's major conglomerates, with revenue of $4.5 billion in 2006. The company operates in six industry sectors: autos, including utility vehicles and light commercial vehicles; small-goods three-wheelers; farm equipment, primarily tractors; IT and IT-enabled services; financial services; auto components such as castings, forgings, sheet metal, gears, steel flats, and composites; and infrastructure development.

Since 2001, M&M has boasted a compound annual growth rate (CAGR) of 17 percent and an annual increase in operating profits of 29 percent. This remarkable success has stemmed in large part from the company's willingness to enter into joint ventures and collaborations and its ability to capitalize on the virtuous cycle that such deals set in motion. With every acquisition, joint venture, and collaboration, a company not only expands the value it offers customers, it also learns important lessons and beefs up its capability to make additional and similar plays. The process feeds on itself, something that many incumbents who view growth-expanding deals as one-off events don't realize.

But M&M had to wait until the tsunami gathered force before it could think as big and act as fast as its leaders wanted to. In 1956, Chairman Keshub Mahindra had a provocative idea. Why not partner with Renault to make and market one of the French company's car models in India? M&M, founded in 1945, already made utility vehicles for the Indian market but had yet to produce a proper passenger car. Rather than develop one on its own, why not tap into the incredible stores of knowledge Renault had accumulated in its many decades of doing business?

To Mahindra, who had a degree from Harvard Business School, the deal seemed like an obvious move. Since the earliest days of the automotive industry, car companies had been forming partnerships, merging, and selling or buying operations and factories. But in 1950s India—recently independent of British rule—such a venture was virtually impossible, as a dense web of rules and regulations barred the country from foreign investment or partnerships.

"My own perception, and it may be wrong, was that the government was fearful of change," Keshub Mahindra says. "Perhaps this had something to do with being colonized for two hundred-odd years. It was scared of foreign capital. So it tied our hands with all these rules and regulations. It was absolutely ridiculous. The result was that we didn't have growth at all."[2]

It would take almost four decades to change the business environment in India. Keshub Mahindra shelved his big idea. But he didn't forget about it. And neither would his successors.

In 1996, M&M formed a joint venture with Ford to introduce the American car company into the Indian market. The project didn't do particularly well, but M&M learned a lot about product design and project management, and it applied its new knowledge to developing its own sport utility vehicle, called Scorpio. Launched in 2002, the model took the Indian market by storm. In 2005, Mahindra began introducing the Scorpio into international markets.

Encouraged by the ultimate benefits of its relationship with Ford, M&M stepped up the pace of its collaborations. It partnered with British Telecom to establish Tech Mahindra, which has bagged some of the biggest telecom outsourcing deals and was valued at $4.5 billion after its initial public offering in 2007. M&M also built its auto forgings business from scratch into the world's fifth largest in just three years by investing some $275 million to acquire companies in India, the United Kingdom, and Germany. In addition, the company has entered into a collaboration with the North American firm International Truck and Engine Corporation to design and launch a new range of trucks in India and export them to its partner's operations overseas.

The decades of work finally came to fruition with the creation of a joint venture between M&M and Renault to produce and market the Logan model in India. The customized Logan was introduced to the Indian market in April 2007 and quickly became a top seller.

M&M is also thinking big about tractors and has set its sights on becoming the largest tractor company in the world in terms of sales volume. With around 260,000 tractors sold in 2006, the Indian tractor market is the largest in the world by volume, followed by the United States and China.

Mahindra Tractors, best known for its sub-80-horsepower machines, has been the undisputed market leader in India for twenty-three years, with a market share of almost 40 percent. Mahindra offers the widest product portfolio in the industry, with tractors starting as low as $10,000, and sells it with a focused, regional approach. It collaborates closely with local banks to offer financing options that suit local needs. And Mahindra possesses the largest distribution network in India for farm equipment, consisting of 510 dealers and 1,175 service points.[3]

Mahindra tractors are designed for the particular circumstances of the small, independent farmer. In India, farms are typically three or four acres in size, in comparison to the farms of several hundred acres that are common in the United States, smaller even than the fields of a local grower of summer produce in the United States. What's more, Indian farmers use their tractors for all kinds of work besides plowing fields. They haul rocks, careen along bumpy dirt roads, "puddle" rice, thresh *jowar* (sorghum), and even sculpt new golf courses. Moreover, India is a country of varied farming conditions, with different soil conditions and different cropping patterns that translate into different requirements for tractors.

Most of India's 306 million farmers do not yet own a tractor. But thanks to favorable government policies, increased mechanization, and new financing options, the market is experiencing 20-percent growth per annum. That's why so many incumbents are working to boost their share in this huge domestic market.

So Anand Mahindra knew that it wouldn't be long before the big global tractor makers would be putting big pressure on his company. Mahindra decided that the best way to protect his tractor business's home base would be to build scale abroad. M&M already had low-cost factories at home. By buying up competitors, it would secure its presence in India as well as extend its global reach. So the CEO set an objective to become the leading worldwide tractor maker (by volume) by 2010.

Soon the company had acquired Jiangling Tractor Company

(JTC) of China, considered placing a bid for Tractorul in Romania (although, ultimately, it did not), entered into a joint venture with Iran Tractor Manufacturing Company (which commands an 80-percent market share in its country), and acquired Swaraj Enterprise Tractors in India. Mahindra's domestic share jumped from 33 percent to 45 percent.

These acquisitions weren't as willy-nilly as they may sound; each had particular potential. The tractor industry changes slowly, in terms of technology, especially in the rapidly developing economies. In China, Mahindra saw that a huge number of farmers were not working with tractors at all, but rather with power tillers—machines that resemble lawn mowers and (in their larger incarnation) golf carts. "China had been at a different level of mechanization," Anand Mahindra told us. "They had a million power tillers that were waiting to be converted to tractors." A year after Mahindra acquired JTC, the Chinese company grew 15 percent, faster than the Indian tractor industry.

"We are going to see the Chinese market becoming a dominant factor in deciding which players retain their scale and their size around the world, and that's why we committed to China," Mahindra said. "We don't believe you can be number one in the world in your industry unless you are a big player in India and China."

CEMEX: THE POWER OF SERIAL ACQUISITIONS

Cemex's core strategy is to achieve profitable growth through acquisition. Notes chief executive officer Lorenzo Zambrano, "Geographical diversification enables us to operate in multiple regions with different business cycles. For the long term, we are trying to ensure that no one market accounts for more than one-third of our business." Besides mitigating cyclical risks, global expansion has given Cemex access to more stable capital markets, enhanced its production capacity, and countered increased domestic competition.

Cemex's sales revenues grew from less than $1 billion in 1989 to nearly $5 billion in 1999, without any loss of profitability. During that time, EBITDA margin ranged between 30 and 40 percent—10 to 15 percentage points higher than the company's leading global competitors. With 2006 sales of $17.4 billion and EBITDA of $4.1 billion (23.6 percent), Cemex is still more profitable than its global competitors. How does it do it? Several ways.

For one thing, the company has standardized its operations, which enables it to quickly assimilate new acquisitions via "the Cemex way" and swiftly capitalize on synergies. As an example, Cemex expects to generate recurring synergies of $360 million from its 2005 acquisition of RMC Group, the UK-based cement maker.

But Cemex doesn't just expect newly acquired companies to conform to its standardized operations. It also learns from the enterprises it purchases and applies that knowledge to further improve operations. Indeed, a continuous improvement philosophy is ingrained in the company's culture and supported by formal processes. For instance, after Cemex learned about petcoke (a relatively affordable energy supply) from a Spanish company it acquired, it began using petcoke throughout the organization. This same philosophy influences decisions about all other aspects of the company's operations, including logistics, plant networks, global procurement, management of quarry life cycles, safety records, and maintenance practices.

Finally, Cemex has found ways to profit from local demand and supply conditions as well as price differences across the many regions where it now operates, thanks to its numerous acquisitions. To illustrate, in the market for ready-mix concrete, contractors often change their orders at the last minute to meet changing customer specifications. By equipping its concrete-mixing trucks with GPS, Cemex has enabled its dispatchers to arrange deliveries within twenty minutes in the Mexican market, compared to three hours for competing vendors. As a result, Cemex has been able to increase its market share, charge a premium to time-conscious contractors, and reduce costs from unused concrete.

Making Haste—Slowly

Challengers think big and move fast to make their acquisitions, but when it comes to integrating newly purchased businesses, they often take their time. The Western view toward acquisitions holds that if the integration is not completed speedily, the benefits of synergy will be lost. Most incumbents plan the postmerger integration and identify the team that will lead the effort well before the acquisition officially takes place.

In some cases, though hardly all, challengers approach integration differently. The Tata Group, for example, does not engage in hostile takeovers. That action is not in line with the Tata philosophy. When the company does make an acquisition, it follows an adaptive model rather than take the traditional prescriptive approach. Says R. Gopalakrishnan, a director of Tata Sons, "I define a prescriptive M&A as one where you have a pretty good idea of your playing field in terms of geography or domain. You then short-list the potential candidates, track them, watch them like a hawk. Once you've acquired the company, you go in with a prescriptive set of ideas of how you want to operate, because that has been part of your acquisition proposal. 'I will do this. I will do that. I will teach them how to run that plant better. I will teach them how to get to markets better.' During the process of acquisition, you have presented the plan, ad nauseam, and you are committed to it, emotionally, psychologically, and strategically."

The adaptive model works quite differently. Instead of prescribing, Tata develops a broad statement about how the acquisition will help the company strategically. "I don't refer to the financials," says Gopalakrishnan. "It is almost like the companies are two patterns, rather than two parts which meet together."

One reason that challengers "make haste slowly" in this way is simply that they are relatively inexperienced in making acquisitions and handling postmerger integrations. However, it is also a question of philosophy and cultural mind-set. Most of the challengers we spoke with talked about trust and cultural fit as the most critical success factors in acquisitions and partnerships. They generally believe it's important to retain the leadership team of the acquired firm. An acquisition, they said, is a marathon rather than a sprint.

So the challengers do not step in immediately after acquisition and shake things up to show who's boss. Instead, they remain inconspicuous and let the local managers run things much as they had before. For the first twelve months, challengers will launch joint efforts to build trust and create a common vision for the merged entity. It is not until the second year that they begin relocating assets and capabilities from high-cost locations to low-cost locations.

In all such collaborations, the challengers demonstrate a keen appetite for learning. "I think our greatest strength is our humility and ignorance," says Gopalakrishnan. "After all, we are not experts in everything."

BUILDING BRANDS

Challengers are also using acquisitions to improve their brand equity at home and abroad. When it comes to iconic brands, the rapidly developing economies have long looked to the West for inspiration. On the list of the top one hundred global brands, as ranked by Interbrand for 2006, not one comes from a rapidly developing economy. Only three—Samsung, Hyundai, and LG—come from the Korean wave of challengers that preceded this tsunami. None come from the Mexican wavelet. And just six are from the Japanese challengers that flowed in before that.

There is (as yet) no Coke, BMW, Nokia, Louis Vuitton, American Express, Gucci, or Google of the rapidly developing world. The best Russian brands of 2006? Such nonhousehold names (in the developed countries) as Beeline, MTS, Baltika, and Slavneft. In Brazil, you might recognize Natura (for more on this company, see chapter 5), but probably not Itaú or Bradesco. In China, China Mobile tops the list, with Lenovo—perhaps the only brand name that most Westerners would recognize—at number ten. Moutai, a distinctive Chinese liquor that confounds many Western palates, ranks eighth.

Creating, establishing, nurturing, and enhancing a brand takes time, expertise, and a keen understanding of cultural nuances. But the effort is well worth it. A well-recognized brand generates tremendous value for a company, not only increasing sales and profits but also giving the enterprise license to expand and innovate. So it's no surprise that the challengers see brand acquisition as a way to expand their field of play as well as enter new markets and attract new customers. The challengers' goal is straightforward: acquire a strong brand, then leverage the brand's promise to quickly spur growth everywhere they operate.

TATA BAGS TETLEY

Tata Tea bought the United Kingdom firm Tetley to gain some immediate name recognition and a platform on which it could build a portfolio of "wellness solutions." Another unit of the sprawling Tata Group, Tata Tea is one of India's most prestigious beverage companies. It's the second-largest branded tea player in the country, after Unilever's beverage business, Hindustan Lever Ltd. In fiscal year 2007, Tata Tea had revenue of more than $1 billion and profit of $138 million.

The company considers itself a tea expert, with extensive knowledge about how to retain freshness through special packaging and rapid shipment of tea from the garden to the consumer. Executives believed they could apply that knowledge of tea freshness in markets around the world. "By redefining freshness to customers, you are able to present a very strong competitive advantage," says chief operating officer R. Krishna Kumar. "That was the logic we were looking at to get into the world market, and to do it through global branding."

But Tata's own brands were not well known outside India, and the company's leaders recognized that the varieties and blends it offered might not suit other markets. Thus, they considered building a new Tata brand for the global market, especially the developed economies. "We realized that spending money on creating a brand, investing in promotion, and creating a market for the Tata brand globally would have been a very expensive exercise and not guaranteed," affirms Kumar. "So we figured that one of the ways in which we needed to grow globally would be to acquire a global brand and then build on it to create a global platform."

What other country besides China is closely associated with tea, tea drinking, tea lore, and tea culture? The United Kingdom, of course. Tata purchased Tetley Tea—a British company founded in 1837 and one of the world's most famous tea brands—for $432 million in 2000.

After that came a rash of additional acquisitions of brands intended to help Tata Tea build on the Tetley platform and leverage "the core properties of tea: health, wellness, goodness, and antioxidants," as Kumar describes them. However, the new brands did not have to be confined to tea: they could be any product that moved consumers toward ready-to-drink beverages seen as herbal-based "wellness solutions."

For example, Tata brought into the fold Good Earth Tea, an herbal brand from California, in 2005; Jemca of the Czech Republic, also an herbal tea specialist, in 2006; the U.S.-based Glaceau, makers of flavored energy drinks, in 2006; and, from South Africa, Joekels Tea Packers, blenders and packers of a wide variety of teas, in 2006. In 2006, 75 percent of Tata Tea's revenues of $1 billion came from outside India. (In 2007, Coca-Cola Co. purchased Glaceau for $4.1 billion, and also bought out Tata, who realized a healthy return on its original investment in the company.)

Tata's brand-driven acquisition push has not only helped it build a global platform, it has also enabled the company to realize greater profits from its high-margin brands. The company has used its excess cash to fund further acquisitions and put even more resources into brand management—activating that virtuous cycle that has benefited so many challengers.

FILLING CAPABILITY GAPS

Another key action of the challengers' acquisitions efforts has been to fill key capability gaps in areas such as technology and market access. In January 2007, China Mobile bought Paktel, a mobile operator based in Pakistan. Valued at $460 million, the deal was China Mobile's first successful international acquisition. In acquiring a small operator in a relatively small market, the company wasn't seeking to accomplish a step change in size. Rather, it wanted to create new value by helping Paktel apply in Pakistan the knowledge China Mobile had gained in China. The two markets share similar challenges and characteristics, such as fast growth and populations with little discretionary income.

In particular, China Mobile had extensive experience in working around China's underdeveloped payment system, which makes it difficult for customers to establish accounts with a mobile provider. The same difficulty exists in Pakistan. As China's middle class has grown and average income has increased, China Mobile has also discovered that consumers' behavior changes as they become more affluent. That means learning how to create products, services, and selling methods to enable customers to trade up to more expensive offerings.

Some challengers have used acquisitions to fill capability gaps that help them attract entirely new customers. Bharat Forge is an apt example. Bharat Forge started out as a manufacturer of large truck forgings for the Indian market, with revenues of $112 million in 2001. Since then, it has acquired forging companies in Germany, Sweden, Scotland, and the United States. These enterprises had supplied parts to passenger-car makers or made forged products for the truck industry that lay outside Bharat's offerings. After acquiring the firms, Bharat Forge integrated its engineering teams into its low-cost engineering center in India to build a global engineering capability of great depth and breadth. It also formed a joint venture with a large automotive group in China. In 2007, Bharat Forge's revenues were over $1 billion. The company now supplies a wide range of highly engineered and complex forging products to makers of trucks and passenger vehicles, companies in the oil and gas industry, and railways.

Huawei Technologies, China's leading telecommunications equipment manufacturer, set up R&D centers in twelve locations worldwide—seven in China and five in overseas locations including the United States, Europe, Russia, and India. The company partnered with a who's who of the telecom equipment industry, including 3Com, Siemens, Microsoft, Motorola, Qualcomm, NEC, Mitsubishi, and Kyocera, to build its own capabilities. Originally a supplier of equipment for fixed networks, by 2006 it had begun serving virtually all areas of the telecommunications industry, including mobile handsets and infrastructure, data communications, and software.

TATA TECHNOLOGIES AND INCAT: FORTUITOUS SYNERGIES

Even M&As that are not so formally targeted can deliver valuable results. For example, Tata Technologies (TT) acquired U.K.-based INCAT in 2005 in response to a challenge from a customer, a large U.S.-based incumbent that manufactured vehicles. At the time, both Tata and INCAT provided the incumbent with a variety of engineering, design, and product life cycle management services—Tata from its low-cost operations in India and Thailand, INCAT from its locations close to the customer's facilities in the United States and Europe.

When this customer downsized its U.S. operations, it needed outside support more than ever but didn't want to consolidate the engineering work with just one of the vendors. Both suppliers brought something important to the table. TT offered quality service at low cost; INCAT, strong customer service and intimate understanding of the business.

So an executive from the manufacturer took Pat McGoldrick,

TT's managing director, out to dinner and asked him, "Do the Tatas have the guts, the money, and the time to come to Michigan? Can you be local, develop customer intimacy, go to swim with the people, go to church with the people, and learn how to do the business? Do you have that?"

McGoldrick didn't think his company could do all that. Then the executive told him he had taken the chief of INCAT out to dinner the night before and posed similar questions to him. The customer had said to INCAT, "Look! Do you think you can keep charging us a hundred and twenty bucks for your services when I can get them for half that from TT? Do you have the time and the guts to go into India and develop a low-cost offshore delivery site?"

The head of INCAT realized that no, his company was likely not in a position to establish an operation in India or Thailand anytime soon. So, McGoldrick told us, "The customer replied, 'If you don't have the time and the guts and the patience, then I think you guys should get together.' And that sparked off the process that led to the acquisition."

After a period of exploration, discussion, and due diligence, the companies decided the merger made sense for both of them, because each offered some capabilities and advantages the other could not. But it wasn't easy. "We had some challenges when it came to integrating the two organizations," admits Warren Harris, chief operating officer of INCAT. "But we've undertaken a number of projects that have validated our value proposition. And we're extremely excited about the next couple of years, not just because it's a grand business, but because customers really value it. They don't want the hassles of having to deal with offshoring themselves in an area that is full of all sorts of challenges."

BAJAJ: REVVING UP THE INSIDERS

Challengers have learned that acquisitions and partnerships, no matter how well intended and carefully thought out, will not have a positive, lasting effect on either party if the companies don't use what they've learned from the experience to improve the way they do business.

Bajaj Auto, for example, seeking to make its motor scooter business more competitive, chose to partner with talented outsiders whose skills and processes it hoped would eventually rub off on company insiders.

In 1985, Bajaj Auto was India's largest manufacturer of Vespa-type motor scooters, with two-stroke engines. The following year, a new wave of Japanese motorcycles entered the Indian market—led by a hot little model called CD 100, born of a joint venture between Honda and Hero Group.

Bajaj, however, kept on making scooters pretty much as it had for twenty-five years. The company seemed to have completely missed the "next thing" in its industry, but, as is often the case in the rapidly developing economies, the reality was a little more complicated than that. "Right through until the early 1990s, our production capacities were controlled by the government," Sanjiv Bajaj told us. "As a result of which, we had a ten-year waiting list for our product. It was not a monopolistic situation, because there were seven or eight other manufacturers of two-wheelers. But we had just the kind of product, at that quality and at that price, that got into consumer's minds. They could not get enough of it."

Even though the Japanese motorcycles were more fuel efficient and snappier looking than the Bajaj scooters, "the consumer overwhelmingly bought the scooter because it was convenient to use and it was cheaper," said Bajaj. "Right up until 1994 or 1995."

Then two things happened.

First, in the wake of the first Gulf War (which ended in early 1991), fuel prices in India started going up significantly. Suddenly, the higher purchase price of the Japanese bikes seemed less important than the total operating cost. Most of the Japanese motorcycles had four-stroke engines, which were 40 percent more fuel efficient than the two-stroke scooters from Bajaj. Second, consumer financing started to become more widely available so the consumer could buy with credit.

Suddenly, everybody in India who drove a scooter (and there were millions who did) wanted a real motorcycle. In the early 1990s, scooters made up as much as 60 percent of the two-wheeler market. By 2000, motorcycles accounted for more than 50 percent, and the Vespa-style, two-stroke scooter had dropped to 15 percent. By 2004, it had sunk to 5 percent.

At that time, Rajiv Bajaj took over as head of product development. Just twenty-eight years old, Rajiv is the grandson of the company's founder and the son of its current chairman, Rahul Bajaj. "We started reworking our entire product portfolio in two-wheelers and three-wheelers," said Sanjiv Bajaj, who is Rajiv's younger brother.

Rajiv faced a formidable task: transforming Bajaj Auto from a local producer of antiquated scooters into a global leader in two-wheeler and small-engine technology. Sure, the company had a team of experienced engineers, but its scooters used Vespa technology, and the team lacked the ability to design motorcycles that could compete with the new Japanese bikes.

As one of his first moves, Bajaj built a new design team led by a talented designer in his early thirties. He engaged a small design outfit called Tokyo R&D, which employed several ex-Honda engineers, to learn more about motorcycle engine design. He worked with Glynn Kerr Design, an independent motorcycle designer and stylist based in Italy, which offered ideas about how motorcycle engines should look, feel, and sound. He consulted with Orbital Engine of Australia Corporation, to help Bajaj understand the direct-injection system for two-stroke engines.

Rajiv Bajaj also changed the way his company sourced components. At the time, the firm manufactured most critical engine components in-house. For components purchased from vendors, the process was handled the old-school way—the specs went out, and the finished products came back in. Bajaj changed all that. Rather than dictating to component vendors, he looked for their input and advice—about everything from headlights to carburetors. The in-house engineers learned to love what the company had long feared: collaboration.

The more it leveraged outside talent to build in-house expertise, the shorter Bajaj's product-development cycle became—from three years to two and then to a mere twelve months. "We got very nimble and quick," says Sanjiv Bajaj. The twelve-month development cycle bests even that of the companies making the bikes that had revolutionized the Indian market: Honda and Yamaha.

Plus, Bajaj's scooters were much cheaper to build. "Even though our bikes are made very well from an Indian point of view, they are still probably one-third the cost of doing the R&D in Japan. Our low-cost R&D allows us to innovate in the space of bikes with below-250-cubic-centimeter engines," Bajaj notes.

Over the years, Bajaj has built such a powerful in-house capability for small-engine design that it has bridged the gap between its own engines' performance and that of its Japanese competitors. Just as important, it has also taken the lead in certain aspects of engine design—such as fuel efficiency for small engines. In fact, companies around the world are now reverse-engineering Bajaj's new DTSI engine technology, a breakthrough, to try to understand and emulate it.

"Through our partners outside India and building our own R&D skills," Bajaj said, "we built the capability to design good motorcycles."

BARTERING

Some challengers get access to technologies that are owned or developed by incumbents by bartering—usually by helping the incumbents improve their market position in the challenger's home economy.

In 2007, the government restrictions against foreign investment had long since been lifted in India, but Renault still chose to team up with Mahindra & Mahindra to create the Logan because the partnership accelerated Renault's entry into an attractive market. M&M had a strong vendor and dealer network, a modern plant, and low-cost engineering capability, all of which enabled Renault to reduce its investment in the Logan by 15 percent. In return, M&M

gained a foothold in the passenger-car industry, where it previously had no presence; built scale in sourcing and distribution; and found opportunities to explore selling its utility vehicles through Renault's global network.

OPENING THE CHINA DOOR

For years, incumbents were not allowed access to local Chinese markets unless they promised to provide technology and capital to their local partners. Until China gained membership in the World Trade Organization in 2001, many industries were restricted, and foreign companies had to form joint ventures with Chinese partners to participate in those industries. The Chinese government often selected the partner for the incumbent or insisted on approving any choice of partner made by the incumbent. The government generally imposed a local content requirement (parts and components made by local companies) of 80 percent and placed restrictions on importing components from outside China.

But many incumbents, eager to set up manufacturing operations in China to leverage the low-cost labor and tap the burgeoning market, accepted these restrictions, creating joint ventures and setting up offices there.[4] During that same period, the Chinese government often ordered Chinese firms to acquire or partner with other local companies. Even if one of the entities was a loss maker, the merger would usually enable the participants to build scale.

Hisense, a state-owned Chinese entity based in Qingdao, grew as a result of both types of government-enforced collaborative activities. Hisense is one of China's largest conglomerates—manufacturing and selling televisions, air conditioners, mobile phones, and refrigerators. In 2006, it had total revenues of nearly $6 billion, over 25 percent of which came from international sales.

Favored by the government, Hisense had absorbed advanced technology from a number of incumbents through joint ventures, most of which were arranged by the government. For example, in the 1980s, Matsushita of Japan provided color-television technology that Hisense incorporated into its popular Qingdao brand. In the early 1990s, Hisense again partnered with Matsushita to produce wide-screen TVs. Hisense also benefited from government-enforced technology transfers from NEC (color televisions), Toshiba (wide-screen color televisions), Sanyo (air conditioners), Lucent (large-scale program exchangers), and Hitachi and Qualcomm (code-division multiple access [CDMA] mobile phones.) Hisense is also collaborating with Lucent, Intel, and Ligent Photonics on 3C technology.[5] In return, of course, these incumbents have been able to expand their operations and sales in China.

In addition to its technology-rich partnerships with incumbent firms, Hisense has steadily built scale through government-enforced acquisitions. Starting around 1993, the company began acquiring a variety of Chinese companies, including Zibo TV Factory, Guizhou Huari Electronic Appliance, and Golden Phoenix TV, and dramatically expanded its manufacturing capacity.

BAOSTEEL: INSIDE DEALS

Baosteel, the Chinese steelmaker, has bartered its considerable insider status for strategic benefit. As a Chinese national champion, Baosteel receives various types of preferential treatment, which has helped the company become a world-class steelmaker, with the largest and most modernized steel mill in China, a wide range of products, and sophisticated R&D operations. But its partnerships with international companies—and the technology transfers that have gone hand in hand with these collaborations—have also played a key role in Baosteel's success.

From its founding in 1978, Baosteel received advanced technology from companies outside China, mainly from the Japanese firm Nippon Steel. The Chinese government contracted the construction of Baosteel's main plant to Nippon Steel, and much of the equipment installed in the first stage of that construction was imported from Japan. The plant, a large-scale tidewater mill located in the coastal city of Baoshan, was built in phases. The initial phase was based on Nippon's Kimitsu Works, and a large expansion was modeled on Nippon's Nagoya Works, its core steel-sheet production center.

In 2003, Baosteel's leaders stepped up their collaboration with international competitors. In that year, they established a Shanghai-based automotive steel joint venture with the steel giant Arcelor, based in Luxembourg, and Nippon Steel that is valued at $785 million. The joint venture is a twenty-year arrangement to manufacture 1.7 million tons of top-quality steel plates to meet the increasing demand from international carmakers for locally produced product.

Also in 2003, a $4.68 million project involving the construction of laser-tailor-welded blanks was jointly launched by Baosteel (38 percent), Arcelor (25 percent), and Shanghai Volkswagen Automotive Co Ltd. (37 percent). The collaboration expects to use an advanced laser welding system developed by a Swiss company to further process steel plates provided by Baosteel.

Several global steel giants, including Nippon Steel, POSCO, and Arcelor, have monopolized the technology for making world-class sedan sheets. Thus, it's hard to imagine that these companies would transfer their core competitive weapon to a rival like Baosteel. However, Baosteel holds some very attractive bargaining chips; namely, the huge size and rapid growth of the domestic Chinese steel market and the firm's highly competitive positioning within the industry.

In the case of the original Baosteel-Nippon joint venture, Nippon Steel has apparently made two major concessions to gain access to that all-important Chinese market. One is a 50-50 equity split rather than a majority stake for Nippon Steel. The other is that Baosteel, not Nippon Steel, is the main supplier of the hot-rolled coils used to make cold-rolled sheets.

Both joint arrangements are intended to meet the needs of all the participants. With the technology-for-market access deal, Nippon Steel and Arcelor may come to accept that a strategic alliance with Baosteel is the most feasible way to make money under current business conditions, even if they feel uneasy about possibly bringing a new member into the global steel giants' club.[6]

IMPLICATIONS: RECOGNIZE AND REJECT YOUR LIMITS

The challengers are in a hurry.

They're unwilling to accept internal limitations. They want to become leading players in their industries and are acquiring, collaborating, and partnering their way forward to realize that vision.

But incumbents need not sit by and watch as the challengers build dominant positions for themselves. They too can think big, act fast, and go outside their current geographical borders and organizational boundaries—by establishing two-way collaborations with challenger companies.

To do so, the incumbents must avoid the arrogance of the big acquirer—the tendency to swallow up smaller companies for a specific tactical purpose, without thinking enough about the strategic value of the acquisition or about the ancillary benefits the acquisition might deliver.

In the pharmaceutical industry, as we saw in chapter 6, drug firms around the world have entered into partnerships with Cipla, the Indian pharmaceutical firm. Through these deals, Cipla gets access to customers and brands, while the incumbents gain entrée to the lowest-cost manufacturer of generic drugs. Even the big global pharma players, like Astra Zeneca, are engaging in such partnerships.

Yet these collaborations are the exception, not the norm. Most incumbents still have a "go it alone" or "be monogamous" mind-set in terms of their partnerships, except perhaps in China, where government regulations may dictate otherwise. But as new clusters of capabilities emerge in the rapidly developing economies—from drug discovery and auto-component design in India to material sciences in Russia or Brazil and electronics in China—incumbents must forget their hesitation and aggressively build linkages with challengers.

Incumbent-challenger collaboration can be driven by broad strategic needs, such as gaining distribution or building scale. For example, big established players benefited from Hisense's growth by expanding their own customer base and sales in China. Nippon Steel and Arcelor transferred technology to their joint venture with Baosteel to increase their scale in the fast-growing Chinese automotive market while leveraging Baosteel's preferential position in that market.

Partnerships can also lead to valuable outsourcing or subcontracting arrangements. Hisense is the world's largest supplier of 40-inch LCD TV sets; it also produces for NEC, among others. Wipro, Tata Consultancy Services, and Tata Technologies have served as outsourced partners for IT infrastructure, product development, engineering and industrial services, and R&D for large incumbents.

And finally, partnerships can be R&D driven. Examples include Bajaj's interactions with Kawasaki as well as Cipla's focus on drug discovery and development for incumbents while its partners handle drug marketing, sales, and business development.

Play Many Roles

In such collaborations, challengers often play many roles—as suppliers for, and customers of, the incumbents. Bajaj, for example, sells its products in the Philippines under the Bajaj brand name, using Kawasaki's sales and distribution infrastructure. In most markets, Kawasaki is an archrival of Bajaj; in the Philippines the company is a partner.

"We told Kawasaki that, in products below 250cc, we now make motorcycles as good as or better than theirs," says Sanjiv Bajaj. "So there is a real opportunity for them to source from us and sell in different parts of the world. The Philippines is the pilot. Kawasaki started in its own plant there and now they sell around 100,000 a year in a market that is about 400,000 but growing at 20 percent year on year. Our relationship with them has gone around full circle now.

At first, Bajaj was buying technology from Kawasaki and branding our products as Kawasaki in India. Now they buy products branded Bajaj from us."

Similarly, ZTE has collaborated with incumbents like Motorola, Intel, Qualcomm, and Texas Instruments. While the incumbents have won most of the big contracts for the telecom infrastructure build-out in China,[7] they have also invested in the domestic market and thus fueled the growth of challengers, including ZTE.

THINK STRATEGICALLY

When incumbents contemplate entering into a collaboration, merger, or acquisition, they have a tendency to get bogged down in protracted discussions and soul-searching about "who we fundamentally are" and "what our purpose is."

As we've seen, challengers tend to ask more forward-looking questions, like: "Will the acquisition give us access to important new customers? Will it provide technologies that we could not develop ourselves or obtain in another way? Will it improve our ability to defend ourselves in an industry consolidation, downturn, or competitive attack? What do we want to be? What *could* we be?"

Many analysts were surprised when Videocon, an Indian conglomerate, bought the cathode-ray tube (CRT) business of Thomson Group of France. CRT was already a mature technology, rapidly being replaced by plasma and LCD screens. Growth in the consumer markets in Europe and the United States, where Thomson operated, was slower than in other parts of the world. But Videocon saw the Thomson acquisition as a way to learn the business, become a major player in global electronics components, gain access to technologies it didn't have and didn't want to develop, and connect with a valuable set of new customers.

Mahindra & Mahindra follows a similar strategy. "What we are doing with acquisition is leapfrogging our place along," Anand

Mahindra explained to us. "The competitive advantage is ultimately in India. But the question is how do we get customers, how do we get channels of distribution, and how do we get technology—without going into it in such a manner and such a large degree that we are saddled with all the reasons that the West is uncompetitive. That is the fine balance. You won't find us buying up on an accumulation strategy, to be number one. We don't want to inherit the problems of the current Western dominators of the business."

As the challengers pursue acquisitions for the purpose of leapfrogging, they often move very quickly and downplay the acquisition's potential for generating profits in the short term. As a result, they sometimes pay a higher price than an incumbent might pay (based solely on its judgment about the deal's immediate impact on profits). Instead of instant gains, challengers focus on using the acquisition to support a long-term strategic objective.

Incumbents are now thinking more strategically about acquisitions in the rapidly developing economies. Global firms like IBM and EDS have acquired local business-process outsourcing companies in India to jump-start their own low-cost operations as well as take on their Indian challengers.

Incumbents can also take a page from the challengers and buy local companies with strong brands to gain faster access to RDE markets. One major deterrent to such acquisitions is the high valuations of the challenger companies. Incumbents, still focusing on hard financials rather than long-term strategy when eyeing possible acquisitions, find it difficult to make a high-cost purchase in a low-cost country. For example, The Boston Consulting Group (BCG) made a valuation for an incumbent—a global player in electrical equipment—of a potential acquisition target in India. By evaluating the acquisition strategically in terms of market access and opportunity to drive the evolution of the market, we determined that the local firm had nearly double the typical valuation, which is based on a multiple of cash flow.

Evaluate the Value Chain

Challengers tend to enter each collaboration or acquisition with a clear view of which elements of the value chain they can strengthen as a result of the action. Incumbents should do likewise. They need to take a harder look at their own value chain and decide which parts to defend, which parts to strengthen, and which parts to divest. This isn't easy, but it's the best way to craft a strategy for collaborations and acquisitions regarding challengers—co-opting them where it makes sense, divesting them where necessary, and acquiring them where they can strengthen the incumbent's business.

As we've said, global pharma majors are testing the waters of drug discovery and development with Indian partners. Should they buy the challengers while they're still small, on a learning curve, and relatively inexpensive? Should they wait until they are large, more experienced, and have more developed capabilities—as well as higher valuations?

Organize to Go Outside

Finally, incumbents have to decide how to organize for collaborative arrangements, partnerships, and acquisitions with challengers. Decisions about organizational structure will determine the success or failure of these partnerships. What role should the corporate center play? How should the company manage operational and organizational processes? What values should be espoused in the new entity? How should the participants in the deal leverage the available talent? How can incumbents learn from challengers and put their new knowledge to work?

Incumbents should not copy the business model of the leading challengers. Rather, they need to develop their own versions of thinking and acting fast—and finding their own ways to go outside.

CHAPTER 8

INNOVATING WITH INGENUITY

> "When people ask me 'What is your competitive advantage?'
> I say, 'The quality of our engineers.'"
> *Mauricio Botelho, Embraer*

We are and remain the world's leader in innovation," said John Engler, president of the National Association of Manufacturers in 2005. Engler was speaking about the United States. But he warned, "We do not enjoy that status by divine right, and we cannot assume that we are safely ahead of the world. Other countries are climbing the technology ladder just as eagerly as we are."

Perhaps even more eagerly. Leading challengers are investing heavily in innovation to power their already-rapid rise. The Chinese telecom equipment maker ZTE—widely regarded as an innovation leader in its home country—spent an impressive 12 percent of its $3 billion 2006 revenue on R&D.

The contenders are creating institutes and research parks. BYD, for example, established its Central Research Institute, where hundreds of scientists and engineers grapple with issues ranging from materials research to vehicle engineering. And Goodbaby has its Infant Research Institute, where some two hundred designers work to design and create "Safe, comfortable, convenient and fashionable baby products which help babies' physical and intellectual development."[1]

Venture funds, too, attracted by the prospect of getting in on the ground floor of the next generation of challengers, are actively courting small technology firms in the RDEs. Venture capitalists invested $1.89 billion in Chinese companies during 2006, a three-year high, according to VentureOne. Early-round investments accounted for about 62 percent of all those deals. Investments in Chinese information technology firms, in particular, rose 34 percent in 2006 over the previous year, according to a study by Dow Jones, VentureOne, and Ernst & Young.[2]

Governments, keenly aware of the central role innovation plays in their modernization agendas, are also fostering creative thinking in their countries. As part of President Vladimir Putin's New Deal, for example, $1.1 billion is earmarked for grants to innovative schools, teachers, and pupils.

Universities, too, are offering more courses than ever in design, innovation management, and entrepreneurship, as well as collaborating with corporations to develop study programs. China-based Suntech Power, one of the world's top ten manufacturers of photovoltaic cells, not only operates its own technology R&D center but also has established cooperative relationships with academic institutions, including the University of New South Wales in Australia and Zhongshan University in China.

The challengers understand that innovation is key to their continued rise. As Anand Mahindra puts it, "I am obsessed with our comparative advantage on innovation." But even with all these efforts, the challengers are far behind the incumbents when it comes to the size of their investments in innovation.

Yes, ZTE spends 12 percent of its annual sales on R&D. But Motorola's 8 percent expenditure is bigger than ZTE's total annual revenue. Sure, Ranbaxy, one of India's leading pharmaceutical companies, had a total R&D budget of $87 million in 2006. However, that's almost laughable by the standards of the global pharmaceutical industry: GlaxoSmithKline spent $5.2 billion on R&D in 2004, sixty times that of Ranbaxy. True, BYD spends about 1.5 percent of its revenues on R&D. But that's small in comparison to the big Japanese and Korean electronics firms. Sanyo, for example, allocates 8 percent of its revenues to R&D. (Still, low cost makes a difference in R&D, as in everything else. BYD employs ten times as many engineers as Sanyo does.[3])

The annual number of patents filed is another (imperfect) indicator of how the challengers have lagged behind the incumbents. From 1999 to 2003, all the companies based in the five largest rapidly developing economies—China, India, Russia, Brazil, and Mexico—were granted a total of 3,900 U.S. patents. In that same period, American companies were granted 399,000—a hundred times more.

And so, without much in the way of labs, inventors, R&D budgets, or intellectual property, the challengers have had to find their own ways to develop new products and services for their markets.

They have done so mainly through three actions:

• *Adapting the Ideas of Others*
• *Leveraging*
• *Rapid-fire Inventing*

ADAPTING

In the early days of the tsunami and right up through the 1990s, the majority of challengers built their success by adapting—borrowing and imitating—the ideas, business models, technologies, products, and services of other companies, usually incumbents based in the developed economies. But these companies are not the pirates, rip-off artists, and intellectual property thieves that have received so much media attention in the past decade. After all, in every industry and country, there are products and services that look remarkably similar to ones that originated elsewhere. The ideas were there; the challengers leveraged them.

B2W of Brazil became the largest online retailer in Brazil by imitating the methods of amazon.com and Homedepot.com. Baidu, the dominant Internet search engine in China, with more than 69 percent market share, out-Googled Google by building a search engine similar to Google's but providing much better performance with Chinese characters. The company took in $108 million in 2006, a Google-like growth explosion of 163 percent in 2005.

China's 51job got to be the top recruiting and human resources service provider by creating a job-search engine that looks a lot like Monster.com. Not only is 51job the top such service in China, it's the only national job-search site in China. With a presence in Shanghai, Beijing, and twenty-six other Chinese cities, it's still growing in terms of sites, visitors, and revenues.

Li Ning is the number one provider of sports footwear, accessories, and apparel in China's second- and third-tier cities, boasting roughly 20-percent market share. It patterns itself after Nike by providing a full range of sports gear and fashion and building an extensive distribution network throughout China's small- and medium-size cities. Its revenue jumped 30 percent from 2005 to 2006.

China's Home Inns & Hotels Management models itself on such American chain hotels as Courtyard by Marriott and Hampton Inns. Home Inns offers a high standard of cleanliness and comfort to both business and leisure travelers, with rates ranging from RMB159 ($21) to RMB299 ($39) a night. But the company does not own its buildings, and it relies heavily on leasing and also franchises some of its properties, while most of its competitors manage leased hotels. Although Home Inns wasn't the first to imitate the economy-traveler model, it has done so more successfully than its competitors. Established in 2002, it had opened one hundred eighty-two hotels in more than thirty-nine Chinese cities by 2006, with plans to open as many as ninety-five more in 2007. Occupancy rates climbed from 87 percent in 2005 to 90 percent in 2005 and 93 percent in 2006.

In each of these cases, the challenger looked beyond its own organizational and geographic boundaries for business models and processes, strategies, and product and service ideas it could tailor to its own unique business conditions. The result was an innovative and remarkably successful enterprise in its own right.

The Roewe: Roots in the Rover

In China, up-and-coming automobile makers have borrowed, bought, or adapted much of the technology and design savvy of the global auto industry. Many Chinese automobile makers accumulated their knowledge by learning from the foreign auto companies they supplied and by reverse-engineering systems and components from the incumbents. They began imitating the products they helped build and, eventually, created their own designs.

You may or may not have heard of Shanghai Automotive Industry Corporation (SAIC), China's government-backed, highly profitable, number one automaker. For many years, SAIC has manufactured cars for General Motors and Volkswagen for sale in China.

Now, SAIC seeks to become a world-class producer of its own cars and is starting out at the high end with a new luxury brand it calls Roewe (pronounced row-wee). In 2006, SAIC purchased the rights to several technologies and designs from Rover, the renowned British marque. (Ford bought the brand name itself, which is why SAIC had to come up with a new one.) SAIC's first model, the Roewe 750, is based on the Rover 75, a midmarket model, with a few significant modifications to take it upscale—a longer wheelbase, redesigned interior, and a signature grille that features two lions clutching a scepter that forms the backbone of an elaborate letter R.[4]

To create the Roewe 750, SAIC hired several of the Rover engineers who had worked on the model in previous years. They also outsourced some of the work to Ricardo Inc., based in the United Kingdom, one of the world's largest automotive engineering companies. Ricardo set up an R&D center dedicated to the SAIC project, and several hundred SAIC engineers worked alongside the Rover and Ricardo people on the Roewe program. When the work was done, ownership of the R&D center was transferred to SAIC.

Now SAIC had its own state-of-the-art R&D design capability as well as a hot new car model it could call its own. The Roewe 750 debuted at the end of 2006, and in its first five months on the market, ten thousand units had been sold.[5]

SAIC is working on additional variants of the 750, including one with even more luxurious appointments, as well as other new Roewe models. Left-hand-drive versions will be sold into European markets, probably through the dealer network of SAIC's Korean subsidiary, SsangYong Motors. The company has announced plans to produce 200,000 passenger cars and 400,000 buses and trucks under its own brand name by 2010.

Roewe has its roots in the British Rover brand, but adaptation is likely to lead quickly to genuine invention as SAIC's squad of designers and engineers gain experience with their new brand and confidence in their ability to connect with the market.

LEVERAGING

Sometimes the challengers have built their innovations by getting a tremendous amount of leverage out of what looks like not very much. This is true of many of the Chinese companies we've discussed in this book—including BYD, Johnson Electric, and Goodbaby—but is not exclusive to them or to China. The Brazilian aircraft maker Embraer, for example, transformed itself from a nearly bankrupt state-owned enterprise into the world's third-largest producer of commercial aircraft by leveraging a very small fleet of planes, a little capital, and a great deal of ingenuity.

THE EMBRAER ERJ 145: INNOVATING OUT OF CRISIS

In 1945, Brazil had emerged from a dictatorship, and a democratic government took office with big plans for developing the country's economy. Two resulting projects laid the foundation for the creation of Embraer. The country's first steel mill, the basis of any industrialization effort, was set up. And the government decided to create its own aircraft. To that end, in 1946, the Brazilian government established the Aeronautical Technical Center (CTA) in São José dos Campos for the study of aeronautics, and in 1950, the Aeronautical Technological Institute (ITA) was created to develop a cadre of trained aeronautical engineers.

Over the next twenty-five years, the two institutions accumulated a considerable body of knowledge and trained a generation of engineers. Their work enabled the government to establish the Empresa Brasileira de Aeronáutica—better known as Embraer—as a state-owned enterprise in 1969. For the next two decades, Embraer practiced the arts of innovative (sometimes adaptive) design, producing propeller and turboprop planes such as the EMB 110 Bandeirante, a nineteen-seat, nonpressurized, regional propeller plane, and the EMB 120 Brasilia, a thirty-seat pressurized turboprop. The Bandeirante was largely based on a prototype designed in the CTA, but the Brasilia was a clean sheet design by Embraer.

In the late 1980s, Embraer tried its hand at invention by developing regional aircraft—small, short-haul planes designed to carry passengers from Brazil's smaller cities to its major airlines' big hubs. The company experimented with new technologies. The CBA 123, for instance, was based on the push propeller, which is mounted at the rear fuselage rather than at the wings and makes the plane more stable and fuel efficient. But even in low-cost Brazil, production costs for the CBA 123 would have been so high that Embraer could not interest any airlines in further development. The model would have been too expensive for their budgets.

The Overlooked Regional Jet

Embraer continued using adaptation to create fresh designs. The company's engineers learned of a new engine design that would enable them to produce a cost-effective regional jet that could fly faster and higher than a turboprop—with less noise, vibration, and turbulence.

Although Embraer had little experience with jets, in 1989 it began developing the ERJ145, a forty-five-seat regional jet. But before the company could introduce the airplane, it and the industry encountered difficulties. Embraer's bread-and-butter model, the Brasilia, was aging and losing sales to newer designs sporting superior technology. The first Gulf War dampened sales worldwide. Embraer saw its cash flow dry up. The Brazilian government pumped in enough cash to see Embraer through the crisis. But, as is often the case in such situations, most of the money went into supporting the manufacture and sale of existing products. Research and development went hungry.

The Brazilian government itself was not in particularly robust condition. To relieve its financial obligations, it privatized many of the country's state-owned enterprises—including Embraer. In December 1994, Brazilian investors put $161 million into the company, the Brazilian government retaining 44.6 percent of the shares. That year, Embraer endured a R$161 million loss on R$170 million in revenue. It had R$240 million in debt and an order backlog worth only about R$775 million. For all practical (if not legal) purposes, the company was bankrupt.

In 1995, Mauricio Botelho took over as chief executive officer. (He is now chairman of Embraer.) He bet the company's future on innovation and threw resources into completing the development and production of the ERJ 145, even though he knew the aircraft would come to market after Bombardier had launched its regional jet, the CRJ (Canadian Regional Jet). However, it soon became clear that the demand for regional jets was much greater than the industry had anticipated and Embraer's rivals, including Bombardier, did not have sufficient capacity to meet it. So there were customers waiting, if Embraer could deliver an aircraft that offered at least as attractive a value proposition as the others in its segment.

"Airlines were using bigger aircraft than the market requires," Botelho told us. The niche for jets that carry 35 to 50 passengers had gone largely unexploited. Before 1992, no company had successfully manufactured commercial jets containing fewer than 50 seats. Embraer became the second player in this niche market, where demand far outweighed supply. The ERJ 145 proved good enough. Launched in 1996, it quickly scored a resounding success. In the following years, new smaller versions were launched, the 37-seat ERJ 135 and the 44-seat ERJ 140. The success of the ERJ 145 family spread out to other markets through derivatives, including three intelligence, surveillance and reconnaissance (ISR) versions for the defense market, and the Legacy, an executive jet suitable for corporations, entrepreneurs, and charter companies.

The Double Bubble Beats the Stretch

The market's warm reception of the ERJ 145 family emboldened Embraer to consider developing the next generation of regional jets. One idea looked especially promising—a craft based on the ERJ 145 but with capacity to carry 70 to 110 passengers. But the company worried about encroaching on the turf of Boeing and Airbus, two global players that could crush Embraer if they chose to. "We didn't want to fly too close to the sun," explains Satoshi Yokota, Embraer executive vice president, technology development and advanced design. But the new design would have less capacity than most of the jets offered by Boeing and Airbus, so Embraer decided to take the risk.

According to conventional wisdom in aviation design, the best way to increase a small plane's passenger capacity is to lengthen the fuselage. If you've traveled a lot, you've no doubt found yourself at least once aboard the "stretch" version of a well-known aircraft. But there were problems with stretching the EMB-145. The aircraft was fitted with rows of three seats. To keep this seat arrangement and boost carrying capacity by twenty to fifty seats, the fuselage would have to be extended so much that economics would suffer.

There was another factor: comfort. "You must bring the customer perspective to the engineer," notes Luís Carlos Affonso, head of Embraer's 70- to 110-seat E-Jets design program from 1999 to 2005, "or else he will optimize what he already has." An extra-long fuselage would be uncomfortable for passengers, with its lengthy, narrow center aisle and scanty headroom.

Some of the rival aircraft, such as Bombardier's fifty-seat CRJ, had wide-body designs that could accommodate four-seat rows. But the seats were still cramped, and there was not enough overhead bin space to accommodate even 22-inch wheeled suitcases, the frequent traveler's bag of choice.

So Embraer's engineers worked on a new design they called "double bubble." The most structurally effective shape for a fuselage is round, because that shape minimizes pressurization loads. But roundness creates a lot of unusable space, especially at the sides of the plane's body. The standard solution is to shape the fuselage into an oval. This works well for large planes, but in smaller aircraft, it leaves less cargo space in the belly of the plane.

The traditional solution for regional jets is to go with an oval that is closer to round, which provides more cargo space and a little more headroom. But it still makes things tight for people seated at the windows. For its new jet, Embraer used two frames, a larger one on top for the passenger part of the fuselage, and a smaller one on the bottom for cargo and systems. This freed up more room for the window seats and provided enough overhead bin space to take wheeled baggage. The smaller frame below accommodated checked luggage and revenue-producing cargo to be carried. By using two circles with different radii, Embraer made the new craft as large as possible where it matters for passenger comfort but not so round as to increase wind resistance and thus fuel consumption, as well as providing enough space for baggage.

The company shared its ideas for the new jet with airlines around the world that were likely buyers, soliciting and incorporating their feedback. More than forty airlines provided input. The result was the Embraer 170 series, which offers buyers the economics of a regional jet and the passenger comfort of the larger commercial jets.

The E-170s have been a major success—they're best-sellers, the company has a large order backlog, and, along with other models in their class, they've helped to transform the industry. Indeed, since

1995, the number of regional jet routes has expanded 1,000 percent in Europe and 1,400 percent in the United States. Much of that increase comes from commuter airlines that the majors own or contract with to connect smaller markets with their hubs.

The success of the Embraer commercial jets has led the company into the more profitable and even more competitive market for executive jets—more luxurious aircraft aimed at the well-heeled jet-setter or business executive.

As before, Embraer showed its penchant for design ingenuity. Although aircraft makers often stretch their small planes, they rarely shrink their large ones. Designers tend to believe that the heavier, bulkier frame can't be successfully adapted to a smaller, lighter craft. Embraer disagreed. The company took its larger regional jets and downsized them to create the Phenom and Lineage lines of executive jets, which seat six to eight and seven to nine passengers, respectively. Then it engaged BMW's design center to create a luxurious interior. With the new portfolio of aircraft, Embraer is able to offer customers state-of-the-art jets with greater comfort and fuel efficiency at a lower cost—without sacrificing the safety and reliability found in its large, world-class commercial jets.

Today, Embraer is the world's largest aircraft manufacturer of commercial jets up to 120 seats, having produced more than 4,200 aircraft for customers on six continents. It is a global company with $4 billion in revenues, and offices, industrial operations, and customer services facilities worldwide. With nearly 24,000 employees and an order backlog of $15.6 billion, the company designs, manufactures, sells, and provides after-sales support and services for the commercial and executive aviation markets, as well as for the defense and government segment.

Was ingenious innovation the foundation of Embraer's success? Yes, but not entirely. Brazil's low wages—less than a third of those of developed-country manufacturers—have helped Embraer keep costs low. Also, currency differences work in Embraer's favor: the company's income is U.S. dollar–based, but a significant portion of its costs are in the cheaper local currency. Embraer also has the Brazilian government to thank for its enthusiastic support of the domestic aviation industry and for developing the local engineering talent that drives its innovation.

Despite these advantages, Frederico Curado, Embraer's president and chief executive officer, thinks of his company's achievement as deriving primarily from the ability to listen to customers and design innovative aircraft for their needs. "Brazil still produces lower labor costs than those in the developed countries, but labor represents just 10 to 15 percent of the cost of an aircraft," he told us. "The real issue is the ability to develop a product in a very short time in a very efficient way—from conception to delivery—that meets the customer's needs."

RAPID-FIRE INVENTING

Whether they are adapting, leveraging, or starting from scratch, the challengers have a great curiosity, a sensitivity to market needs and demands, a willingness to try anything and also abandon an idea or prototype that's not working, and the inventiveness to create many iterations—all at remarkable speed.

These qualities enable the challengers to introduce to the marketplace reimagined, reinvented, and reconfigured technologies, products, and services that can win. And, if they don't win, they can cook up another ten possibilities in rapid-fire succession.

GOODBABY AND THE MAMA-PAPA STROLLER

When we met with Song Zhenghuan, it didn't take long for him to pull out his company's 700-page catalog, bursting with every kind of product and service for children. As he flipped through the pages, pointing out strollers and diapers and swing sets, we had the sense that he could tell a story about each and every product there.

The ingenious improvisers at Goodbaby have deep knowledge of what their customers want, what resources they have available to create new products, and which offerings to develop and leave on the shelf, given their limitations—all marks of a high "indigenous IQ"; that is, understanding of the local environment, culture, and consumer.

If indigenous IQ could be tested, Song would score in the top percentile. He is a natural inventor. A former schoolteacher, Song set out to develop and patent a baby stroller that could be easily converted into a car seat. He figured that Chinese parents, financially stretched by the costs of raising and educating a child, would appreciate this clever and affordable product that offered two functions for the price of one. The stroller would "grow with the child until he is ten." Thinking he could sell the patent for this innovation, Song displayed the stroller–car seat at a local consumer goods exhibition, hoping to find a buyer. The design captured the imaginations of baby-product manufacturers who saw it, and they worked themselves into a frenzy trying to outbid one another for it. When the bid reached 60,000 RMB—with no upper limit in sight—it dawned on Song that he had hit on something big, that he had a talent for creating products that people wanted. At that moment, his patent seemed more valuable in his own hands than somebody else's. He turned down all bidders and decided to produce and sell his inventions himself. Goodbaby was off and running.

The company's commitment to innovation and product design has endured for seventeen years, with top priority given to the development of its R&D capabilities. Goodbaby spends, on average, 4 percent of its revenue every year on R&D, well above the industry average. In addition to its China-based Infant Research Institute, Goodbaby also operates R&D centers in Germany, France, the United Kingdom, the United States, and Japan. Locating these product-development sites in its customers' markets helps Goodbaby to stay current with design, fashion, and quality trends. Since 1990, Goodbaby has been awarded more than 2,300 patents, 40 of them from outside China.

Goodbaby Group has become the biggest manufacturer and seller of baby carriers in China and is popularly known as "The King of the Baby Carriage." The group held an 80-percent share of the Chinese market from 1996 to 2006 and has had top place in the U.S. market for five years running—2001 through 2006. An estimated 400 million households worldwide use Goodbaby products.

In 2005, Goodbaby's annual revenue amounted to RMB 2.5 billion ($321 million), 80 percent of which came from its overseas customers. Thanks to its R&D prowess, the company innovates a new product every twelve hours. Industry insiders call this uncanny quality the "Goodbaby Phenomenon." "The major reason Goodbaby is successful," says Song, "is that it attaches great importance to technological development and innovation."

ARAVIND EYE CARE: INGENIOUS DELIVERY

For some challengers, innovation is more about coming up with better business processes than with new products or technologies. Take Aravind Eye Care, the world's largest provider of cataract surgery. Founded in 1976 in India by Dr. Gorindappa Venkataswamy, the company performs 250,000 surgeries and treats 1.5 million outpatients per year. Dr. V (as he's known to the poor in India) says his goal is to "wipe out needless blindness," and Aravind is well on its way there. Fully 60 percent of the company's patients are treated gratis, and the company still makes a profit.

How is this possible? Dr. V has transformed the cataract-surgery model to suit market conditions in the rapidly developing economies. Expensive medical equipment is scheduled for around-the-clock use to drive down the cost per surgical procedure. Doctors and staff are extraordinarily efficient and productive, carrying out more than 4,000 cataract surgeries per doctor a year, in comparison to an average of 400 performed by other surgeons in India. Like the cost-efficient use of equipment, this task specialization is an innovation in this industry. In a traditional hospital, a surgeon admits the patient, orders tests, synthesizes the resulting information, plans the surgery, coordinates the team, and monitors postoperative care. The surgeon acts like an orchestra conductor, overseeing the entire operation and taking individual responsibility for its success. At Aravind, a surgeon moves from one operating table to the next, performing only the cataract procedure itself, while teams of nurses remain at each table and oversee the patient's care before and after the surgeon does his or her work.

To further drive down costs, Aravind's subsidiary company, Aurolab, reverse-engineers high-quality lenses and surgical supplies. The consequent savings enable the company to expand and further refine its delivery system.

Altogether, Dr. V's ingenious adaptations of business processes and his reverse-engineering of materials have positioned his company to provide cataract operations at one-fiftieth of what patients typically pay in the United States.

THE 1 LAKH CAR: A VISION OR A DREAM?

Tata Motors also embodies challengers' savvy approach to innovation. Just a decade ago, few auto industry insiders and observers took the company seriously. Tata had only a few hundred million dollars to invest, and it lacked the sales volume to achieve those all-important economies of scale. Even more ludicrous, it was located in India, a country with rudimentary road systems.

Fast-forward to today, and Ratan Tata, the chairman of Tata Motors, has pulled off quite a feat. The company's foray into the car business started in 1998, when it launched the Indica. The car looked good but had initial quality problems. Consumers, however, liked what they saw and quickly placed orders for some 100,000 vehicles. Over the nine years since the Indica's debut, Tata has steadily addressed the quality issues and launched improved versions—the V2 and the Indigo, a sedan. Sales have grown steadily, and Tata is now India's largest auto manufacturer. It cranks out 450,000 cars and commercial vehicles a year, recorded revenue of $5.5 billion in 2005–2006, and owns 18 percent of the Indian car market. The company has already beaten the odds by meeting Europe's high-quality standards and seeing its international exports grow.

It has gotten this far with a blend of borrowed competence from abroad and homegrown invention. But it's what Tata has in the pipeline—a work of true ingenuity—that traditional car manufacturers fear most. Tata is well on its way toward launching the "1 lakh" car—a good-quality, reliable automobile originally intended to be priced at the equivalent of about $2,500. (A lakh is 100,000 rupees.) The goal of this project is to meet the transportation needs of the "next billion," the mass of customers in developing countries who currently drive motorcycles or three-wheelers. Designing and prototyping is progressing well, although the retail price is likely to be closer to $3,500, and Tata has committed to bringing the car out in 2008.

According to outside observers, the car will be like nothing on the road in the developed countries. It is not meant to be an "urban-centric" car, but will be able to travel virtually wherever people themselves would travel, either by motorized vehicle or on foot. The car will be available with a 660-cc, two-cylinder gasoline engine or 800-cc diesel engine—possibly with a direct-injection, turbocharged variant. In internal Tata tests, the car has achieved fuel efficiency of 26 kilometers per liter. The engine resides in the rear of the vehicle, rather than in the front. Headlights are set into the bumper.

Tata has developed the car in close association with both local suppliers and global specialists. Bosch, the world's largest independent parts supplier to the automotive industry, designed a fuel injection system especially for the 1 lakh car and also provides alternators, brakes, and other systems. To keep costs low, Tata negotiated favorable terms with key suppliers such as Sona Koyo/Rane (steering), Gabriel (suspension parts), Lumax (lights), Shriram Pistons (pistons), and Ricoh Auto (clutch), as well as Bosch. Tata has also been supported in its effort by the government, which provided various concessions and tax breaks for its new plant.

Thanks to its low-cost assembly operations and its existing channel network, Tata can expect to shave off significant manufacturing and distribution costs. Even so, Tata will probably realize a low margin on the car, probably around 5 percent. But with a projected volume of one million units, even those slim profits will add up.

The global auto majors said it couldn't be done—and for them, they're right. It's an unachievable price point for business models grounded in high-cost consumer and manufacturing markets. Only a challenger could have dreamed it up.

IMPLICATIONS:
DO WHATEVER IT TAKES

The incumbents have built castles of intellectual property, but these bastions are not unassailable. India has strengths in software development and outsourcing. Russia has built expertise in large-scale system integration and long-range, high-bandwidth networking. China, thriving on the hybrid model of capitalism and central planning, now has impressive technical resources.

Today, when we think of the greatest innovators, few challenger company names come to mind. But in just a few years, we'll be telling a different story. Ingenious challengers will enjoy equal billing alongside the great product and technology wizards of the West. Some challengers will win renown for their own homegrown intellectual property. Others will become famous for their clever recombination of existing ideas from East and West to satisfy customers in novel, admirable ways. To stay in the running, incumbents will need to take a few pages from the challengers' book of innovation. Collaborating, synthesizing, borrowing, rapid-fire inventing, contributing to developing nations' welfare, and anticipating obstacles can all help.

COLLABORATE

Many incumbents have found that their product portfolio doesn't quite satisfy the price points and functionality desired by customers in the developing economies—particularly in the midmarket. When they try to fill these gaps in their portfolio, they realize just how hard it is to rethink their products and services. They're not prepared to make radical departures from their traditional expertise, invested capital, and established position. They see the disjointed infrastructure and frustrations of doing business in the rapidly developing economies as obstacles rather than sources of innovation. And they don't always have the experience or the will to make do with what's around them.

So, eager to tap into pools of creativity in China, India, Brazil, Russia, and Mexico, incumbents are building or have already built research and development facilities in these countries, either on their own or in collaboration with challengers.

AT&T, for instance, formed a joint venture with Tech Mahindra, a Mahindra & Mahindra subsidiary, to open an R&D lab in Bangalore for telecommunications research. Randall Stephenson, chairman and chief executive officer of AT&T Inc., attended the opening ceremony—it was his first visit to India.[6]

Intel collaborated with Haier to establish the Haier & Intel Innovation, Research and Development Center in 2006. The center brought together Intel and Haier's R&D staff, personnel, and systems and is dedicated to a single task: developing new products. Among other things, developers there are working on a PC for rural consumers and a computer that motorists can use while driving.

Intel and Haier have also brought Suning, a leading retailer of home appliances in China, into the collaboration. Suning is responsible for sales and service platforms, Intel produces the CPUs and supplies marketing resources, and Haier Computer provides branding, industrial designs, and production capacity. This arrangement enables Haier to market its own name-brand computers designed specifically for local markets at low prices but still incorporate cutting-edge technology.

Pursue Diversity

Getting wiser to the ways of the rapidly developing economies doesn't require abandoning one's roots. Rather, it means intertwining them with others'. That's what challengers have been doing for the past twenty years—borrowing, recombining, adding, subtracting, improvising. Managers who can synthesize Western know-how with Eastern ideas, practices, and viewpoints—combining the best of each—will find that innovation opportunities spring up everywhere.

Incumbents can more easily spot and capitalize on these opportunities by locating their innovation facilities in the rapidly developing economies. For example, Motorola's R&D center in China operates independently of the company's R&D headquarters and develops products and services in response to both global and local demands. Engineers at the Chinese center are dedicated to finding better ways of inputting Chinese characters into mobile phones. Many other companies have been working on the problem and have imported a variety of Western-developed technologies, including styluses and motion-sensitive screens. But Motorola's R&D people decided that those methods would always be too expensive for low-end, affordable products. So the company adopted an Eastern value: simplicity. It designed a phone with a large keypad that enables people to enter the characters with their fingers, rather than use a stylus or touch screen. Motorola describes the new model, the Motorola A668, as "a natural combination of technologies and Chinese calligraphy." Consumers love it, and the phone won a gold medal at the Asian Innovation Awards in 2005.

BORROW

Ingenuity in innovation is not solely about developing products especially for the rapidly developing economies, but also about mining those markets for ideas that can be exported to the rest of the world. Bajaj, for example, has incorporated many midrange technologies into its entry-level motorcycles. With the launch of a new platform in 2007, Bajaj intends to change the value proposition that its vehicles offer worldwide—new suspension technologies, advanced engines, and affordable prices.

In 2007, Motorola introduced the Motofone F3 handset. Costing less than $40, the phone nevertheless boasts advanced technology that includes a battery life of four hundred hours; voice-activated calling with a user-friendly, icon-based interface; and local-language voice prompts for new users or those with limited literacy.

Indian companies have come up with some interesting new takes on retail distribution that could also be adapted for developed markets. For example, using an open-distribution approach, these challengers can tailor their products to customers and deliver them directly. These techniques, originally developed to reach poor and rural customers in India, may offer even greater potential when used to reach affluent, urban customers in the developed markets.

CONTRIBUTE

In many developing countries, the government has clear priorities: strengthening the nation's economy and improving citizens' living standards. These governments regularly intervene in the marketplace and involve themselves in company operations to further those objectives. Incumbents that align with the innovation agenda of such governments and that tailor their business model and value proposition appropriately will improve the odds of building sustainable relationships with the country—and its consumers.

It pays to cooperate with governments of rapidly developing economies, as well as industry associations and universities, to help develop technology standards and ease the country's problems. Issues such as energy shortages and environmental degradation translate into commercial opportunities for innovative foreign companies that devise solutions. In the fast-changing business environment of the rapidly developing economies, such investments also position foreign firms to become shapers rather than followers.

PROCEED WITH CAUTION

For incumbents seeking to innovate in rapidly developing economies, we advise proceeding with caution. Many institutions in these economies, while improving, still don't provide an environment conducive to innovation. For example, nations may lack a competitive and open system for R&D funding as well as effective intellectual-property protection.

In some cases, a gold rush mentality for quickly making profits postpones real invention. Companies make short-term investments in promising-looking enterprises, only to pull out when the payoff doesn't materialize immediately. But innovation can happen only when investors make a long-term commitment to research and development and are willing to tolerate an uncertain payback. Worsening the situation, senior researchers with the experience and skills to lead major projects are in short supply in these economies, a limitation that can further stymie innovation.

And sometimes, government policy aimed at fostering native intellectual property fuels piracy instead. In a high-level fraud case in China during 2007, Chen Jin, a dean at Jiaotong University in Shanghai, received more than $14 million in government research funding and won a national innovation prize for developing a series of made-in-China integrated-circuit chips. He was later revealed as a fraud who had only modified existing Motorola chips.

At other times, the breakneck pace at which challengers scale the intellectual property curve hides flaws. In 2003, British Telecom (BT) announced a plan to develop a twenty-first-century network called 21CN. In a series of strict appraisals and tests over a period of two years, BT evaluated some three hundred suppliers, including Huawei Technologies. Managers at Huawei felt confident that the company would meet BT's requirements. After all, they had successfully completed several quality improvement programs, including an integrated product development project in 1998 and Integrated Supply Chain initiative in 2000, developed by IBM. When a delegation from BT scrutinized Huawei's products and operations, however, they found a number of faults—but eventually chose Huawei as one of BT's key suppliers.

Innovation in the rapidly developing economies can be a risky business, no matter how ingenious your company is.

CHAPTER 9

EMBRACING MANYNESS

"Somehow, the centipede needs a hundred legs to move."
R. Gopalakrishnan, Tata Group

The seventh struggle of globality is operating and organizing successfully in an environment of "manyness."

Globality, after all, implies many countries, economies, markets, locations, and facilities, each a unique window onto the world, each a unique combination of customers, competitors, suppliers, resources, infrastructures, and cultures. The struggle is determining where to have presence in the world, of what type, at what level, with which purpose, and how to get there.

Cemex, based in Mexico, operates in fifty countries on four continents, with 66 cement plants, almost 2,000 ready-mix concrete facilities, nearly 400 quarries, 260 distribution centers on land, and 80 marine terminals. And that's not even counting the sales and executive offices or the trade relationships the company maintains with more than 100 countries worldwide.

The rapidly developing economies embrace many corporate forms, units, structures, operating entities, and legacies. The economies and the companies that play in them have far greater diversity and texture than in those developed countries. Relationships among and between them are different. What works with one may backfire with another.

Challengers range from heavily regulated, state-owned entities like Baosteel in China and Gazprom in Russia, to young and nimble entrepreneurial companies, like Sisecam in Bulgaria and Cavincare in India and Tencent in China. They represent a range of businesses and industries that may require distribution networks and retail shops or big factories and research institutes.

Doing business in globality presents a great variety of competitive situations and collaborative possibilities that may require different strategies and approaches at different times. There are endless opportunities and many ways to play each one. The struggle is to be clear about the purpose of pursuing each opportunity—talent? cost? market position?—and to embrace variety as required.

Finally, globality is composed of many kinds of managers, processes, systems, management styles, and states of being. No single site of operations can be the center in the way that incumbents have traditionally thought of "world headquarters." It's a world of polycentricity.

Orascom, the Egypt-based mobile telecom provider, is composed of a remarkable set of units and operations, each one different, each a center of its own. There is Mobinil in Egypt, Djezzy in Algeria, Mobilink in Pakistan, Tunisiana in Tunisia, Banglalink in Bangladesh, Telecel in Zimbabwe, and IraQna in Iraq. (Naguib Sawiris, chairman and chief executive officer, travels to Baghdad regularly. "I take a small car from the airport," he said. "I sit next to the driver. I choose a hotel at random. And I try not to stay more than one or two days."[1])

Manyness can be an unfamiliar concept for incumbents that are more used to seeking for the single best way, the ideal organizational structure, the signature leadership style. It can be uncomfortable for those with a bias toward standardization. It can frustrate those who believe in one-world strategies, centralized authority, home offices, and the alignment of people and ideas.

It's not that the challengers are much more experienced than incumbents in operating in an environment of manyness. The number of challengers with a large global footprint is quite small in comparison to the number of incumbents that have an international presence. But their very lack of experience enables them to see the world differently.

In some respects, the challengers' organizations that have globalized look quite similar to those of the incumbents. After all, incumbents are the most expert at standardizing global processes and using shared services. Many incumbents, particularly those with multiple business units, have mastered the use of matrix organizations and have developed effective mechanisms to coordinate across business units and geographies.

But in other ways, the challengers' global organizations look quite different. They have taken from the knowledge and wisdom that's been accumulating for nearly a century in the developed markets, adapted it to the operating models of their own economies, and created syntheses that are particularly suited to an environment of manyness.

Some of the challengers' ideas and practices can seem a little mysterious, even unfathomable. "If somebody asks us to draw an organizational plan," said Dr. Amar Lulla, chief executive officer of Cipla, "we have to sit and work it out. Because we don't really have one."

Gaining through manyness is a struggle that involves these key actions:

- *Choosing Global Presence*
- *Retaining Local Character*
- *Polycentralizing*

CHOOSING GLOBAL PRESENCE

Where should a company have presence? Many companies, incumbents and challengers alike, have gone abroad willy-nilly, with little

intent, only to discover that the manyness of locations and operations does not bring them any gain at all.

M&M: THE ACCIDENTAL GLOBALISTS

When Anand Mahindra, chief executive officer of Mahindra &
Mahindra, returned to India from Harvard Business School in 1981
and joined the company that his grandfather had founded in 1945,
he was animated by a single idea: to take his company global. "You
are not safe at home unless you can compete abroad," he told us.
"Every business unit in our group has to have a global texture to it
and a global aspiration to it."

At that time, M&M had two small entities overseas: one in the
United States, one in Greece, both in trouble. The American subsidiary, based in Texas, was mired in litigation for alleged nonde-
livery. The Greek subsidiary existed only because a Greek importer
had gone bust and left M&M with worthless receivables. At the
time, write-offs were seen by the Reserve Bank of India as a telltale
sign of illegal trade transactions, so M&M converted the receivables into equity instead. Both operations were, as Mahindra put it
to us, "acknowledged within the group folklore to be pretty much
disasters."

A third expansion effort—in South Africa—had quickly fizzled
after a promising start when it came to light that M&M's affluent
local business partner was a celebrity criminal wanted by Interpol.

So, for all intents and purposes, Mahindra & Mahindra was an
India-only company with some great strengths in its home market—
good product, sizable volumes, economies of scale, and cost leadership. These attributes were sufficiently robust that Anand Mahindra
believed the company could overcome its past misadventures and
successfully build an overseas business.

And so Anand Mahindra chose the United States as the country into which M&M would establish a successful presence. "If we
hadn't had that failure in Texas," he said, "I wouldn't have chosen

America as the first area to compete. But I figured that I had so much intellectual property about how *not* to do business in the United States, that I could convert it into something positive." Mahindra used the same reasoning to choose the leader of the new America expedition—the manager of the South African debacle. "We said to each other, 'Now let's do it right.'"

They did it right. Today, M&M is the fourth-largest tractor maker in the world, with a major presence on five continents. Sales have been growing 17 percent a year since 2001, with operating profits increasing at 29 percent annually. The company has a leading domestic market share of 45 percent in utility vehicles (UVs), 33 percent in tractors, and 41 percent in large three-wheelers. Exports of tractors and UVs have been strong in regions such as western Europe, South Africa, Malaysia, the Commonwealth of Independent States, and Latin America, with UV exports expanding 80 percent and tractor exports growing 30 percent in 2006 alone.

The U.S. operation has flourished. Mahindra USA opened its second assembly plant and distribution center in Calhoun, Georgia, in 2006 and achieved revenues of $150.4 million for that fiscal year, up from nothing.

The key to the company's global success, Mahindra explains, has been devising a business strategy that works for the company as a whole, a basic pattern on which each branch of the company, anywhere in the world, can base its activities with comparable success.

The need for such a strategy was a lesson hard learned by the failure of M&M's previous enterprises abroad, which proved that, without adequate organization, the individual branches of the company would flounder helplessly on their own limited resources or else fail entirely under the influence of incompetence.

"You have a picture of the accidental tourist," says Mahindra. "This is what Indian exporters were. There was no road map or strategic intent, no real passion or goal behind going abroad. There was no method at all, there was no process by which you did it." So Mahindra recognized those missing elements—passion, goals, and a method—and around these he built a globally viable business model.

He began with the basics: instituting due diligence, the evaluation of partners and dealers, market assessment, and new business evaluations in his plans for international expansion. He also took into account M&M's success at home in India, and sought ways to duplicate the conditions of that success in the company's ventures overseas. One of India's core strengths is its low-cost, low-tech manufacturing: forgings, castings, and the like. Another of its strengths is the considerable abundance of raw materials. A third is the obvious advantage of a home operation: managerial talent, good local reputation, a significant presence in the community as an employer and provider.

Mahindra knew these attributes must have some value from a global standpoint; after all, they were what had made India a leader in the market. "So, in fact, it would be criminal if an Indian company that enjoyed a leadership position in the world's largest tractor market did not actually go out and exploit that home-market advantage to become a global leader," he said.

Mahindra took a fledgling product division and is working toward creating a global network of competencies. He has persistently moved across geographic borders, pressing each business to think about globalizing and moving across business borders, through continual innovation. He has capitalized and built on his misadventures—of which there were many—to move the business forward. Now the company has the global presence that Anand Mahindra sought.

RETAINING LOCAL CHARACTER

Much of the strength of the rapidly developing economies is to be found in their diversity, and companies can build success by working to retain the character and cultural identity of their local operations.

As Pratik Kumar, executive vice president of human resources at Wipro, put it, "An important element is cultural continuity. How do we allow space for subcultures to thrive and exist and be comfortable? Because, in nuances, each will be very different, depending on where the centers are and where those folks are. When you grow to a size of a hundred thousand or two hundred thousand people, how does that happen?"

BHARAT FORGE: SEMI-INDEPENDENCE

In 2001, Bharat Forge was a small Indian company that produced forgings, primarily for the local auto industry. It had revenue of about $112 million and faced a rather uncertain future because of the severe downturn in the Indian commercial vehicle industry.

By 2006, Bharat Forge had become the second-largest, fastest-growing, and most profitable automotive forgings company in the world, supplying not only the major truck manufacturers but the biggest makers of passenger cars as well. Its revenue soared from $112 million in fiscal year 2001 to over $1 billion in fiscal year 2006, and market capitalization climbed from $82 million in 2001 to $1.6 billion in 2006.

The company was able to make this quantum leap by executing a series of diverse acquisitions in the United States, Europe, and, more recently, China. While an acquisition-driven growth strategy is not unique to Bharat Forge (or to challengers), what stands out about Bharat Forge is the way it has handled the acquisitions.

Bharat Forge acquired six manufacturing facilities from 2004 to 2006, creating a collection of facilities and operations in the process, and the company believes that the key to its success is its approach to managing the companies it has acquired. Rather than integrating them, Bharat Forge operates them as a system of semi-independent operations. In most of them, the management team has remained in place, and the company has kept its own board of directors. Most important, decision rights have been left with the management of each company.

Many companies that buy factories as part of their pinpointing efforts will quickly start to fiddle with the plants' capacity and capabilities, most often downsizing them as much as possible. Bharat Forge, however, has not downsized a single one of its acquired companies in Europe or the United States. Rather, it has invested to increase capacity in the plants so that they will be better able to replace the production of low-margin products (once it has been migrated to the distant-shore plants in India or China) with products that are more technologically complex and that can earn higher margins.

Bharat Forge might have chosen to integrate its operations and create "one Bharat Forge" globally. Instead, it has chosen to leave these operations with a high level of autonomy, enabling them to become thinking centers of activity.

Why?

Bharat Forge's view is that the world economy, while increasingly global, actually comprises a multitude of highly diverse regions, each with unique characteristics requiring local knowledge and fast, informed decision making. As operations away from the center grow larger, they carry more weight in making decisions and take on more significant roles in the organization. Bigger and more complex bets require on-the-ground experience and judgment. As the distant units become more important, the executives that are chosen to lead them tend to be more senior. Suppliers, customers, and government officials also expect to deal with real decision makers, and the executives themselves expect autonomy commensurate with their responsibility. For a host of reasons, authority naturally shifts away from the center toward what was the periphery but has now become the core.

Another company that has a bias toward diversity and autonomy is Suzlon Energy. When the board of Suzlon meets outsiders, it is not immediately obvious that the company is Indian-owned. Alongside Tulsi Tanti, the chairman, can be found executives from Denmark, Germany, the Netherlands, North America, and Australia—the result of overseas purchases that have turned the group into the world's fifth-largest maker of wind turbines.

"Each division of the company is led by a local chief executive officer and is managed there," says Tanti, an entrepreneur from India's mercantile Gujarat State, who is the force behind the group that last year paid $521 million for Hansen Transmissions International, a Belgian gearbox maker.

POLYCENTRALIZING

Because the challengers view the world not as one increasingly common "global" entity, but rather as a collection of highly diverse regions—each requiring strong local leadership with the autonomy to act knowledgeably, quickly, and decisively—these companies adopt organizational forms in which responsibilities and decision-making rights are widely shared throughout the company, with rich debate going on across regional viewpoints, from well down in the managerial ranks all the way up to the board. In these organizations it's often hard to determine where, if anywhere, the "center" is. Often, they have not one center but many.

"Being global means that you have to think globally and have to be present globally," said Frederico Curado, chief executive officer of Embraer. "Embraer will be present globally, and that involves sharing our decision-making process, which means that decisions will often be formulated elsewhere. This will fundamentally change the concept of headquarters—it may no longer exist."

TATA: A CENTER OF CENTERS

Tata is a polycentric organization that has an unusual entity—the Group Corporate Center (GCC)—that acts like a center in some ways, but in other ways does not.

Tata Sons is a holding company with 96 business units that form its polycentric organization, and in order to keep the many centers connected, Tata operates the GCC, which has five important functions: setting broad direction, identifying opportunities, assisting with finance for the occasional large project, increasing the "liquidity of ideas," and providing the occasional push when a push is needed.

Equally significant is what the center does not do. The GCC does not attempt to enforce one uniform global approach on all its businesses. It does not put its finger into the activities of individual companies. It does not mandate group business targets or require that every company follow common processes.

The GCC played a key role in Tata's efforts at global expansion, which began in 2003, when Ratan Tata, chairman of both Tata Group and Tata Sons, articulated a broad vision of internationalization for the entire company. He knew that the individual companies, most of which were based in India, did not have the capability to scout the world for investment or acquisition opportunities, so he created a focus point within the GCC for this work, appointing Alan Rosling, a British national who had diverse senior-level international management experience, as the executive director charged with working with the operating companies on their internationalization plans. Once Tata began acquiring new companies and bringing them into the group, the GCC facilitated learning across the businesses and across regions. In some cases, when the GCC identified an opportunity that would require an existing business to think and act beyond its immediate priorities, the GCC gave it a nudge.

Tata recognizes the inherent differences in its many businesses and across regions and gives managers freedom to act as entrepreneurs, build their organizations, and establish the external relationships required to realize new opportunities. The unusual latitude given to management helps Tata attract and retain talented local executives whose roles might otherwise have been diminished to the point where they would leave the company. Although other companies offer local executives the chance to participate in leadership development programs and to take positions at other of their businesses around the world, nothing compares to the opportunity to run your own show.

One might think that an organization as diverse as Tata would be in danger of flying apart without the binding force of a strong central organization, but Tata does have its own kind of glue—at the board level. The board of each business unit includes a number of directors who sit only on the board of that unit, directors who are members of the GCC, and directors from boards of one or more of the other Tata business units.

This arrangement—which R. Gopalakrishnan, a director of Tata Sons, refers to as the "biological fusion of the Group Center and the companies"—makes manifest two beliefs that lie at the heart of the Tata organizational model. The first belief is that all of the boards must possess a perspective that is elevated enough to provide long-term direction for group management. The second is that the judgment of each board member will be broadened and improved by exposure to the scope and complexity of the group's activities and markets. This kind of multibody, representative membership also enables each board to become a mechanism for the sharing of resources, expertise, knowledge, and best practices across all the businesses of the company. An item on the agenda of every board meeting is connecting people across the group with the right skills, experience, and power to get things done.

ORGANIZATIONAL GLASNOST

A company with many centers can be like a centipede that successfully moves forward—if a bit laboriously sometimes—or it can become disjointed and uncoordinated and unable to move coherently. The difference is openness—"glasnost," to borrow the Russian term from the early days of the tsunami.

There is a famous quotation from Mahatma Gandhi that seems to apply to many important situations in India, and Anand Mahindra quoted it to us about the importance of openness in global organizations. "I do not want my house to be walled in on all sides and my windows to be stuffed," Gandhi said. "I want the cultures of all lands to be blown about my house as freely as possible. But I refuse to be blown off my feet by any."

Openness is about "unstuffing the windows" of the company to allow in the wealth of ideas and capabilities that exist "out there" in the fuzzy-edged cloud of suppliers, customers, and competitors. It's about a belief that no matter how talented your own people are, the majority of talent will always be outside your company's borders, and that you need to take advantage of it.

One way to do so is to make the boundaries of the organization as porous as possible. For incumbents, this can be a very difficult and even painful undertaking, primarily because it can mean surrendering some control over the access to intellectual property. Organizations resist such IP glasnost. After years of research and investment to gain a proprietary edge, years of building walls to keep the inner workings of the company safe from prying eyes, how can we simply open the doors and let our best secrets walk out? How can we hand over responsibility for innovation to outsiders?

Challengers have fewer of these problems, simply because the majority of them are IP-poor. They have less to lose and are therefore more willing to make their boundaries porous so that they can build complex webs of relationships with outsiders.

One reason that challengers are particularly adept at creating and operating in such fluid organizations is their emphasis on trust. Relying more on trust and less on policies and procedures to exercise control is particularly important in fast-moving environments with multiple centers, porous boundaries, constant tensions within the matrix, and leaders who are mercurial builders.

Trust is a guide that informs every action. To trust someone in a given situation is to ask him or her to judge what to do—and for that it is never sufficient to look back at established procedure. One has to inquire into the current situation to discern how to act according to principle.

At Tata, trust manifests itself as respect for individuals, decentralized decision making, and the acceptance of local adaptation. Tata Group values are core to group operations: they influence how decisions are made, how the company operates, and how it is organized. Because of these strong values, employees at all levels know what is expected of them, and hence they are empowered to take independent action. This enables Tata to exercise fairly loose control—without losing control.

CIPLA GOES FLAT

Some challengers believe so strongly in the importance of glasnost and the trust that underlies it that they have done away with organizational structure and policy altogether.

In 1985, the Indian drugmaker Cipla decided to make itself flat by reducing the layers of hierarchy and pruning away as much management bureaucracy as possible. People were made responsible for directing their own actions—policy committees were abolished. An employee's perspective was encouraged to be holistic rather than limited to the narrow functional or operational silos that he or she used to inhabit. "We made this organization completely flat," said Dr. Amar Lulla of Cipla. "There is no hierarchy, no structure, no organizational rank. We say, 'Let's get the business, get the work done.'"

There are no titles. "We saw that titles were becoming a limitation. People would say, 'I am a QC analyst and I will not think about cost, I will not think about engineering, I will not think about process, I will not think about anything except what I must think about as a QC analyst. I am not supposed to think! I am just supposed to analyze!'," said Lulla. "But we said, 'You can do much more than that. You are a human being who is capable of a lot. You are not just a QC analyst.'"

The process of flattening and removing titles took time; it confused some people and ran counter to cultural expectations. "Young men would come to us and say, 'Sir, I want to get married, but what do I tell my prospective in-laws about my title? What am I in Cipla?' We would say, 'Tell them what you want. Tell them the title you want to tell them. That is what you are.'"

There are, according to Lulla, no committees at Cipla. If a Cipla manager wants to initiate a project, he can do it. "We don't have to send presentations, or go to a meeting at the head office in London," Lulla said. "I was talking with the head of a large pharma company about different models of mobile phones. He told me that, in his company, they have a committee to make the choice of which mobile phone the executives will use. Can you imagine? I find that extremely suffocating."

The company also did away with annual appraisals and salary reviews. "We completely threw that away," said Lulla. "We said, 'You can ask for whatever compensation you want, whenever you want, as frequently as you want. You will either get it or you go home. No negotiations about it.'"

Cipla instituted a program to support employees in their pursuit of entrepreneurial ventures—especially if the employees wanted to become suppliers to the company. This emphasized the company's desire to see its people as more than employees—as co-partners in growth. "We have an open policy. If an employee wants to get into business, we will help and support him," said Lulla. "We helped give birth to a number of businesses, took care of them during their infancy, and supported them as they grew to very reasonably sized companies in various fields, including construction, software, finance, and engineering."

The organizational style at Cipla is such that some people, especially at the junior level, do not find a fit, and there is a fair amount of turnover. But senior managers tend to stick, and many of them have been with the company for twenty-five years or longer. "Cipla is so flat," Lulla said, "that we enjoy managing ourselves!"

IMPLICATIONS: SYNTHESIZE

Just as the challengers have synthesized Western business practices with those of their own cultures (and their own devising), incumbents need to adapt, adopt, and synthesize ideas from everyone and everywhere.

The layers of middle management that have built up over time in many incumbent organizations can create a lumbering, centralized bureaucracy that increases costs, reduces flexibility, slows responsiveness, and hinders a company's ability to develop an organization across the rapidly developing economies. "Global IT companies may not be the right partners to win business in emerging markets because of their legacy business models," said Sudip Nandy, chief strategy officer at Wipro. "But Wipro can apply our successful India strategy to other low-cost locations like Southeast Asia, the Middle East, and maybe eastern Europe, and be far more competitive and far more successful than the larger global vendors."

Go Polycentric

In a world in which the economic center is shifting from a single geography to many geographies, each with highly diverse characteristics, where resources are pinpointed in multiple economies, where commerce flows in every direction, and where competitive advantage is constantly shifting, polycentric organizations increasingly make sense.

Incumbents, coming as they do from developed-economy centers, will need to confront issues that are specific to them. As with the challengers, the incumbents' organizations will want to devolve control to be able to respond more quickly and accurately to the local environment.

The typical incumbent corporate headquarters wants to retain control to better perceive and manage its internal and external risks, of which the rapidly developing economies present a bewildering array—including political upheaval, intellectual property encroachment, competitor actions, and ineffective execution. And risk is inherent in the fact that incumbents often enter rapidly developing economies with untested strategies and tactics administered by young, equally untested organizations.

Incumbents tend to be more adept than challengers at pursuing global scale and standardization, motivated by a rather large stick and an increasingly alluring carrot. The stick relentlessly beating on their backs is the high-cost structure that is inherent in their countries of origin. With the rise of the challengers, the beatings have grown even more intense. The carrot is the opportunity to build knowledge about how to win in an increasingly diverse set of markets and to harness global competencies and scarce resources increasingly located in the rapidly developing economies.

There is an important assumption that often underlies the incumbents' efforts to avoid the stick and grab the carrot—that the world is essentially flat and untextured, and that the differences between markets in rapidly developing economies are negligible and even irrelevant. There is what we call a mind-set bias toward oneness— "global" strategies, "global" products, and hence "global" organizations. Therefore, some incumbents conclude, there is not much need to customize strategies, products, or organizations for these markets. As a result, they tilt too far toward global relative to the very real and compelling need to be local. They put more resources into, and place higher importance on, centralization to drive scale and control efficiencies than they do on differentiations that could achieve growth and share in local markets.

When this happens, sources of growth and competitive advantage may concentrate in the periphery of the rapidly developing economies, while power and resources stay in the center, a center that is far away from the new global economic centers. Strategies continue to be formulated using developed-economy assumptions by people with developed-economy frames of reference, resulting in products and marketing programs continuing to be created in the developed countries and pushed into markets in the rapidly developing economies.

CVRD recognized the difficulty of going global while retaining local texture. In all its many locations, CVRD sought to balance the composition of its leadership to reflect the multiculturalism it believed to be important. It created a mix of directors, with people from Brazil, the United States, South Africa, Canada, France, and Norway. At its offices in Asia, New Caledonia, and Indonesia, local people work alongside Brazilians, Canadians, and others.

ALIGN STRUCTURE WITH PRESENCE

Corning has long embraced a polycentric view of the world due to the combination of its significant presence and experience in numerous developed and developing economies and the mind-set of its senior leadership.

In China, Corning has several business units selling products that range from the traditional (such as copper cables and coaxial interconnect systems) to state-of-the-art technologies (such as specialty materials that deliver advanced optical solutions or glass for LCD displays). Corning has established these businesses in China over a period of many years, so they currently are at different stages of development.

Corning's operations are headed by a country manager who is empowered with full profit-and-loss responsibility. The country manager has input into decisions about local-market issues and facilitates the transfer of knowledge across business units. He has joint responsibility with worldwide business unit leaders on strategy, investment, external relationships, people, and organization.

This structure is unique for Corning, whose regional managers typically are responsible only for incubating new businesses, which are then transferred to established business units once they're well established; P&L responsibility generally lies with the global business organization.

To help manage this matrix of business units and country management, Corning runs an internal China Business Council that promotes cross-business-unit coordination. The problem with matrix structures, of course, is that (often) they don't work. On paper, everything seems clear. In practice, it's hard to judge where authority resides for this or that unexpected decision. Competing agendas and internal politics fill the void. The reporting and coordination requirements burden already overstretched management capacity.

Rather than throw out the matrix, however, Corning adds management resources to support it. This involves defining where authority lies, clarifying roles and responsibilities at each level, giving local teams more autonomy when making decisions in which local adaptation and flexibility are important, and giving complete authority to some organizations in the rapidly developing economies.

EMBRACE MANYNESS

The economic center is shifting from a single geography to many, each one an ocean apart from the others in wealth, growth, resources, and society. It is a business world defined by diversity, where growth comes from multiple markets, resources are best pinpointed in multiple economies, and commerce flows in every direction. Amid so much difference, many heads are better than one.

Devolve more and more control to your organization, and make it as open as possible. Value the complexity that arises for the communication flows it forces upon the organization. But also look for opportunities to standardize where variety does not add value, to centralize where diversity is counterproductive, and, very important, to emphasize a clear set of values that will keep manyness from becoming the equivalent of organizational chaos.

For incumbents, to do so may mean vesting a new center of executive influence that possesses the capability to reshape the company's direction and creating governance entities that support and represent the organization's multiple centers—while still leveraging global scale. For challengers, to do so may mean putting more effort into learning how to standardize and globalize core processes—without sacrificing variety where it creates value.

"You know," said R. Gopalakrishnan, "when you see that centipede trying to move, you say, 'Maybe if we chop off ninety-six legs, it could move much faster on just four.' But we have come to the conclusion that somehow, that centipede is structured in a funny way. It needs those hundred legs to move in its own particular way."

CHAPTER 10

COMPETING WITH EVERYONE FROM EVERYWHERE FOR EVERYTHING

"We still have a long time to go."
Xie Qihua, Baosteel

Does globality represent an opportunity or a threat? Is it a good phenomenon or a bad one?

We have talked mostly in this book about the business opportunities that await in the rapidly developing economies and about the successful, even admirable, practices that the challengers are employing to take advantage of them. We have talked less about the threats and downsides, but these are impossible to dismiss. If you're already doing business in India or China, Russia or Brazil, you've experienced them, and if you've traveled to any of these places, you've witnessed them. Even if you haven't, the media are so filled with stories, every day, about the many problems of rapid growth and industrialization— tainted products, pollution, human rights violations, corruption, disparity of income, and on and on—that the issues are very much a presence in everyone's lives across the world.

So it's important to say that it will be unlikely, if not impossible, to compete in the age of globality without coming up against these issues, in both one's business and personal life. Doing business in the rapidly developing economies, and with the companies whose origins are there, will be fundamentally different than it is in the developed markets with incumbent companies.

In Delhi, you'll have to cope with the intense traffic that is a fact of everyday existence there. The Institute of Road Traffic Education estimates that there are 110 million traffic offenses committed *daily* in this city of 4 million vehicles and 16 million inhabitants. Although many parts of the subway system are running, some parts are still under construction and won't be completed until 2021. The 3,500 city buses are generally jam-packed with passengers.

In Beijing, the air pollution is so bad that two runners are said to have died during the 2004 marathon there. The neighboring provinces are filled with coal mines and heavy industries that burn coal, and the resulting air pollution not only clouds Beijing but drifts across the world and affects neighboring countries. Yet even with all that pollution, a report by Chinese academics predicted that by the middle of the century, average life expectancy in China will jump thirteen years to eighty-five years, and that all Chinese households will be lifted out of poverty. Is this state-encouraged misinformation, or merely the wild optimism that the Chinese are known for, or a combination of both?

The list of woes in the rapidly developing economies is long.

India is saddled with a national debt that equals 82 percent of its gross domestic product.

In China, as many as twenty million kids are left at home alone for weeks and months at a time while their parents take jobs in the cities or at distant work sites.

The countries of eastern Europe are struggling with wage and price inflation, worker migration, a low birth rate, a lack of skilled laborers, and antiquated laws.

Mexico is overly dependent on oil revenues, plagued with drug trafficking, and has a weak educational system.

Brazil's economy is sluggish and its government is riddled with corruption.

Throughout the rapidly developing economies, great numbers of people are poor, hungry, out of work, undereducated, and sick.

Apart from these issues and a few others, the rapidly developing economies are doing just fine. And besides, the developed economies also have their problems, from aging populations and income disparities, to corporate wrongdoing and overconsumption of the world's resources.

So we do not argue that globality will be all joy. It will be as frustrating, chaotic, inexplicable, and exhausting as it will be exhilarating, enlightening, and enriching.

NOKIA: CONTROLLING ITS CHINA DESTINY

Nokia, the world's largest supplier of mobile handsets, went through a period of struggling with both the exhaustion and the exhilaration characteristic of the rapidly developing economies to reach its current condition of prosperity. Today, Nokia sells about a million handsets a day, worldwide. At an average selling price of $150, that's $150 million in sales every day—or about $55 billion during the year. In July of 2007, Nokia's share of global handset sales had risen to 36.2 percent, far ahead of second-place Motorola, which slid to 18 percent, just about even with Samsung.

As recently as 2004, however, the outlook for Nokia was not so rosy, especially in China, the world's largest mobile market. This was surprising, because Nokia had arrived early in China, in 1991, when it supplied equipment for Asia's first global system for mobile communications (GSM) to the Hong Kong–based mobile telephony company Hong Kong CSL Limited. A couple of years later, in 1993, Nokia introduced the first GSM handset to appear on the Chinese market. Throughout the 1990s, Nokia took a year-by-year, "let's test the waters" approach to China. It was the standard model for foreign enterprises at the time. Identify a small handful of distributors in the relatively affluent, large cities. Sell them product by the container load, and let them take care of the rest. It was a sensible way to tap emerging market opportunities while limiting risk and avoiding the dizzying complexity, and the unfamiliarity, of the Chinese retail marketplace.

And it made sense. In volume and value, China was still a small market. Europe was well on its way to mobile saturation, but North America was smack in the midst of mass mobile adoption. Globally, Nokia's leadership team focused company strategy and resources on winning the big prizes. But all the while, and with minimal marketing effort, Nokia accumulated an enviable market share in mainland China, selling its sexy foreign-made models to the up-and-coming, brand-conscious Chinese consumer. Demand was there, and it was pent up for want of a good product. All Nokia had to do was keep the containers coming and run the occasional national advertisement to let households with a TV know it was there.

By the turn of the millennium, Nokia's China market share hovered around 30 percent—the largest of any handset maker, domestic or foreign. It was a good beginning that gave Nokia the time to assemble the basics of a solid China operation: manufacturing, organization, and people.

Then came the challengers. Local players brought out handsets with popular designs at lower prices. Armed with blueprints and kits purchased from second-tier mobile players abroad, the Chinese companies assembled low-cost handset models and ventured into their native countryside. The government had connected many of China's smaller cities to the mobile network, and consumers there were ready to plug in. The local players got wider and better distribution because they knew how to work with the distributors and provided them with generous profit-sharing plans.[1]

The Chinese-made phones began appearing in retail outlets deep in the countryside, where Nokia and other foreign makers had little or no presence.[2] Nokia's market share dropped from a high of 30 percent in 1999 to the low teens in 2003. The challengers' share jumped from just 2.5 percent in 1999 to nearly 30 percent by 2002. Analysts predicted that the domestic players would own half the market by

2005. They told global vendors like Nokia to stick to the high-end segments that they understood.

Nokia China's management team took a deep breath, stepped back, and looked carefully at the company's position. There was nothing fundamentally wrong. Nokia had a spectacular brand name, a legacy of success in China, the ability to manufacture in enormous quantities, and a portfolio of high-quality, popular products. There had to be a way to compete with the challengers.

REACHING DEEP IN CHINA

Nokia decided to reach deeper into the market. This would require a fundamental change of course. Nokia had danced into China, hoping to tap the big opportunity without exposing itself to too much risk. It had offered the same phones to the Chinese that it offered to the rest of the world—feature-laden, sleek designs, at prices that were high in comparison to locally made phones.

It didn't take long for China to become an incredibly competitive market for mobile handsets. The big global players—Motorola, Sony Ericsson, and Samsung—all joined the fray. And dozens of Chinese companies began to churn out hundreds of homegrown models, names that most Westerners have never heard: TCL, Ningbo Bird, Legend, Haier, Konka, Eastcom, Kejian, CECT, Panda, and Amoisonic. The market overflowed with handsets offering endless varieties and combinations of shapes, sizes, colors, functions, features, and price.

As a result, it became very difficult for manufacturers to secure shelf space in big stores or in tiny shops. The demand at these outlets is so great that electronics retailers lease their shelf space to manufacturers and, naturally, give the best positions and most profitable shelf real estate to the companies that offer them the juiciest deals and most attentive service. Without shelf space, a manufacturer can barely get the consumer's attention—even with a popular global brand like Nokia.

The challengers, however, knew all about the distribution system and were expert at establishing and nurturing relationships with the tens of thousands of retailers across the country. Nokia didn't even know who its retailers were. Since the beginning, the company had worked with a handful of large distributors, each of which served a region and handled the retail relationships there. Nokia had little leverage with its distributors and virtually no ability to affect what happened in the stores themselves.

Not only did this distribution approach put Nokia at a disadvantage on the shelves, it also meant it was suffering from the too-little-information syndrome. The management team just didn't know what was happening out there. If sales dropped in a region, they had to ask the distributor for an explanation. Maybe he could identify the underperforming districts in the region, describe the issues involved, even offer a solution or two. But was he right?

Nokia realized that it could not grow the business in China without really doing business in China. If the retailer was the gatekeeper of the midmarket consumer, then Nokia would have to find ways to get him to open the gate.

The management team took a new approach to distribution that involved more clearly defined responsibilities for specific activities and individual geographies as well as greater accountability. From ten cities, Nokia expanded into a hundred, then two hundred, then four hundred. Nokia took responsibility for the sales function itself and built its own sales force to manage the retail relationships. Nokia renamed the distributors as fulfillment distributors to make it clear that they were the logistics specialists, not the sales guys.

As part of the change, Nokia faced the task of developing a whole new set of retail skills. How do you manage large retail client accounts? How much margin should you give to them, and how much do you keep for yourself? How do you influence consumers to buy your product once they're in the shop? How do you influence retailers to influence them? These were all issues that Nokia had not confronted before in China, ones on which Nokia China set about becoming experts.

They learned, and the new distribution approach gradually enabled Nokia to exercise much greater control over its market presence. With its own sales force, Nokia was able to get a handle on market conditions and consumer behavior for the first time. It could also build real relationships with retailers, influence their stocking decisions and promotional activities, and position Nokia's products favorably against the endless flood of competitive phones.

At last, Nokia began to really see and understand the consumers it wanted to sell to. As the company learned more, Nokia revamped its product portfolio to include more competitively priced phones with the features (or lack of features) that the midmarket consumer wanted.

Gradually, Nokia built a market information system that was large enough to manage the enormous volume of new retail and market data coming into the company and could provide executive support for a whole new set of retail performance indicators. Today, the company maintains more than forty thousand points of presence across the mainland. Every sales district has a track record, a sales plan, and a person accountable for results. If market share starts to fall in a certain area, Nokia now learns about it quickly, has the ability to find out the causes, and has people on the ground to devise and execute a plan to turn things around.

"You have to understand where people live, what the shopping patterns are," says Kai Oistamo, Nokia's executive vice president and general manager for mobile phones. "You have to work with local means to reach people—even bicycles or rickshaws."

REACHING OUT FROM CHINA

Nokia not only turned around its business in China—it also reclaimed the top spot in 2006, selling 51 million mobile phones to achieve over 35 percent of the market volume—it learned how to deal with the struggles involved in achieving success throughout the rapidly developing economies.

Nokia recognized the importance of minding the cost gap. In order to gain volume and compete with the challengers' offerings, Nokia lowered its prices. Today, the number of handsets that Nokia sells at prices under $65 has almost doubled, rising from 23 percent of its total volume to 42 percent in 2006. According to Nokia's research, about 60 percent of handset sales worldwide in 2007 will be in emerging markets.

Nokia's manufacturing presence in China enables it to constantly narrow the cost gap worldwide. In 2006, Nokia's exports of best-cost handsets and networking gear—made in China, destined for the world—leapt 67 percent from the previous year, to $6.2 billion. Since 2000, the company has registered total exports of $23.6 billion from China. Analysts estimate that Nokia's economies of scale translate into a 3- to 4-percent advantage over archrival Motorola in manufacturing and distribution. This may seem small, but it's enough to make a crucial difference when operating in the low-margin developing markets.

Nokia recognized that it had to grow its own people so they could be effective in the local market. It recruited, trained, and deployed a new sales force. It established a separate China business unit (carving it out from the Asia-Pacific organization) and gave the management team, many of whom were Chinese, more leeway in decision making.[3] Nokia also created a year-long leadership development program to help its Chinese engineers learn to collaborate better. The first graduates of the program were able to develop four new Nokia models, from conception to production, in just twelve months—fast even by Nokia's own benchmarks.

Nokia reached deep into the Chinese market. Not only has that increased its volume and improved its ability to gather information, it has also put the company in a good position for the future. As consumers become wealthier, Nokia will be able to follow them up the value chain to more expensive, higher-technology handsets and services.

Nokia has pinpointed its operations so it can respond to the ever-increasing demand for mobile handsets in the rapidly developing economies (Nokia shipped twice as many phones in 2006 as it did in 2002). Nokia operates mobile-phone factories around the world—in Finland, Germany, Great Britain, Brazil, Mexico, Hungary, India, South Korea, and China. Collectively, Nokia's plants handled more than 100 billion parts in 2006—that's about 275 million every day—and assembled them into hundreds of millions of finished phones.

Nokia has recognized that, in addition to volume, it must also be able to meet the demand for customization from its main customers, the operators of mobile telephone networks. As the competition heats up among these suppliers, they seek to differentiate themselves by offering phones with unique combinations of software capabilities and hardware features. And they want Nokia to come up with the variations and deliver the phones ready to sell at retail.

Nokia has learned that the painstaking, time-consuming innovation process of the incumbents will not always work the best—ingenuity is required. So Nokia has developed a two-stage production process. In stage one, the core components are built. In stage two, which is called "assembly to order," Nokia rapidly churns out an array of custom components—faceplates, buttons, software—in tens or hundreds of thousands of units at a time, designed to meet the current demands of the market.

This is not to say that Nokia is not investing in more traditional research and development activities. In fact, the rapidly developing economies have become important venues for Nokia's innovation efforts. Nokia operates five R&D centers in China, employing more than six hundred staff members, 90 percent of whom are Chinese. The company's Beijing Product Creation Center, set up in 2003, is one of four handset R&D labs that the Finnish phone maker operates worldwide and where about 40 percent of Nokia's global handset portfolio is developed.

The start-up of the Beijing center, however, involved a little struggle with the issue of manyness. The idea of a corporate culture that valued innovation above hierarchy required the Chinese engineers to embrace "a completely new way of thinking," said Steven Marcher, head of the center.

Today, Nokia is the market leader in mobile handsets not only in China but in most of the rapidly developing economies. Across most Southeast Asian countries, its market share tops 55 percent. In the Middle East and Africa, it's well over 60 percent. And in India, Nokia rules an estimated 70 percent of the GSM phone market.

Nokia has achieved its success in large part by learning to behave a little more like the challengers that went after its market in China. Nokia has learned, sometimes the hard way, what it means to compete with everyone from everywhere for everything.

THE MEANINGS

What, more exactly, does that phrase—competing with everyone from everywhere for everything—really mean?

For starters, who is everyone? And why must we be *competing* against all of them? What about collaboration? Social networks? Sustainability and win-winning?

Jeff Immelt, chief executive officer of General Electric, read our list of the BCG Challenger 100 Companies when it was first published in 2006 and did something unexpected with it. With his leadership team, he divided the companies on the list into four categories: customers, suppliers, competitors, and nonaligned. After they had studied the list for a bit, Immelt said, "Our goal is to have lots of customers, lots of suppliers. And no competitors."

That phrase "no competitors" struck us. What did he mean by that? Perhaps it has to do with the meaning of the word *with*. We generally think of competing with another company as battling *against* it for markets, customers, and profits, but it also means working with customers, with suppliers, and with other partners to reduce costs, improve development, gain new resources and capabilities, and interpret and demystify local markets. In globality, entities will often be competing in both senses of the word *with*—in some situations, an enterprise will be your friend and ally; in others, it will be your antagonist and opponent.

For example, Gazprom, Russia's energy giant, competes with other energy companies to produce and deliver natural gas to businesses and countries. But it also partners with them, providing access to its gas fields to companies that are usually competitors in exchange for links into the now-partners' distribution systems in markets where Gazprom has no presence.

In China, it's sometimes tricky to tell who beer maker Anheuser-Busch (AB) is competing against and who it's working with. AB launched its Harbin 1900 and Harbin Ice brands into about thirty Chinese markets in 2006 and has announced plans to roll out both brands to another twelve Chinese markets in the next year. The AB brands found themselves in competition with another new brand, called Snow, which was created by CR Snow, a joint venture between SABMiller and China Resources Enterprise Ltd. CR Snow became the number one brewer in China in 2006, topping Tsingtao Brewery in both volume and revenues. This was a curious situation for AB. It owns a 27-percent stake in Tsingtao Brewery, and its Harbin brand competes with Tsingtao's signature product. Does this sound confusing? Did AB think of its ownership stake as a conflict? Not really. "The more focus on premium beer the better," said an AB executive.

Such relationships may get confusing at times, but they can also be highly rewarding.

And where is everywhere? Are we suggesting that every company must have a presence in every market that has a few living, breathing customers with a few pesos or yuan or rupees to part with?

No, but it means that meaningful markets will be springing up and growing in every corner of the world, and companies must constantly consider whether to have a presence in them. Central China. Southern India. Ukraine. Ghana. Iran. Chile. Malaysia.

In Zambia, two entrepreneurs are building a low-cost airline, Zambian Airways, that offers flights from Lukasa to Johannesburg, South Africa, targeted at the thousands of traders and migrant workers who travel that route regularly. The fare is $100, less than it costs to ride the bus. Today, the company flies three aircraft, which is three more than it had two years ago.

In Macao, the island off the south coast of China (and the only place in the country where casino gambling is legal), there's a battle shaping up involving billions of dollars of revenue to be had from casinos, resorts, and upscale shopping malls. Stanley Ho, a Hong Kong entrepreneur who held the exclusive gambling rights in Macao for fifty years, now finds himself competing with Las Vegas super-star developers Sheldon Adelson, Steve Wynn, and Kirk Kerkorian.

Merger and acquisition fever is spreading into countries and regions that might not immediately spring to mind as locations of valuable properties. Russian companies have been acquiring in nearby Armenia, Belarus, Kazakhstan, and Uzbekistan, and they have also been buying companies in the United Kingdom, South Africa, Canada, and the United States (eight acquisitions in 2006). The Czech Republic, Poland, and Hungary closed a total of 101 deals in 2006, compared with 74 in 2005. That number would make a slow year (or month) for the investors and lawyers in the United States, but it has risen fast and is likely to continue growing.

Everywhere also means that you'll be competing in markets that you thought you had already won: the United States, for example.

And what about everything? What does that include?

For starters: customers, suppliers, partners, capital, intellectual property, raw materials, talent, ideas, space, distribution systems, manufacturing capabilities, and natural resources.

In India, for example, publishers are vying for magazine readers. Since 2005, ten foreign consumer magazines have launched Indian editions, and another twenty or so say they will begin putting copies on the newsstands in 2007. You can already pick up Indian versions of *Maxim, Marie Claire*, and *Good Housekeeping*. They're all after the 300 million or so English-speaking, middle-class Indians (equal to the entire population of the United States) who have an interest in what's going on in the world beyond their own country.

In Brazil, the government has begun to auction timber rights to large tracts of the rain forest in an attempt to create a coherent pol-icy that will allow for logging and development but also protect the environment and the country's incredible natural assets. Companies will be competing with each other to win the rights to these precious and limited timber resources (they won't own the land, however, or have the right to exploit any other resources), and they'll also be competing against each other in the world market.

So competing with everyone from everywhere for everything in the age of globality will be as tumultuous as it was in any of the great eras of expansion and change that preceded this one. For most companies, it will require making some fundamental changes in order to move forward and succeed.

EMERSON: TIME FOR CHANGE

That's what Emerson discovered some years ago, in the early days of the tsunami. Emerson's corporate offices in St. Louis, Missouri, are a seven-minute ride from the airport, Lambert–St. Louis International. That's important because as Charlie Peters, senior executive vice president, a twenty-five-year Emerson veteran, likes to say, "If you don't go, you don't get." Peters knows all about "going": He's traveled to China and throughout the Asia-Pacific region a dozen times a year for many years.

Emerson may seem an unlikely model of globality. The company was founded in 1890 in St. Louis as a manufacturer of electric motors and fans. It soon expanded into sewing machines, dental drills, player pianos, and power tools. During World War II, Emerson supplied the U.S. Army Air Force and became the world's largest manufacturer of gun turrets. In the 1950s, the company embarked on a program of growth and diversification, growing from two plants and 4,000 employees in 1954 to 82 facilities and 31,000 people in 1973. Five product lines had mushroomed into hundreds, and the company had nearly $1 billion in sales.

In 1973, Charles (Chuck) F. Knight became chief executive officer, and he continued the development of a disciplined management process that would enable Emerson to successfully expand overseas. As sixteen-year veteran Craig Ashmore, senior vice president of planning and development, explains, "Planned opportunism got us where we are today." And that's a company with sixty divisions; regional corporate headquarters in St. Louis, Hong Kong, London, and Dubai; other offices in Europe, Asia, and Latin America; and a marketing presence in more than 150 countries on six continents.

Emerson's international journey began in earnest in the early 1980s, when the economy slowed down in the United States, and inflation soared. Competition from lower-cost players had intensified. Emerson got a wake-up call when the company lost a significant piece of business to a Brazilian competitor. "The retail prices they were charging for their goods were far below our costs for similar products," Ashmore recalled. Emerson decided to do something about the situation. In particular, it would have to find a way to cut costs in order to match the retail prices made possible by its rivals' low-wage operations.

Chuck Knight, by then famous for his demanding management style and relentless focus on improving Emerson's performance, defined the company's new agenda: best cost. In a best-cost world, Emerson's offerings would have the lowest possible cost, highest possible quality, and be made anywhere in the world that could meet all criteria simultaneously.

Not surprisingly, the idea of offshoring production for a century-old, American-heartland company that sold most of its products in the United States was a difficult one and met with significant resistance from just about everyone—managers, employees, suppliers, and customers. Those were the years, after all, of the rise of Japanese products—especially cars—in U.S. markets, and the call to "Buy American" was everywhere. But Knight knew that Emerson had to make the move offshore to sustain its success and continue to grow.

Knight had a bit of a globality mind-set, even then, in part because he had spent a good deal of time in Europe in his younger days, working in his family's business. So offshoring did not seem as foreign to him as it did to many Americans in the 1980s and he was ready to give it a try.

Getting the leaders of fifty different business units on board with the plan wouldn't be so easy, however. One piece of evidence that Knight used to convince them was the company's previous success with a manufacturing operation outside of the United States. In the early 1980s, Emerson had set up a plant in Mexico to manufacture temperature controls and it had been an important success for the company—achieving operating profits that were significantly higher than in Emerson's U.S.-based factories. Knight kept referring to the Mexican plant as a model of what Emerson could achieve and prodding his managers to "get on the program." One by one, they embraced the idea of offshoring some or all of their production to Mexico. Between 1983 and 1988, Emerson closed some fifty plants and created 5,000 jobs in low-cost countries. All of the business units involved found that their operating profits increased.[4] (Emerson also became quite celebrated during this period; it was one of the companies featured in the seminal management book *In Search of Excellence*, published in 1982.)

These successes in Mexico and elsewhere helped to change the mind-set of Emerson's managers, and they began to consider the idea of going even farther afield with their operations. The next step was to make some acquisitions in Europe in order to build scale. One of the first, in 1989, was of Leroy-Somer, a French industrial automation company based in Angouleme, a small town in the southwest of France, that had annual revenues of $450 million. The deal was Emerson's second-largest acquisition in its history and its largest ever in Europe.

Not only did Emerson acquire a valuable business, it also gained new talent for its leadership team—notably Jean-Paul Montupet, chairman of Leroy-Somer. Today, Montupet is executive vice president of Emerson, head of its Industrial Automation Group, and has overall responsibility for Emerson in Europe. Montupet earned his MBA from the École des Hautes Études Commerciales in Paris, attended the Harvard Business School's International Teachers Program, and had held a number of executive positions before joining Emerson.

When he first arrived at Emerson, Montupet could not help but notice that some members of the corporate staff had a rather distinct lack of experience in managing international operations. "Emerson was very U.S.-centric," he said. "I could even say, very Midwest-centric. One time when it looked like Leroy-Somer might exceed its capital budget by 5 percent, I was told by the director of corporate manufacturing that I had to cut the budget, even though the slight increase was entirely a result of the exchange rates." The frustrated director remarked to Montupet, "Someone should tell Chuck to quit buying these foreign companies."

Montupet says that Knight deliberately adapted his leadership approach to accommodate cultural differences, and that was key in getting the leadership team beyond its U.S.-focused mind-set. For example, Knight realized that his confrontational management style did not work as well in Europe as it did in the United States. "Performance review meetings with Chuck were always tough," Montupet told us. "He could be very challenging, and out of these exchanges came valuable new ways to operate the business. But Chuck's experience in Europe made him recognize that the same approach would not work in Europe. He toned down his behavior to get the right impact when he traveled overseas."

While Emerson sought to grow through acquisitions in Europe, it also spotted an opportunity to gain additional cost savings with the opening up of central and eastern Europe in the early 1990s. Once again, however, there was resistance—this time to the idea of offshoring, specifically in eastern Europe—and it came mostly from Emerson's managers located in Europe. As Montupet put it, "European management raised lots of reasons why 'job shifting' could not happen in Europe. Yes, you could do it, but not in the way it was done in the United States. In Europe, you can't just shut a plant quickly. The process has to be much more gradual."

Knight found a way to bring the managers around, by running small pilots of the proposed operations, and he eventually prevailed. "In 1991, when we started the process, 100 percent of our production was in 'high-cost' Europe," Montupet said. "Now 40 percent is in 'low-cost' Europe."

In the early 1990s, Emerson anticipated that Asia—specifically China—could further fuel the company's growth, and, happily, it already had a leg up in that region. Rosemount, a company that Emerson had acquired some years before, had established a position in China in 1975. Rosemount's leader, Vern Heath, was a warm guy with a talent for cultivating deep relationships. He had established a close bond with the mayor of Shanghai, who had helped Rosemount to enter China in the days before anyone could see the tsunami coming, and had guided it through the governmental red tape.

To build on the foundation that Heath had established, Emerson sent some of its most experienced and successful executives—including future chief executive officer David Farr—to set up a corporate office in Hong Kong in 1993. From the beginning, Emerson took a hands-off approach with its country-based managers. As Ashmore explains, "At Emerson you run your own ship. The P&Ls are pushed down to the businesses. They make the decisions and are responsible for performance. We at corporate don't issue edicts. We raise issues and ask questions. They try it, and if it works, they do more. It's their decision."

David Farr's responsibility in the Asia corporate office was to build the capabilities and contacts needed to help Emerson divisions succeed when they moved there. According to Peters, "When a division tells us that they want to expand into Asia, we try to give them a solution on a silver platter. If a division wants to go into the Philippines, for example, we can tell the business unit leader who to call there to get office space, fifteen managers, and experts for moving their processes and capabilities to the Philippines. You just have to have the willingness to go, and we'll help you make it happen."

In 2001, Emerson acquired Avansys from Huawei, the Chinese telecom network provider. Charlie Peters describes Avansys as the "ultimate Chinese company. It had the smartest people, who worked extremely hard, and because it sold power-supply systems to the telephone infrastructure, it was everywhere in China, with offices in twenty-eight cities." From the Avansys workforce, Emerson managers learned a lot about the distribution system in China and how to reach even deeper into Chinese markets. Today, about $1.5 billion of Emerson's total worldwide sales—or about 7 percent—comes from China.

As Emerson built its sales throughout Asia, it built up its local manufacturing and procurement capabilities to support them, and it also began to move some of its engineering and back-office work into China, as well as into eastern Europe. In 2007, Emerson employed twice as many engineers as it did in 1997, but its engineering costs were lower in 2007 than they were in 1997.

Emerson has come a long way from those first tentative steps into Mexico. Emerson's fundamental strategy is to fully leverage opportunities around the globe, pinpointing operations, sourcing from advantaged locations, leveraging engineering talent, and creating growth in new markets through its global operations—meeting its customers' needs with presence in countries throughout the world as sourcers, makers, and marketers.

TOWARD GLOBAL TRANSFORMATION

The struggles that Emerson has experienced over the past two decades are similar to those that many incumbents (and would-be challengers, too) are just beginning to face. When we talk with leaders of such companies, we find they are asking questions like "What should we be doing to move forward globally?" or "We've already made major investments in globalization, but are we still going in the right directions?" or "Are we making changes fast enough?"

We usually respond by saying that there are many ways forward and that no one of them is always right or completely wrong. However, whatever your situation is—just starting the journey or looking at a long track record of international activity—for most companies, to accomplish the breadth and depth of changes we have been describing in this book will entail more than business-as-usual or incremental change; it will require a global transformation. By global transformation we mean a significant (and, usually, rapid) change to multiple dimensions of your company's business model to fully address threats and opportunities.

There are seven actions you can take to help you move toward a global transformation:

- *Evaluate Your Competitive Position*
- *Shift Mind-Sets*
- *Assess and Align Your People*
- *Recognize Your Full Set of Opportunities*
- *Define Your Future Global Shape*
- *Encourage Ingenuity*
- *Lead Your Transformation from the Front*

Evaluate Your Competitive Position

The first step in moving forward is to gain an understanding of where you are. Step back, and take a dispassionate look at your company within the industries in which you compete and where you are and where your competitors are—both incumbents and current or potential challengers.

Threats and opportunities will vary markedly by industry. Some industries are already feeling the full heat of global competition, while others are still relatively unaffected. This is due to differences in the nature of competitive advantage within each industry. First, is it labor intensive, R&D intensive, or marketing intensive? How important is proximity? Is there a great need for customer interaction? Second, each industry is differently affected by the forces of globality—country origins, global access, and hunger. Third, your position depends on where you started and the capabilities you have in the domains in which you compete. For Emerson, knowing that its cost position was not competitive was enough to sound the alarm. Evaluating your competitive position today will likely require you to do some additional work to come to a clear point of view. Ask yourself:

What are the threats and opportunities within my industry, given the unique combination of the nature of competitive advantage, challenger-country origins, global access and hunger, and our own starting position and capabilities?

Where have our competitors built relationships, positions, and advantages that we don't have? In which of our current businesses, markets, products, and services do we have a sustainable competitive advantage?

Which challengers are, or could become, competitors? Suppliers? Customers? Which ones might we collaborate with?

Are we capitalizing on low-cost sources for procurement, production, and research and development? Are we leveraging global scale in R&D, sourcing, manufacturing, marketing, and other functions?

Do we have positions from which we can sell into the most important rapidly developing economies? Do we have the distribution systems we need to go deep into those markets?

Shift Mind-Sets

Our goal in writing *Globality* has been to help companies shift their mind-sets in the light of the new global realities so they can successfully take advantage of the vast opportunities that globality offers—while avoiding, or at least mitigating, some of the threats.

At Emerson, according to Charlie Peters, the change to a best-cost strategy could only be made with a shift in mind-sets. Chuck Knight already had a penchant for globality, but he needed to get the leaders of fifty different business units on board. To do so, he leveraged the company's previous success in Mexico, acquired new companies that addressed competitive needs and exposed Emerson's leaders to business outside the United States, and got his managers out to see firsthand what was happening in other markets.

Competing with everyone from everywhere for everything can require an even greater shift than was needed at Emerson twenty years ago. How do you get enough people in your company—a critical mass—to understand that reality?

See for Yourself

It's important to understand what's going on in the countries where you have presence and to get firsthand experience of what the markets, businesses, cultures, and people there are like—and the speed at which they're changing. Visit your RDE operations regularly. If you don't have any, visit your customers'. Don't go alone. Connect with as many people as you can. Plan to listen much more than you talk.

Listen to your suppliers: What are they doing? What are they thinking? What are they planning? How do they view you as a customer? As a partner? As a competitor?

Listen to your people in the markets: What can they tell you about the needs and wants of the customers there? What concerns do they have about current operations? What ideas do they have for future opportunities? Do they see partnership or acquisition opportunities?

Listen to people throughout the distribution system: Are you meeting their needs? Are your competitors outflanking you? Are you missing big opportunities? How could the distribution system be changed or improved?

Listen to your partners: Are you living up to their expectations? Are they the right people for you to be partnering with now? What could you do together to radically improve your collective position? Will they become competitors? Are they already?

Leverage Successes

Leverage the voices of leaders in the company who have experienced the new order firsthand. Martin over in robotics cut 30 percent off his materials cost by sourcing from São Paulo. Rachel hit her stretch sales target by trialing a prototype in India. Tony increased yield by 18 percent by building a route-optimization competency center in Bangalore. Celebrate and publicly acknowledge achievements that stem from a new way of looking at the company and its markets.

Build a Fact Base

Resistance to transformation is sometimes emotional, but it is often rational, too. Case studies, business model benchmarking, taking apart competitors' product, and tracking fluctuations in global market share are all tools that can educate and inform management and directors about the reality of the post-tsunami world and the need to set a new course. Put challenger stories in the leadership-development curriculum—or better yet, move the classroom to Buenos Aires.

Convert Your Top 200

Change of this type must begin at the top. In our experience, it requires commitment from the folks who would be considered senior management—heads of businesses, geographies, and functions, plus key influencers. This is the group that must buy in, and to do so, they need the conviction that comes from firsthand experience. They should have the opportunity to participate in leadership-development programs; personal visits; interactions with competitors, customers, and suppliers; and line experience in one or more of the rapidly developing economies. Shift the mind-sets of your top 200 people and you will be well on your way toward transforming the entire company.

ASSESS AND ALIGN YOUR PEOPLE

People are the lifeblood of the company, and to succeed in globality, that blood needs to comprise the right set of characteristics and must circulate vigorously and constantly. If yours is like many companies, you will probably find that you need more people than you currently employ who possess the right mind-set, have the right skill set, and are in the right places.

At Emerson, Chuck Knight knew that the transformation would require leaders who would be open to new ideas and new ways of doing things. Assessing his people led him to conclude that he needed people who would bring different experiences and who were used to viewing the world through different lenses. As a result, he reached outside to bring in fresh blood and then made sure that it kept circulating around the globe.

A starting point in the assessment process is to run through the following global talent management checklist.

Embrace a New Global Talent Mind-Set

Have you shifted from a West-centric to a polycentric view? Are you locating operations to capture global talent pools? Are you overinvesting in people required to capture growth in RDEs? Are you balancing global and local programs to win the talent battle?

Elevate Global Talent Planning

Are you planning for the global talent you will need where you need it—now and five years out? Are you managing talent on a global basis?

Hire Potential, Build Bench Strength

Are you accessing hidden talent pools through innovative recruiting methods? Are you building a strong brand and localizing your offering to attract high potentials? Are you developing talent through locally tailored training and development?

Accelerate Careers and Create Global Leaders

Do you have the right senior people—leaders who are builders—in your RDE operations? Are you rotating your key people from RDEs and from developed economies through countries with different characteristics? Are people from the rapidly developing economies playing important, global roles in your enterprise? Does your board reflect your aspirations in terms of geographic mix?

RECOGNIZE YOUR FULL SET OF OPPORTUNITIES

Companies often approach doing business in the rapidly developing economies with a particular bias. They seek to leverage low cost, or to tap the large markets, or to take advantage of talent or other resources. This makes sense in the early stages, but to transform globally it's important to move beyond this starting point and to recognize your full set of opportunities.

Emerson's first steps were taken in response to the threat from a lower-cost RDE-based challenger. But unlike companies that take that first step and then stop, Emerson kept going and recognized a much broader set of opportunities. Its forays into Mexico were followed by acquisitions in western Europe, which led to expansion into eastern Europe to leverage lower-cost operations. Then came expansion into Asia, with an emphasis on China. Along the way, Emerson broadened its objectives—moving from lower-cost manufacturing to global sourcing and then to talent development—and achieving growth throughout the process.

You can continue to reduce costs in many ways. You can increase your procurement and manufacturing activities in the rapidly developing economies. You can outsource some or more of your back-office functions (such as accounting) or establish new RDE-based call centers. You can shift your mix of high-end functions so that more of them are accomplished by RDE-based companies. As a result, you may be able to double your engineering output at half the cost.

The revenue opportunities may be an even greater source of profit increases. In the coming years, the billion people who are already consumers in the rapidly developing economies will steadily be increasing the number and value of their purchases. What's more, a billion more customers will be entering the market, looking for basic products like telecommunications, financial services, and consumer goods.

An added benefit of serving these markets is that the low-cost products designed for the consumers and companies in the rapidly developing economies can be brought back to the developed markets—often with very little modification—to establish a new lower-cost value proposition and accelerate growth.

The rapidly developing economies also represent opportunities to tap talent pools and other resources, such as raw materials, energy, and increasingly rich sources of ideas and knowledge. The key is to ensure that you take a broad perspective when assessing the potential opportunities and to be open to pursue an even broader set of them.

DEFINE YOUR FUTURE GLOBAL SHAPE

For most companies, the resulting set of opportunities will be very broad and diverse, which will require segmentation—and then making choices about markets, sources of cost advantage, talent pools to tap, and where to locate operations and source resources. It will also require choices about the sequence in which to pursue the opportunities. Taken together these choices will define the pace of transformation and the future global shape of your company.

Emerson, as we've seen, did not tackle everything at once. In the early days, it moved from region to region, using different regions to accomplish different objectives. It segmented the opportunities—Mexico for cost, western Europe for growth, eastern Europe initially for cost and later for engineering talent, China for growth and low-cost manufacturing and then sourcing and talent. Today, the company's strategy is multidimensional, with cost, sourcing, engineering, and logistics needs all factored in as it positions itself to meet customer needs in any region.

Incumbents are used to relatively homogenous markets in the developed world, but the rapidly developing markets are much more heterogeneous, with a rich array of segments that change rapidly. It's critical to choose which segments you want to focus on now (and which ones you'll approach later) and determine what it will take to succeed with each targeted segment.

It's important to identify the best segments for the long run, not just the ones that are easy to understand and reach right now. As we've discussed throughout the book, many companies content themselves with picking off the high-end customers and ignore the rapidly growing mid-tier segments. When they do this for too long, competitors (challengers or incumbents) are often able to build their reputations, brands, and customer loyalty and establish a strong position to take advantage of much larger and longer-term opportunities.

Markets, however, are only part of the opportunity. It is also important to segment opportunities to leverage the rapidly developing economies for low cost, talent, and other resources. In making choices, don't be overly constrained by the resources available within your company. Many incumbents have been able to develop quickly by reaching outside to acquire, partner, and collaborate with external parties.

Encourage Ingenuity

Segmenting opportunities and making choices are necessary but not sufficient; to transform, you also need to be open to new creative approaches. Ingenuity, as we have seen, is one of the key advantages of the global challengers, but it need not be theirs exclusively.

By acquiring Avansys, for example, Emerson was able to broaden and deepen its distribution—and to learn up close about Chinese ingenuity in product development, manufacturing, and distribution. When the deal was announced, many analysts were skeptical about the fit and the value of the product portfolio. However, for Emerson, the real value of Avansys went far beyond a set of products.

Pursuing markets in and leveraging resources from rapidly developing economies creates opportunities for everybody, but they may not always look that way to incumbents. Use the ingenuity you see in the rapidly developing economies to stimulate your people located in the developing economies. Encourage them to look for all kinds of possibilities, develop ways to take advantage of them, try out a variety of approaches, modify them if necessary, and try them again. If they work, bring them back to the developed markets.

Ingenuity knows no boundaries.

LEAD YOUR TRANSFORMATION FROM THE FRONT

Companies cannot succeed in the age of globality without strong leadership, so what you do as a leader is very important.

Emerson would not have achieved its transformation without highly visible leadership—first from Chuck Knight and his team, located both at the center and in the far-flung regions, and then by David Farr as a key player, first in the expansion into China and subsequently as chief executive officer. Throughout the transformation journey, Knight, Farr, Peters, Montupet, and many others carried the torch in front of the troops, igniting passion in others as they traveled the globe.

So ask yourself, are you spending the right amount of time struggling with the right things? Are you acting as a role model for a shift in mind-set? Are you creating the right incentives—and the right consequences—for your top two hundred business leaders to embrace and lead change? Are you operating in a polycentric way? Are you ensuring that investments are being made in the right locations at the right pace? Are you doing enough to mind the cost gap? Are you moving the right people to the right places? Are you getting ahead of the trends? Are you spending enough time in the rapidly developing economies? Are you recognizing the full set of opportunities? Are you looking at alternative ways of doing things and trying to apply them in your existing business? Are you paying enough attention to managing change? Are you learning fast enough to have answers to critical questions?

Are you too jet-lagged?

Not jet-lagged enough?

Are you demonstrating your commitment so that others follow?

Are you preparing your company to succeed in the era of globality?

SUCCESS IN GLOBALITY

That final question, of course, raises another one. How do we define success in globality?

Once a company has faced the struggles and mastered them to some degree, then what? What will success look like in the age of globality? Will it still be about financial performance, as it so long has been in the developed economies? Or will it be about something else? Sustainability, perhaps. Or the ability to "give money away," as Tata does. Maybe we'll follow the lead of the state of Bhutan, whose ultimate measure of success is happiness.

Certainly, everyday life will look different. One safe bet is that it will involve a lot more traveling. That has certainly described the authors' lives for the past twenty years as we have worked with a steadily increasing number of companies with endeavors in countries around the world. For this book, the authors traveled constantly to meet with clients and conduct interviews. The author team collectively gathered once a month in whatever city seemed the most convenient for the most people at the time—we convened in Chicago, London, Prague, Delhi, New York, Hong Kong, Frankfurt, and back in Chicago again—logging at least six hundred collective hours of travel time and more than 300,000 miles in the air.

But the number of miles traveled will not define success in the age of globality any more than will the number of flags tacked into the map of the world.

Throughout this book, we've described the struggles that companies face when doing business in the rapidly developing economies and the actions they can take to overcome these struggles—creating low-cost, high-quality, and ingenious products; growing their people; thinking big and acting fast; reaching deep into big markets; pinpointing their operations wherever it makes the most business sense; and embracing manyness in their organizations.

That leaves the important and larger question of personal and corporate success, achievement, and contribution. During the course of working on this book, we asked many challengers about their goals and got some amazing responses. Many executives in challenger companies deeply believe that they are working for the good of their countries and their future.

This sense is very strong in India, perhaps because the country is so large, and the need there is so great. Subramaniam Ramadorai, of Tata Consultancy Services, said, "Internationalization and globalization was a natural happening, because we decided to create something for the future with a very clear mind-set that someday it would be beneficial to this country. That is completely different from traditional companies in the United States and Europe, where you start something there, build a market, take it to the international market, and apply it there. It is completely opposite of that. In 1972, 1974, who would have heard of an IT industry for India? Who would have even imagined that we have been doing something for the future which is very substantial not only for the industry, but for India as a brand?"

The desire to improve one's position in the world is not restricted to India. Challengers in China, eastern Europe, and South America see globality as a way to create success for their countries. "There are huge opportunities for big countries such as the United States, India, or China, but those countries have a good chance of surviving on their own," said Juan Antonio Alvarez, of CSAV. "If they don't go global, they are missing something. But for Chile, that's not the case. We must do it. We have that imperative. We have that passion. And I think that's an advantage."

The challengers also think about their place in the world, about sustainability and scarce resources. "We operate in places that are very sensitive in terms of environmental issues," said Tito Martins of CVRD, "the Amazon forest, New Caledonia, Australia, even in some parts of Canada. So we have to show the world, not only the capital markets but all the stakeholders, that we are concerned about environmental issues and social responsibility. Not because everybody's doing it, but because we already are doing it."

Some challengers think about how best to help and serve people. "The Tata Group's fundamental belief is that you have to create wealth in the communities you serve," said Patrick McGoldrick of Tata Technologies. "For us, for many years, that meant just India. Today, it is the world. And is this philosophy that the Tatas have internationalizable? The answer is absolutely!"

Over the years, we have talked with many people whom we consider to be heroes in the business world and asked them similar questions about the role they believe that their company—and they themselves—should play in society. Like the challengers, they don't talk about meeting quarterly earnings targets or cutting costs or beating rivals. They always talk about their dreams. They speak about people they have known, in their factories and boardrooms, retail outlets and warehouses. They talk about their companies as if they are families. Above all, they say they want their personal and professional lives to be meaningful and rich journeys. They want to build something. And they want it to endure.

Those measures of success will not change in the age of globality. In fact, experience with the people, businesses, and cultures of the rapidly developing economies is likely to inspire us all to an even broader, deeper, and more fulfilling view of our industries, our companies, and ourselves.

Now, as the tsunami surges, it's both an honor and a responsibility to act as decision makers doing business in a world that has moved beyond the physical limitations of the past and has become an ecosystem of opportunity for everyone from everywhere for everything.

What you do, what you decide, how you think, how you behave will affect people's lives and change the world, either for the worse— or for the better.

Acknowledgments

Writing *Globality* involved the commitment and contributions of many people, and we are grateful to those who have participated in the project—and the work that laid the foundation for it—over the past several years.

Thanks to our partners and associates at The Boston Consulting Group (BCG), who have supported the Global Advantage initiative and the development of this book. You have acted as mentors, thought partners, and collaborators on numerous projects, and we think of *Globality* as our collective achievement. We especially want to thank Hans-Paul Buerkner, our chief executive officer, whose support, encouragement, and assistance helped bring the book to life.

Thanks to the many senior executives around the world who spent time with us during the research phase of this book and who shared the stories of their companies and insights about globality gained from years of experience that we have included in the text. Thanks, too, to the many senior executives of companies whom we did not quote directly in the book but whom we have worked with and learned from over the past twenty-five years and who, over the past five years, have been especially helpful in decoding the meaning of globality.

Thanks to John Butman, an independent writer who has collaborated with several BCG authors, who worked closely with the *Globality* team to develop a successful proposal, conduct research, shape ideas, and write the text. John flew around the world to meet with us—in Chicago, New York, Hong Kong, Frankfurt, London, Prague, and Delhi—to brainstorm, cajole, encourage, and help mold our collective ideas as the book took shape. His touch with the written word is truly a gift. He has contributed much to shaping the ideas and to the writing of the book, and we are very grateful that we were able to collaborate with him. John was supported by a team that included researchers Janine Evans and Emily Donaldson, editors Lauren Keller Johnson and Martine Bellen, and received valued assistance from Patricia Lyons, Alex Aderer, and Nathaniel Welch.

Before there was a book or even the idea of a book, there was a small group of people who took a passionate interest in the topic of globalization, the forces that were shaping globality, the growth of the rapidly developing economies, and the rise of the challengers. This pioneering group played a vital role in developing our ideas, starting in 2003, and it included Thomas Bradtke, Kathleen Lancaster, Jean Lebreton, Bill Matassoni, David Michael, Xavier Mosquet, KC Munuz, Josef Rick, George Stalk, Dave Young, Jésus de Juan, Kevin Waddell, John Wong, Pascal Cotte, Christopher Mark, Zafar Momin, Francois Rouzaud, Immo Rupf, Alison Sander, Barry Adler, and all three authors of this book, Hal Sirkin, Jim Hemerling, and Arindam Bhattacharya. We are particularly grateful to David Young and Josef Rick, practice-area leaders, who sponsored the Global Advantage topic in the early days.

Special thanks go to David Michael, who has been deeply involved in Asia for the past twenty years, first as a student studying Mandarin, then as a consultant working with clients throughout the region, and now as a member of BCG's Asia-Pacific leadership team as the managing director of our Greater China system. We also feel great gratitude to Thomas Bradtke, who was a core member of the Global Advantage team from its inception and now helps lead our work with clients in the Middle East. David and Thomas were the lead authors of a report called *The New Global Challengers: How 100 Top Companies from Rapidly Developing Economies Are Changing the World,* published in May 2006 and revised and updated in 2008, that served as the springboard for this book. David has continued to be an extraordinary thought partner and his ideas are woven throughout *Globality.*

BCG's Global Advantage initiative, now led by Bernd Waltermann along with Arindam and Jim, includes James Abraham, Marcos Aguiar, Sandra Bell, Andrew Clark, Martha Craumer, Laurent de Vitton, Ralf Dreischmeier, Daniel Friedman, Susumu Hattori, Brad Henderson, Hubert Hsu, Vinoy Kumar, Christopher Kutarna, Kathleen Lancaster, Nikolaus Lang, Michael Meyer, David Michael, Yutaka Mizukoshi, Christoph Nettesheim, Josef Rick, Hal Sirkin, George Stalk, Carl Stern, Arvind Subramanian, Alan Thomson, Kevin Waddell, Lauren Whitehurst, John Wong, Tom Hout, and Benjamin Pinney.

As the early research work evolved into the creation of a book, we formed a dedicated research, writing, and support team that included at various times and in varying capacities Sandra Bell, Jeff Bill, Kevin Chan-a-Shing, Bin Chen, Martha Craumer, Chris Croker, Mike Gaffney, Eric Gregoire, Melissa Griffith, Guillermo LopezVelarde, Michael Meyer, Adrian Monsalve, Jyoti Nigam, Laurent de Vitton, Lauren Whitehurst, and Eric Stuckey. We would like to offer particular recognition to Michael Meyer and Christopher Kutarna, both of whom made significant contributions to the research and the writing of the book.

We have been fortunate to have the help and advice of our agents, Todd Shuster and Esmond Harmsworth, of the Zachary Shuster Harmsworth Literary Agency, who helped us connect with our publisher and have faithfully supported the development, launch, and global distribution of *Globality.* Rick Wolff, our publisher at Business Plus, encouraged us to write a book that would appeal to a broad audience and has given us insightful feedback and guidance throughout the process. We would be remiss if we did not acknowledge the valuable contributions made by Rick's assistant, Tracy Martin, and Robert Castillo, the Hachette Book Group managing editor.

Our administrative assistants Paula Daly, Deepti Punni, and Jane Wu supported us throughout the process, helping us juggle our schedules and manage our travel plans as we crisscrossed the globe, conducting interviews and brainstorming together.

As the book neared its final form, we reached out to a few trusted friends and colleagues who offered to read the manuscript and who provided helpful feedback and insights that enabled us to sharpen our messages.

Finally, we would like to thank the many people whom we have learned from and worked with on these topics over the years, and who have helped to shape BCG's Global Advantage practice and this book, including Thomas Achhorner, Rose-Marie Alm, Jim Andrew, Britney Ateek, Cameron Bailey, Christine Barges, Stephanie Barker, Jorge Becerra, Lucy Bellisario, Andy Blackburn, Laurent Billés-Garabedian, Rolf Bixner, Marcus Bokkerink, Michael Book, Stépan Breedveld, Susan Brigham, Willie Burnside, Gary Callahan, Steven Chai, Thierry Chassaing, Catherine Cherry, Kristin Claire, Darrin Clements, Maritza Colon, Corey Coosaia, Leroy Coutts, Angèle Craamer, Thomas Dauner, Rob Davies, Joe Davis, David Dean, Filiep Deforche, Fernando Del Rio, Frank Dietz, Sebastian DiGrande, Patrick Ducasse, Mary Egan, Anders Fahlander, Christine Fasquel, Alastair Flanagan, Mark Freedman, Danny Friedman, Joerg Funk, Gerardo Garbulsky, Margarita Garijo, Marc Gilbert, Peter Goldsbrough, Antoine Gourevitch, Emile Gostelie, Steven Gunby, Philippe Guy, Per Hallius, Gerry Hansell, Hans Michael Hauser, Lee Haviland, Arif Janjua, Dan Jansen, David Jin, Nicolas Kachaner, Perry Keenan, Ken Keverian, Wookyung Kim, Tom King, Kim Wee Koh, Mathias Krahl, Carsten Kratz, Matt Krentz, Monish Kumar, Maureen Kwiatkowski, Harry Kwon, Irina Lazukova, Corry Leigh, Li Gu, Jenna Lim, Roland Löhner, Tom Lutz, Sheri Macatangay, Marcos Macedo, Heather Mac Millan, Andy Maguire, Tomoko Maki, Joe Manget, Sharon Marcil, Franz-Josef Marx, Akiko Masumi, Dave Matheson, Andreas Maurer, Kathleen McCoomb, Marie-Pierre Milliez, Yves Morieux, Maria Morita, Jean Mouton, Roanne Neuwirth, Ron Nicol, Rebecka Nilsson,

Thomas Nordahl, Carlos Novaes, Naoki Ota, David Pecaut, Walter Piacsek, Heidi Polke, Patricia Powers, Collins Qian, Byung Nam Rhee, David Rhodes, Naoki Shigetake, Michael Silverstein, Larry Shulman, Delaney Steele, Oliver Stähle, Georg Sticher, Peter Strüven, Tjun Tang, Olivier Tardy, Miki Tsusaka, Seppa Tukka, Joseph Wan, Meldon Wolfgang, Andre Xavier, Byung Suk Yoon, and Yu Liang.

Thanks to all the people mentioned here as well as to others who made a contribution and whom we may have inadvertently omitted; you all have helped to create this book and make it a success.

Appendix

THE BCG CHALLENGER 100

Company and Country	Industry
ARGENTINA (1)	
Tenaris	Steel
BRAZIL (13)	
Braskem	Petrochemicals
Coteminas	Textiles
CVRD	Mining
Embraer	Aerospace
Gerdau	Steel
JBS-Friboi	Food and Beverages
Marcopolo	Automotive Equipment
Natura	Cosmetics
Perdigão	Food and Beverages
Petrobras	Fossil Fuels
Sadia	Food and Beverages
Votorantim	Process Industries
WEG	Engineered Products
CHILE (1)	
CSAV	Shipping

Company and Country	Industry

CHINA (41)

Baosteel	Steel
BYD	Consumer Electronics
Chalco	Nonferrous Metals
Changhong	Home Appliances
Chery Automobile	Automotive Equipment
China Aviation 1	Aerospace
China Minmetals	Nonferrous Metals
China Mobile	Telecom Networks
CIMC	Shipping
CNHTC	Automotive Equipment
CNOOC	Fossil Fuels
COFCO	Food and Beverages
COSCO Group	Shipping
CSCL	Shipping
CSIC	Shipbuilding
Dongfeng Motor	Automotive Equipment
FAW	Automotive Equipment
Founder	Computer / IT Components
Galanz	Home Appliances
Gree	Home Appliances
Haler Company	Home Appliances
Hisense	Consumer Electronics
Huawei Technologies	Telecom Equipment
Johnson Electric	Engineered Products
Lenovo	Computers / IT Components
Li & Fung Group	Textiles
Midea	Home Appliances
Nine Dragons Paper	Paper-packaging
Petro China	Fossil Fuels
SAIC	Automotive Equipment
Shougang Group	Steel
Sinochem Corporation	Chemicals
Sinomach	Engineered Products
Sinopec	Fossil Fuels

Company and Country	Industry
TCL Corporation	Consumer Electronics
Techtronic Industries	Engineered Products
Tsingtao Brewery	Food and Beverages
VTech	Consumer Electronics
Wanxiang	Automotive Equipment
ZPMC	Engineered Products
ZTE Corporation	Telecom Equipment

EGYPT (1)

Orascom Telecom	Telecom Networks

HUNGARY (1)

MOL	Fossil Fuels

INDIA (20)

Bajaj Auto	Automotive Equipment
Bharat Forge	Automotive Equipment
Birla Hindalco	Nonferrous Metals
Cipla	Pharmaceuticals
Crompton Greaves	Engineered Products
Dr. Reddy's	Pharmaceuticals
Infosys Technologies	IT Services / BPO
Larsen & Toubro	Engineering Services
Mahindra & Mahindra	Automotive Equipment
Ranbaxy Laboratories	Pharmaceuticals
Reliance Industries	Petrochemicals
Satyam Computer Services	IT Services / BPO
Suzlon Energy	Wind Energy
Tata Consulting Services (TCS)	IT Services / BPO
Tata Motors	Automotive Equipment
Tata Steel	Steel
Tata Tea	Food and Beverages
Videocon Industries	Consumer Electronics
VSNL	Telecom Networks
Wipro Technologies	IT Services / BPO

Company and Country	Industry

INDONESIA (1)

| Indofood | Food and Beverages |

MALAYSIA (2)

| MISC | Shipping |
| Petronas | Fossil Fuels |

MEXICO (7)

América Móvil	Telecom Networks
Cemex	Building Materials
Femsa	Food and Beverages
Gruma	Food and Beverages
Grupo Bimbo	Food and Beverages
Grupo Modelo	Food and Beverages
Nemak	Automotive Equipment

POLAND (1)

| PKN Orlen | Fossil Fuels |

RUSSIA (6)

Gazprom	Fossil Fuels
Inter RAO UES	Energy
Lukoil	Fossil Fuels
Norilsk Nickel	Nonferrous Metals
Rusal	Nonferrous Metals
Severstal	Steel

THAILAND (2)

| CP Foods | Food and Beverages |
| Thai Union Frozen Products | Food and Beverages |

TURKEY (3)

Koc Holding	Home Appliances
Sebanci Holding	Chemicals
Vestel	Consumer Electronics

Notes

CHAPTER 1. What Is Globality?

1. Jo Johnson, "Report Says India to Grow 8% until 2020," *Financial Times*, 24 January 2007.

2. Norihiko Shirouzu, "Obscure Chinese Car Maker Seeks U.S. Presence, Changfeng's Vehicles Will Be On Display at Detroit Show; Communist Lauds Competition," *The Wall Street Journal*, 3 January 2007, 1.

3. Tal Barak, "World Series? Wait a Minute…" *NPR* page, 1 June 2005. <http://www.npr.org/templates/story/story.php?storyId=4675711>

4. Ben Shpigel, "NY Times Taking Another Global Step, Minaya Leads Group to Ghana," *The New York Times*, 27 January 2007. <http//www.nytimes.com/2007/01/27/oporto/baseball>

5. Jared Sandberg, "'It Says Press Any Key. Where's the Any Key?'," *The Wall Street Journal*, 20 February 2007. <http://online.wsj.com/article/SB117193317217413139.html>

6. Infosys Technologies Limited, Infosys signs agreement to set up software development centers in China (Bangaolre, India: Infosys Technologies Limited, 2005).

CHAPTER 2. Tsunami

1. Peter Hessler, "China's Boomtowns," *National Geographic*, June 2007. <http://www7.nationalgeographic.com/ngm/0706/feature4/index.html>

2. Pete Engardio, "Live-Wire Management at Johnson Electric," *BusinessWeek*, 27 November 1995.

3. Chris Prystay, "India's Boom Is Boon for Business Schools," *The Wall Street Journal*, 30 March 2007, B4B.

4. Joe Leahy, "Unleashed: Why Indian Companies Are Setting Their Sights on Western Rivals," *Financial Times*, 7 February 2007.

5. Yin Ping, "Schools Unite for Global CEO Programme," *China Daily English*, 25 October 2005.

6. Jason Bush, "Russia's New Deal: The Kremlin Is Pumping Money into Education, Housing, and Health Care," *BusinessWeek*, 9 April 2007, 40–45.

7. Irina Vyunova, "Putin Says Russia Needs Own Base to Train High-Grade Execs," ITAR-TASS World Service English, 21 September 2006.

8. Surojit Chatterjee, "Birla's Hindalco Buys Aluminum Giant Novelis for $6.4 billion," *International Business Times*, 13 February 2007. <http://in.ibtimes.com/articles/20070213/birla-039-s-hindalco-buys-aluminum-giant-novelis-for-us-6-4-billion.htm>

9. Zubair Ahmed, "India Attracts Western Tech Talent," *BBC* News, 5 Sept 2006. <http://news.bbc.co.uk/2/hi/south_asia/5272672.stm>

10. Nandini Lakshman, "India's Got a Job for You," *BusinessWeek*, 19 June 2007.<http://www.businessweek.com/globalbiz/content/jun2007/gb20070619_062414.htm>

11. The Baker Institute Energy Forum, "The Changing Role Of National Oil Companies In International Energy Markets," (Baker Institute Energy Forum). <http://www.rice.edu/energy/research/nationaloil/index.html>

12. Peter Hessler, "China's Boomtowns," *National Geographic*, June 2007. <http://www7.nationalgeographic.com/ngm/0706/feature4/index.html>

13. "Office Workers Take to Streets of Shanghai," *China Daily*, 18 May 2007.

14. "70% of Chinese Workers Overworked," *China View*, 8 May 2007.

15. Jack Ewing and Gail Edmondson, "Rise of a Powerhouse," *BusinessWeek*, 12 December 2005.

16. "It's Back-Breaking For India Inc. Bosses," *The Financial Express*, 30 May 2007. <http://www.financialexpress.com/old/latest_full_story.php?content_id=165649> (accessed 20 September 2007)

17. International Iron and Steel Institute, World Steel in Figures. 4 September 2007. <http://www.worldsteel.org/?action=storypages&id=23> (accessed 19 September 2007).

18. Pei Sun, "Industrial Policy, Corporate Governance, and the Competitiveness of China's National Champions: The Case of Shanghai Baosteel Group," *Journal of Chinese Economic and Business Studies* 3, No. 2 (2005): 173–192.

19. Ibid.

20. Ibid.

21. "Fortune Global 500 #296," *Fortune Magazine*, 24 July 2006. <http://money.cnn.com/magazines/fortune/global500/2006/snapshots/1964.html> (accessed 19 September 2007); Baosteel, Introduction to Products. <http://www.baosteel.com/plc/english/e04customer/e040102.htm> (accessed 19 September 2007); "Fortune 50 Most Powerful Women in Business #2," *Fortune Magazine*, 14 November 2005. <http://money.cnn.com/magazines/fortune/mostpowerfulwomen/2005/international/2.html> (accessed 19 September 2007);

22. The Boston Consulting Group, "Baosteel Company Profile," (Boston: BCG, 2007).

23. Pei Sun, "Industrial Policy, Corporate Governance, and the Competitiveness of China's National Champions: The Case of Shanghai Baosteel Group," *Journal of Chinese Economic and Business Studies* 3, No. 2 (2005): 173–192.

24. Knowledge@Wharton, India in the Global Supply Chain: Can Domestic Demand and Technology Skills Help It Catch Up? (Philadelphia, PA: Knowledge@Wharton, 15 February 2007).

25. Ibid.

26. Ibid.

27. Jack Ewing and Gail Edmondson, "Rise of a Powerhouse," *BusinessWeek*, 12 December 2005.

28. "Outsourcing in Eastern Europe," *The Economist*, 1 December 2005.

29. Ibid.

30. Bill Roberts, "Beyond the China Mystique," *Electronic Business*, 1 March 2006. <http://www.edn.com/index.asp?layout=article&articleid=CA6310932>

31. James Carbone, "No Place Like Home For High-End Electronics," *Purchasing*, 16 November 2006. <http://www.purchasing.com/article/CA6389605.html>

32. Bill Roberts, "Beyond the China Mystique," *Electronic Business*, 1 March 2006. <http://www.edn.com/index.asp?layout=article&articleid=CA6310932.

33. Johnson Electric Holdings Limited. Annual Report 2006.

34. The Boston Consulting Group, *The New Global Challengers: How 100 Top Companies from Rapidly Developing Economies Are Changing the World* (Boston: The Boston Consulting Group May 2006).

35. "China Port Handling Capacity Seen at 8 Bln Tons in 2010—Xinhua," *ABC Money* page, 23 May 2007.

36. "India Calls for Port Capacity to Double," Port World page, 25 June 2007 <http://www.portworld.com/news/2007/06/68246?gsid=e1e8350b2377db7aebdd49c9711a5009&asi=1

37. "Installed Capacity of Power Plants Totals 508 Gigawatts," *Xinhua News Agency*, 18 January 2006.

38. Richard McGregor, "China's Power Capacity Soars," *Financial Times*, 6 February 2007.

39. Paolo Hooke, "China's Power Sector: Can Supply Meet Demand?" *Asia Times Online*, 7 October 2005.

40. Ministry of Communications, "2001 Statistics on Road Transportation" (Ministry of Communications, 6 June 2007). <http://www.fdi.gov.cn/pub/FDI_EN/Economy/Investment%20Environment/Infrastructure/Highway/t20070606_79566.htm>

41. Ministry of External Affairs, "India in Business, ITP Division" (Ministry of External Affairs, India). <http://www.indianbusiness.nic.in/industry-infrastructure/infrastructure/road.htm>

42. Federal Highway Administration, Department of Transportation. <http://www.fdi.gov.cn/pub/FDI_EN/Economy/Investment%20Environment/Infrastructure/Highway/t20070606_79566.htm>

43. Steve Hamm, "The Trouble with India: Crumbling Roads, Jammed Airports, and Power Blackouts Could Hobble Growth," *BusinessWeek*, 19 March 2007, 48–58.

44. Ibid.

45. Ibid.

46. Ibid.

47. "China's 15-Year Science and Technology Plan," *Physics Today*, December 2006.

48. Harold Sirkin, "India and China Wise Up to Innovation," 30 January 2007. <http://www.businessweek.com/globalbiz/content/jan2007/gb20070130_742264.htm> (accessed 19 September 2007).

CHAPTER 3. MINDING THE COST GAP

1. Jack Ewing and Gail Edmondson, "Rise of a Powerhouse," *BusinessWeek*, 12 December 2005.

2. Shahid Javed Burki, "The Post-MFA Scenario," 24 August 2004. <http://www.dawn.com/2004/08/24/op.htm> (accessed 19 September 2007).

3. Mercer Human Resource Consulting: Salary Survey, 2005.

4. Aaron Ricadela, "VC Players Look East, to China," *BusinessWeek*, 15 February 2007.

5. Nathan Koppel and Andrew Batson, "A US Law Firm Takes a New Route into China," *The Wall Street Journal*, 30 January 2007.

6. The Boston Consulting Group, *The New Global Challengers: How 100 Top Companies from Rapidly Developing Economies Are Changing the World* (Boston: The Boston Consulting Group May 2006).

7. Zhou Susu, interview by Jim Hemerling, tape recording, 5 March 2007.

8. Joe Havely, "Rural Citizens Fighting Back," CNN page, 2 May 2005. <http://www.cnn.com/2005/WORLD/asiapcf/05/02/eyeonchina.rural/index.html>

9. Dexter Roberts, "China Mobile's Hot Signal," *BusinessWeek*, 5 February 2007, 42–44.

10. Interfax Information Services, B.V., *China's Largest Battery Maker BYD Industrial to Issue 130 Mln Shares on HK Gem* (Interfax Information Services, B.V., 26 July 2002).

11. "Japan Resisting Battery Assault," *South China Morning Post*, 26 February 2005.

12. Thomas Bradke and Jim Hemerling, *The New Economics of Global Advantage: From Lower Costs to Higher Returns* (Boston: The Boston Consulting Group, 2005).

13. India Supply Chain Council, *BMW Look to India for New Procurement Centre*. 8 January 2007. <http://www.supplychains.in/en/art/?367> (accessed 24 September 2007).

14. James Fallows, "China Makes, The World Takes," *The Atlantic* July/August 2007, 94.

15. Yeda Swirski de Souza, "Getting Theory and Practice Closer in Organizational Learning," Universidade do Vale do Rio dos Sinos, Brazil.

16. Honda, *Honda Automobile (China) Co., Ltd. Begins Auto Exports.* 24 June 2005. <http://world.honda.com/news/2005/c050624.html> (accessed 24 September 2007).

17. Li and Fung Group, "Industrial Clusters" (Li and Fung Research Centre, May 2006).

18. GE company page, http://www.ge.com

19. "Industry Updates: Hisense's Wonder Chip," *China Daily*, 30 Oct 2006.

20. "Hisense Plans to Grab More International Shares," *SinoCast China IT Watch*, 30 November 2006.

21. Goodbaby page, <http://www.goodbabygroup.com/> (accessed 12 March 2007).

22. GE Healthcare, *GE Healthcare Invests US$37.5 Million in Chinese Bio-Sciences Manufacturing Facility.* 23 September 2005. <http://www.gehealthcare.com/company/pressroom/releases/pr_release_10322.html> (accessed 24 September 2007).

23. Investment & Trade Promotion Center, *Canon Completes World's Largest Printer Factory in Vietnam.* 26 December 2005. <http://www.itpc.hochiminhcity.gov.vn/en/business_news/business_day/2005/12/folder.2005-12-26.3782039751/news_item.2005-12-26.6897964193> (accessed 19 September 2007).

24. Andrew Tanzer, "The Quick and the Dead," *Forbes*, 8 November 1993.

25. Pete Engardio, "Live-Wire Management at Johnson Electric," *BusinessWeek*, 27 November 1995.

26. Louis Kraar, "The Overseas Chinese: Lessons from the World's Most Dynamic Capitalists," *Fortune* 130, No. 9, 31 October 1994.

27. Johnson Electric Holdings Limited. Annual Report 2006.

28. HSBC, "Johnson Electric," (HSBC, 9 February 2007).

29. Euromonitor International, "Major Appliances Market Research Reports," (London: Euromonitor International 2007).

30. Miriam Jordan and Jonathan Karp, "Washing Machines for the Masses—Whirlpool Develops Inexpensive Model Aimed at China, India, Brazil," *The Asian Wall Street Journal*, 10 December 2003.

31. Robert Malone, "IBM Moves Global Procurement to China," *Forbes*, 13 October 2006.

32. India Supply Chain Council, *BMW Look to India for New Procurement Centre.* 8 January 2007. <http://www.supplychains.in/en/art/?367> (accessed 24 September 2007).

33. Ellen Byron, "Emerging Ambitions—Global Target: Shelves of Tiny Stores," *The Wall Street Journal Online*, 16 July 2007, A1.

34. Pete Engardio & Bruce Einhorn, "Outsourcing Innovation," *BusinessWeek Online*, 21 March 2005.

CHAPTER 4. GROWING PEOPLE

1. Philip Shishkin, "Rising Tide Boat Builders Help Transform Turkey into a Regional Star," *The Wall Street Journal*, 14 September 2006.

2. Jim Yardley and Lin Yang, "In City Ban, a Sign of Wealth and Its Discontents," *The New York Times; Guangzhou Journal*, 15 January 2007.

3. Swati Lodh Kundu, "China's Impending Talent Shortage," *Asia Times*, 6 July 2006.

4. "Most Romanian Men Abroad Worked in Construction Field Before Leaving the Country," *Rompres*, 15 December 2007.

5. "Invest Romania—Performance of SMEs," *Romanian Business Association News*.

6. Damien Whitworth, "The Polish Dream: Beyond the Army of Nannies and Plumbers, Poles Have Embraced the British Job Market Like Never Before—From the City to the Clubs to the Delis, They Are Out to Win," *The Times*, 16 June 2007.

7. Cris Prystay, "India's Boom is Boon For Business Schools," *The Wall Street Journal*, 30 March 2007, B4B.

8. "If in Doubt, Farm it Out—India Business Survey," *The Economist*, 1 June 2006.

9. James Surowiecki, "India's Skills Famine," *The New Yorker*, 16 April 2007.

10. The Boston Consulting Group, "RDE 100," (Boston: BCG 2007).

11. Howard W. French, "In China, Children of the Rich Learn Class, Minus the Struggle," *The New York Times*, 22 September 2006.

12. Anita Chang, "College Exam Impacts All of China," *Washington Post (Reuters)*, 8 June 2007.

13. Bruce Einhorn and Dexter Roberts, "Now College Grads Can't Find a Job," *BusinessWeek*, 11 October 2004.

14. The Boston Consulting Group, "RDE 100," (Boston: BCG 2007).

15. "Hisense's Wonder Chip," *China Daily*, 30 October 2006.

16. "Opening the Doors," *The Economist*, 5 October 2006.

17. Ibid.

18. "Tata Consultancy Opens Training Centre in Uruguay," *Indo-Asian News Service*, 4 February 2007.

19. Christopher Power, "Davos: Demographics, Economics, Destiny," *BusinessWeek*, 25 January 2007.

CHAPTER 5. REACHING DEEP INTO MARKETS

1. Donald N. Sull and Alejandro Ruelas-Gossi, "The Art of Innovating on a Shoestring," *Financial Times*, 24 September 2004.

2. China Daily, *Huiyuan Juices Up Market After IPO*. 1 March 2007. <http://en.ce.cn/stock/marketnews/200703/01/t20070301_10544182.shtml> (accessed 25 September 2007).

3. "The Coming Boom," *The Economist*, 3 May 2007.

4. Larry Rohter, "In the Land of Bold Beauty, a Trusted Mirror Cracks," *The New York Times*, 14 January 2007.

5. Natura Company page. <http://natura.infoinvest.com.br/static/enu/linhas_produtos.asp?language=enu>

6. "Case study—Natura: Going back to Natura," *Brand Strategy*, 8 September 2005.

7. Larry Rohter, "In the Land of Bold Beauty, a Trusted Mirror Cracks," *The New York Times*, 14 January 2007.

8. Itau Corretora, "Natura," *Hold*, 4 January 2007

9. Natura market share based on the total size of the Brazillian market for Cosmetics, Fragrances, and Personal Hygiene from Sipatesp/ ABHIPEC—the Brazilian Association of the Cosmetic, Toiletry & Fragrance Industry.

10. Peter Marsh, "Natura Looking for Growth Outside of Brazil," *Financial Times*, 2 October 2006.

11. "Natura Eyes Expansion," *Beauty Business News*, 20 March 2006.

12. "China's Top Stroller Maker Enters 400m Homes Worldwide," *Xinhua News Agency*, 21 February 2006.

13. "ARC Capital Holdings—First Day of Dealing," Share Crazy page, 26 June 2006. <http://www.sharecrazy.com/share2607share/share.php?disp=news&epic=ARCH&news_item=060626arch1431f.htm> (accessed 13 March 2007).

14. "China Firms Urged to Go More High-Tech," *China Daily* page, 20 June 2002, <http://www.china.org.cn/english/BAT/35082.htm> (accessed 13 March 2007).

15. Goodbaby page. <http://www.goodbabygroup.com/> (accessed 12 March 2007).

16. "Goodbaby Plans More Openings in China," China Franchiser page, 7 March 2007. <http://www.chinafranchiser.com/2007/03/07/508-goodbaby-plans-more-openings-in-china/> (accessed 12 March 2007).

17. BCG calculation based on data from the Economist Intelligence Unit (EIU) and Datamonitor.

18. China Daily, "Leadership to Adjust Growth Model," 10 October 2005. <http://www.chinadaily .com.cn/english/doc/2005-10/10/content_483662_2.htm> (accessed 25 September 2007).

19. "China Industry: Foreign Firms Dominate Telecoms Equipment Market," *Economist Intelligence Unit*, 28 September 2006.

20. "China Set to be the Number One Broadband Market by 2007," Ovum <http://www.ovum .com/go/content/c,377,66667> (accessed 6 March 2007).

21. "China Industry: Foreign Firms Dominate Telecoms Equipment Market," *Economist Intelligence Unit*, 28 September 2006.

22. Zhou Susu, interview by Jim Hemerling, tape recording, 5 March 2007.

23. Zhou Susu, interview by Jim Hemerling, tape recording, 5 March 2007.

24. BAL Holdings Ltd, "2006 BAL annual report," (BAL, 2006).

25. Sanjiv Bajaj, interview by BCG, 2006.

26. David A. Ricks, *Blunders in International Business* (Blackwell Publishing, 1993).

27. Julie Jargon, "Can M'm, M'm Good Translate? Campbell Rethinks Soup as it Prepares to Enter Russia and China," *The Wall Street Journal*, 9 July 2007, A16.

CHAPTER 6. PINPOINTING

1. Jackie Range and Rumman Ahmed, "Wipro to Acquire Infocrossing," *The Wall Street Journal*, 7 August 2007, B4.

2. Bradley R. Staats and David Upton, "Lean at Wipro Technologies," (Harvard Business School case), 16 October 2006.

3. American Power was acquired by Schneider in 2007. After this acquisition, the merged firm is not pinpointed as APC on its own was.

4. "Hungry Tiger, Dancing Elephant," *The Economist*, 4 April 2007.

CHAPTER 7. THINKING BIG, ACTING FAST, GOING OUTSIDE

1. "Rubles Across the Sea," *BusinessWeek*, 30 April 2007. <http://www.businessweek.com/ magazine/content/07_18/b4032056.htm> (accessed 25 September 2007).

2. Joel Kurtzman, "Thought Leader: An Interview with Keshub Mahindra, Chairman of Mahindra & Mahindra, Bombay, India," *Strategy + Business*, Summer 2007.

3. ABN AMRO, *Mahindra & Mahindra*, (Mumbai, India: ABN AMRO, 11 October 2006).

4. Ya Dong Luo, "Partnering with Chinese Firms: Lessons for International Managers," Ashgate, Aldershot et al. Michael F. Roehrig, *Foreign Joint Ventures in Contemporary China* (New York: St. Martin's Press, 1994). Sandra Bell, "International Brand Management of Chinese Companies. Case Studies on the Chinese Household Appliances and Consumer Electronics Industry Entering US and Western European Markets," (PhD dissertation, University of Duisburg-Essen, Shanghai Fudan University, in press 2007).

5. Liu Ling, *China's Industrial Policies and the Global Business Revolution. The Case of the Domestic Appliance Industry* (New York: Routledge, Abingdon, 2005). Sandra Bell, "International Brand Management of Chinese Companies. Case Studies on the Chinese Household Appliances and Consumer Electronics Industry Entering US and Western European Markets," (PhD dissertation, University of Duisburg-Essen, Shanghai Fudan University, 2007).

6. Pei Sun, "Industrial Policy, Corporate Governance, and the Competitiveness of China's National Champions: The Case of Shanghai Baosteel Group," *Journal of Chinese Economic and Business Studies* 3, No. 2, (May 2005): 173–192.

7. "China Industry: Foreign Firms Dominate Telecoms Equipment Market," *Economist Intelligence Unit*, 28 September 2006.

CHAPTER 8. Innovating with Ingenuity

1. Goodbaby page, <http://www.goodbabygroup.com/> (accessed 12 March 2007).

2. Aaron Ricadela, "VC Players Look East, to China," *BusinessWeek*, 15 February 2007.

3. Richard McGregor, "Inside the Middle Kingdom," *Financial Mail*, 8 July 2005.

4. Keith Bradsher, "What Should a Chinese Car Look Like?" *International Herald Tribune*, 22 April 2007. <http://www.iht.com/articles/2007/04/22/business/22auto-china-auto-showASIA.php>

5. Dexter Roberts, "China's Auto Industry Takes On the World," *BusinessWeek*, 28 March 2007.

6. "Tech Mahindra Opens R&D Lab in Bangalore," Network Computing page, 13 July 2007, <http://www.networkcomputing.in/NetInfraJuly-07TechMahindraOpensLabinBangalore.aspx>

CHAPTER 9. Embracing Manyness

1. Stanley Reed, "The Middle East: Where Western Telcos Fear to Tread," *BusinessWeek*, 21 March 2005. <http://www.businessweek.com/magazine/content/05_12/b3925076.htm> (accessed 19 September 2007).

CHAPTER 10. Competing with Everyone from Everywhere for Everything

1. Daiwa Institute of Research, "China Mobile Handset Industry," (Daiwa Institute of Research, 4 November 2002).

2. Ibid.

3. Bruce Einhorn, "A Dragon in R&D," *BusinessWeek Online*, 27 October 2006.

4. Charles F. Knight with Davis Dyer, *Performance Without Compromise: How Emerson Consistently Achieves Winning Results* (Boston: Harvard Business School Press, 2005), 90–95.

Index